Mathematizing Your School

Learn the secrets to getting your entire school excited about math! This book from acclaimed author Dr. Nicki Newton and experienced instructional specialist Janet Nuzzie shows you how to integrate engaging math instruction at every level, from the small group project to the school-wide assembly. With contributions from math coaches, district leaders, and classroom teachers, this book will give you the practical tools you need to boost student proficiency, encourage collaboration between staff members, and make math an important part of school life.

You'll also learn how to:

- Create a safe and inviting environment for mathematics instruction;
- Devote adequate amounts of instructional time to help students develop their skill set as proficient mathematicians;
- Use real-world contexts and hands-on instruction to boost engagement;
- Give students the tools and opportunities to be confident, to question, to take risks, and to make mistakes;
- And much, much more!

Nicki Newton has been an educator for 30 years, working both nationally and internationally, with students of all ages. She has worked on developing Math Workshop and Guided Math Institutes around the country. She is also an avid blogger (www.guidedmath.wordpress.com), Facebooker (Guided Math 123), tweeter (@drnickimath), Pinterest pinner (www.pinterest.com/drnicki7), and YouTuber (Dr. Nicki YouTube channel).

Janet Nuzzie has served teachers and students at the campus, regional, and district level for 23 years. She is the Instructional Specialist for Kindergarten-Grade 4 Mathematics in the Pasadena Independent School District (TX) and works to share the work of her district via Twitter, Facebook, Pinterest, and YouTube (PISDMathematics).

Also Available from Dr. Nicki Newton

(www.routledge.com/eyeoneducation)

Math Problem Solving in Action:
Getting Students to Love Word Problems, Grades K-2

Math Problem Solving in Action:
Getting Students to Love Word Problems, Grades 3–5

Guided Math in Action:
Building Each Student's Mathematical Proficiency
with Small-Group Instruction

Math Workshop in Action:
Strategies for Grades K-5

Math Running Records in Action:
A Framework for Assessing Basic Fact Fluency in Grades K-5

Math Workstations in Action:
Powerful Possibilities for Engaged Learning in Grades 3–5

Daily Math Thinking Routines in Action:
Distributed Practices Across the Year

Mathematizing
Your School

Creating a Culture for Math Success

Nicki Newton and Janet Nuzzie

Routledge
Taylor & Francis Group

NEW YORK AND LONDON

First published 2019
by Routledge
711 Third Avenue, New York, NY 10017

and by Routledge
2 Park Square, Milton Park, Abingdon, Oxon, OX14 4RN

Routledge is an imprint of the Taylor & Francis Group, an informa business

© 2019 Taylor & Francis

The right of Nicki Newton and Janet Nuzzie to be identified as authors of this work has been asserted by them in accordance with sections 77 and 78 of the Copyright, Designs and Patents Act 1988.

Library of Congress Cataloging-in-Publication Data
A catalog record for this book has been requested

ISBN: 978-1-138-32322-3 (hbk)
ISBN: 978-1-138-32323-0 (pbk)
ISBN: 978-0-429-44915-4 (ebk)

Typeset in Palatino and Formata
by Apex CoVantage, LLC

Contents

Meet the Team vii
Foreword (by Dr. Karen Hickman) xi
Preface xiii
Acknowledgments xv

1 **Introduction** 1

2 **Mathematizing Your District: Developing a Common Language** 5

3 **Mathematizing Your District: Building on Shared Knowledge** 33

4 **Mathematizing Your Staff** 73

5 **Mathematizing Your Campus** 101

6 **Mathematizing Your Classroom** 129

7 **Mathematizing Your Students** 185

8 **Mathematizing Your Intervention and Enrichment** 205

9 **Mathematizing Your Parents** 223

10 **Action Planning** 245

Meet the Team

Editors

Nicki Newton has been an educator for 28 years, working both nationally and internationally, with students of all ages. She has worked on developing Math Workshop and Guided Math Institutes around the country. She is also an avid blogger (www.guidedmath.wordpress.com), Facebooker (Guided Math 123), tweeter (@drnickimath), Pinterest pinner (www.pinterest.com/drnicki7), and YouTuber (Dr. Nicki YouTube channel).

Janet Nuzzie has served teachers and students at the campus, regional, and district level for 23 years. She is the Instructional Specialist for Kindergarten–Grade 4 Mathematics in the Pasadena Independent School District (TX) and works to share the work of her district via Twitter, Facebook, Pinterest, and YouTube (PISDMathematics). Janet has presented mathematics professional development sessions at the district, regional, and state level and has held leadership roles in state mathematics organizations.

Contributors

Mariana Breaux has been an elementary school educator for 8 years. She taught first grade and third grade before becoming a Mathematics Instructional Coach for Grades PK–4 in the Pasadena Independent School District (TX). She works closely with teachers and students to foster a deep understanding and love of mathematics. She enjoys sharing reflections of her journey, lessons learned, activities, and tools via Twitter and her blog (www.chroniclesofamathcoach.wordpress.com).

Samantha Cortez is a first-grade bilingual teacher in the Pasadena Independent School District (TX). She encourages her students to be proud mathematicians by identifying their strengths and differentiating her instruction to help make them successful. Samantha has presented mathematics professional development sessions on her data binder and differentiated workstations at the district, regional, and state level and helps write mathematics curriculum for her school district.

Debra Garcia currently serves as the Intervention Teacher for an elementary campus in the Pasadena Independent School district. Before serving as an Intervention Teacher, Debra taught for 13 years in first-grade, third-grade, and fourth-grade bilingual classrooms. She has presented conference sessions for mathematics at the district, regional, and state level.

Jessica Garza is a second-grade bilingual teacher in the Pasadena Independent School District (TX). She avidly works alongside students, parents, and her community to develop and encourage all mathematicians. Jessica has presented mathematics professional development sessions on her interactive journals at the district, regional, and state level and helps write mathematics curriculum for her school district.

Rogelio Guzman has worked in elementary education for 23 years, with the last 21 years being at the same elementary campus. He served as a fifth-grade teacher, then as a third-grade teacher, and currently serves as the Mathematics Instructional Coach for Grades K–4 mathematics in Pasadena, Texas. He shares his passion for mathematics with teachers and students at his campus.

Jacquelyn Kennedy is Mathematics Instructional Coach for a PK–4 campus in the Pasadena Independent School District (TX). Jacquelyn works to inspire the teachers on her campus and throughout her district by sharing her love and passion for mathematics. She looks forward to learning and growing with the outstanding teachers she works with now and in the future.

Kirsta Paulus is a third-grade teacher in the Pasadena Independent School District (TX). She works to engage her students in their learning to foster their sense of understanding, capacity, and enthusiasm for mathematics. She has presented mathematics professional development sessions about her work with anchor charts and interactive notebooks at the district, regional, and state level and helps write mathematics curriculum for her school district.

Lara Roberts has worked in elementary education for 19 years. She began her career as a third-grade and fourth-grade teacher. She is currently a Mathematics Instructional Coach for Grades PK–4 in the Pasadena Independent School District (TX). She works closely with teachers and students, and her efforts center around mathematics instruction and planning.

Foreword

With the current emphasis on STEAM education and with so many mathematics- and science-focused jobs going to folks from outside the U.S., an immediate change is needed regarding how we educate our students in these content areas. We need to have a sense of urgency regarding how we can best prepare our students for these future jobs. Many reports and research findings indicate that employers need employees who can problem solve and find solutions using both innovation and creativity. This shift to create mathematically minded students starts in the elementary classroom.

Embedding and instilling the love of mathematics, reading, writing, science, social studies, healthy living, and the arts in our students can be overwhelming for educators. Finding a balance between teaching all of the curriculum standards while meeting all of the individual needs of our students can be a challenge for teachers, school administrators, and central office leaders who have traditionally had extensive training focused on the literacy standards and minimal training focused on the standards in other content areas. Just as literacy in reading is critical for our students' success, literacy in mathematics and science is also essential for the success and well-being of our students.

Mathematizing Your School paints a picture of the work focused on developing our students' mathematical literacy and delineates in detail the exciting work that is going on in the Pasadena Independent School District (TX) to promote mathematics. The authors include Dr. Nicki Newton, whom we have worked closely with over the course of the past few years, our mathematics specialist, and some of our mathematics coaches and teachers who describe the professional learning journey that has led to a change in the mindsets of our teachers and students regarding mathematics and mathematics instruction. The evolution of instructional practices across our district is allowing our students to realize their potential in mathematics and their capability to become successful mathematicians both in school and in life. Through this work, mathematics continues to grow as an educational priority in the district, on campuses, and in our classrooms.

Pasadena ISD is blessed that our elementary mathematics program is led by a visionary specialist, Janet Nuzzie, who continually dreams of and focuses the district on how things could be regarding mathematics and mathematics instruction. She definitely has a growth mindset, not just for herself, but for all of us around her! She has the ability to utilize systems that are in place to focus the energy around structures such as Math Workshop in order to change the culture of our mathematics classrooms. Janet understands the strength of using professional learning opportunities to empower mathematics coaches and teachers to consider needed refinements to their practice, becoming a champion of those changes, encouraging continued personal growth, and sharing the lessons learned with others. As Janet likes to say, "Mathematicians learn and grow together!"

As our district has worked to refine our practices regarding mathematics instruction, Dr. Nicki Newton has collaborated with our district to help us in our professional learning journey. It is so rare and yet so refreshing to find a consultant who truly has partnered with a district, whether that is through continued face-to-face professional development opportunities or online professional development opportunities, and maintains relationships with administrators, specialists, coaches, and teachers. Dr. Nicki Newton has continually inspired changes to the instructional practices of our teachers and the climate and culture of our elementary schools regarding mathematics and mathematics instruction. This was a much-needed change, and we are forever grateful for her and the support that her many resources have provided us with our efforts.

In this book, the authors share the victories and challenges that come with change, as well as the needed next steps for our mathematics journey. We have not completed the journey, but I am inspired by where we are now compared to where we once were. I hope you enjoy each chapter as real practitioners share about the implementation and use of resources such as curriculum documents, book studies, anchor charts, math journals, math stations, data binders, Math Labs, and family math nights to mathematize our district. Let's also not forget about Mathematician Street and Mathematician of the Month . . . two initiatives that are finding their way onto other campuses in our district and helping us mathematize our schools! I love the pictures that display the work of our teachers and students and hope that these practical suggestions and supports will help you in your journey to mathematize your school and/or district. We hope that the quotes from administrators, coaches, teachers, and students will inspire you to roll up your sleeves and begin mathematizing the world around you. Enjoy!

Dr. Karen Hickman
Deputy Superintendent of Academic Achievement
Pasadena ISD (TX)

Preface

The lyrics are "Come along and ride on a Fantastic Voyage..." those words from a song in the early '80s by Lakeside come to mind when I think about this book. I was in Pasadena, Texas, filming about Guided Math and Math Workshop, and I saw the most amazing things! Math was everywhere, and everyone loved math!

Wow! I immediately asked them to write about it because I think GOOD PRACTICES are contagious. It's our responsibility to spread the news! That is exactly what this book does. Several amazing educators have gotten together, written together, and now published this book about mathematizing schools (which really means making math important). Several different people wrote this book, from many different perspectives of mathematizing a school. We hear from teachers, math coaches, and district specialists all talking about how to make math an important part of school life. I am more than honored to be able to co-edit such a phenomenal book with Janet Nuzzie! Here is how we have organized it:

Chapter 1 is the Introduction. We discuss the blueprint of mathematizing your school and discuss the general components of who, what, when, where, and how.

Chapter 2 and Chapter 3 focus on "Mathematizing Your District." The overall conversation is about how important the district can be in promoting and supporting math for ALL! The district sends messages loud and clear about what is important in the curriculum, and when they are on board, everybody benefits. In Chapter 2 Janet centers her discussion on "Developing a Common Language" using curriculum documents, meetings with campus administrators, and district-wide professional development. Chapter 3 explores how book studies, social media, opportunities for teacher leaders, and campus spotlights provide everyone with ways in which to support the goal of "Building on Shared Knowledge."

Chapter 4 focuses on mathematizing your school staff. In this chapter Lara and Jacquelyn talk about the joys and challenges of getting everyone on board. It *ain't always easy*, but it is definitely worth it! Everybody can teach math with a little help from the Math Coach!

Chapter 5 focuses on "Mathematizing Your Campus." In this chapter Mariana discusses how she first started out mathematizing her school. She discusses the joys and challenges of making it happen. She also gives us a checklist of things to think about and ways to get started.

Chapter 6 focuses on mathematizing your classroom from the teacher's perspective. In this chapter three amazing teachers, Kirsta, Jessica, and

Samantha, describe different things that they do to make math important. We will learn about math anchor charts, math journals, Math Data Binders, differentiated workstations, and more.

Chapter 7 focuses on mathematizing the students in your school! In this chapter Mariana teaches us how to get the kids in on the excitement! Her brilliant idea of Mathematician of the Month (a school-wide initiative) is definitely going to go viral! This is so amazing, and she tells us exactly how to do it! Get ready to get excited!

Chapter 8 focuses on "Mathematizing Your Intervention and Enrichment." Debra and Rogelio describe this amazing Math Lab that they run. They talk about the importance of student's self-monitoring and the *gamification* of mathematics for deep engagement and long-term learning, and they also give us the specifics of how to do it!

Chapter 9 focuses on "Mathematizing Your Parents!" In this chapter we explore what it means to engage our parents so that they too are excited about math, have the tools to help their students learn it, and also have knowledge base to discuss the math that their students are learning.

Chapter 10 focuses on "Action Planning." A goal without a date and actionable steps is a dream. You have to sit down and really plan for the specifics. Throughout the book we give you time to think, reflect, and start planning as different ideas are introduced. However, in this chapter we want you to look at the big picture and think about exactly where and how you are going to get started. We give you ideas, reflection prompts, and some planning templates to start the work!

So, let's get started on this fantastic voyage! You are going to learn and see so many amazing things that will change your mathematical school lives! We sure have. Even as we wrote together and discussed ideas, we continued to learn so many things from each other.

Acknowledgments

Dr. Nicki: I thank God, my family, my friends, and the many colleagues I work with on this great journey! Special thanks to all the educators in Pasadena ISD who worked with me on this project. I am humbly honored that you came along with me on this journey!

Janet Nuzzie: I would like to thank the teachers, mathematics coaches, and administrators in Pasadena ISD who inspire (and humble) me with their willingness to learn and grow as mathematicians. I would also like to thank my parents who worked to provide me with so many opportunities in life, my sister for her continued guidance in my journey as an educator, and my husband who finds a way to make me smile each and every day.

Mariana Breaux: I would like to thank God, my amazing husband, and my family for their constant encouragement and support. I would also like to thank the amazing mathematics teachers at Richey Elementary for embarking on this journey with me!

Samantha Cortez: Thank you Mom for always being my number one supporter and for teaching me how to be the best person I can be. Thank you Dad for always pushing me to be my best and never letting me forget that God is always with me. Thank you also to my loved ones who are always by my side supporting me and encouraging me!

Debra Garcia: Thank you to my administrators and colleagues at LF Smith Elementary and Pasadena ISD for the inspiration, encouragement, and guidance throughout this journey. Thank you to my amazing family and friends for their love and support! Thank you Mom and Dad for all the sacrifices you made to make sure I had opportunities just like this one!

Jessica Garza: Thank you God, my truly incredible husband, family, and friends for your endless love and support. Thank you Mom and Dad for teaching me the value of hard work and inspiring me in more ways than you can imagine.

Rogelio Guzman: I would like to thank God, my amazing wife, my boys, my parents, and family for their unconditional love and support. I would also like to thank my administrators, students, and co-workers for inspiring me to grow into the educator I am today.

Jacquelyn Kennedy: I would like to thank all of the amazing mathematics teachers who have inspired and nourished my love for mathematics. I would also like to thank God, my family, especially my mom, Linda, and my friends who have encouraged me to learn and grow every step of the way!

Kirsta Paulus: The biggest of thank-yous to my family for their constant encouragement and support. Thank you to my school family and my students, who help me see mathematics in a new way each and every day.

Lara Roberts: I would like to thank God, my husband, and children for their support. I would also like to thank my parents for instilling in me the importance of working towards your goals.

1

Introduction

We love mathematics! And it is our mission on earth to get everyone else too as well! Too often we hear, "I don't like math!" or sometimes we even hear "I hate math!" from our colleagues! So we wrote a book to show how math can be so amazing in your school. We want to talk about how to develop a level of comfort with mathematics, how to honor our students and teachers as mathematicians, and how promoting mathematics in our schools can support the development of a mathematical mindset in all stakeholders. We want to discuss ways to encourage all teachers and students to start liking and possibly even loving math. We want to show ways to promote mathematics throughout the school in different ways, from having a Mathematician's Street to having a Mathematician of the Month from every grade level. We want our schools to be mathematized!

What Is It?

Mathematizing your school is about **Making Math Front and Center**. It sits right alongside the Literacy Movement (not behind it)! Mathematizing your school means that everyone is on board (administrators, teachers, students, parents, school staff) with making mathematics accessible (and enjoyable!) to all learners. **Mathematizing your school means . . .**

Mathematizing your school is about creating a safe and inviting environment for mathematics instruction.

Mathematizing your school means fostering a mindset that mathematics is not about getting a right or wrong answer, but it is about different ways of getting the answer . . . it is about thinking . . . the students' thinking!

Mathematizing your school means that students receive adequate amounts of instructional time to develop their skill set as proficient mathematicians.

Mathematizing your school is about clarifying what the end goal is for each student as a mathematician . . . rather than the end goal being solely to pass a test!

Mathematizing your school means that each student is provided with ample opportunities to develop number sense and their own mathematical identity!

Mathematizing your school is a MINDSET shift. It means having expectations that ALL students can be proficient with mathematics. It means that students develop perseverance when tackling challenging problems.

Mathematizing your school means that students understand the role of perseverance in mathematics and use grit and determination when tackling challenging problems!

Mathematizing your school means building a community where mathematics is spotlighted in classrooms and all areas of the school.

Mathematizing your school means that students are a part of a "math movement" where perseverance with mathematics is both welcomed and celebrated!

Mathematizing your school is about empowering all stakeholders to share ideas about how to encourage students as mathematicians and using those ideas to create a positive mathematical environment on the campus.

Mathematizing your school is about getting EVERYONE (students, teachers, campus coaches, campus administrators) to embrace mathematics!

Mathematizing your school creates an environment where mathematics skills are explored through hands-on instruction using real-world contexts.

Mathematizing your school means that mathematics is displayed throughout the learning environment and sends the message that mathematics is valued at your school!

Mathematizing your school means sharing a vision where all students are capable of learning mathematics and finding ways to spark a love for mathematics within administrators, teachers, students, and parents.

> Mathematizing your school means giving students the tools and opportunities to be confident, to question, to take risks, and to make mistakes.

Why Do It?

Mathematizing your school empowers everybody to believe that they are mathematicians. It provides a space where everyone can be comfortable with mathematics and confident in their ability to do mathematics. Everybody loves reading, but a lot of folks fear math. Mathematizing your school addresses that phenomena. **We need to mathematize our school because . . .**

> We need to mathematize our school so that each and every student is empowered to see himself/herself as a mathematician.

> We need to mathematize our school so that students recognize their ability to learn mathematics and are enabled to do so in different ways with different strategies!

> We need to mathematize our school so that students develop a love of mathematics!

> We need to mathematize our school because we want our students to be inspired by mathematics and the opportunities that mathematics creates in their future!

> We need to mathematize our school so that students understand that mistakes are a part of the learning process and that feedback is provided to help students redirect their learning.

> We need to mathematize our school in a way that the environment allows students to feel safe to take risks during instruction.

> We need to mathematize our school because problem solving is all around us and students need to see that mathematics is more than a subject . . . that mathematics is a life skill that will serve them in their daily lives.

> We need to mathematize our school so that all stakeholders recognize the value that the campus administrators and teachers place on the students' learning of mathematics.

> We need to mathematize our schools because a child who is able to think critically, find different strategies, and listen and share ideas can change the world!

Summary

In this chapter we have introduced *Mathematizing Your School*. We have set out to show how school should be a safe space to learn mathematics. Teachers, students, administrators, and parents should understand that it takes perseverance to do mathematics well and that mistakes will definitely happen along the way. Mathematizing your school is about creating a living, breathing, positive environment for mathematics to be promoted and celebrated by all stakeholders in the school and district. Mathematizing a school requires a plan and a coordinated effort that will pay dividends for a lifetime. Mathematizing your school is about creating and fostering a mindset that everyone can and will be successful at math. If we want to truly educate and prepare the next generation to be productive citizens and live successful lives, mathematizing your school should be a non-negotiable for every learning space in our school districts.

Questions to Consider

1. How important is mathematics in your school right now? Do all stakeholders (the students, the teachers, the administration, the school staff [secretaries, cooks, custodians], the parents) realize how important mathematics is?
2. Does your school celebrate teachers' and students' achievements in mathematics? Why or why not? What can be done to further celebrate the efforts of the teachers and young mathematicians?
3. What is one thing about mathematics/mathematics instruction that you would like to change in your school?

2
Mathematizing Your District
Developing a Common Language

Janet Nuzzie is the district instructional specialist for kindergarten through fourth grade mathematics in Pasadena ISD (TX). Her school district has over 55,000 students with 78% of the students being economically disadvantaged. The student population is 83% Hispanic, 8% African American, 6% White, and 3% Asian. Janet has over 23 years of experience in education which includes serving seven years at the district level as an instructional specialist for elementary mathematics, nine years at the regional level as an education specialist for elementary mathematics, and seven years at the classroom level as a fourth-grade teacher. Her synergistic efforts include serving as the president of TASM (an organization of mathematics supervisors in Texas), serving as vice-president (elementary) of TCTM (an organization of mathematics teachers in Texas), serving on numerous mathematics committees at the state and national level, and presenting over 90 sessions at regional, state, and national mathematics conferences. (Connect with Janet on Twitter: @janetdnuzzie)

Introduction

Mathematicians learn and grow together.

—Janet Nuzzie

While one teacher has the ability to make the difference in the life of one child or in the lives of many children, our greatest impact is when we are able to build our expertise together and make a greater impact in the lives of all of the children we serve. The influence and impact that a community of educators can make is powerful and far more reaching rather than just the efforts of one sole educator. The text that follows shares the journey that our district has made . . . a journey to develop a common language regarding what mathematics instruction should look like and sound like. Developing a common language involves all stakeholders (teachers, campus coaches, and campus administrators) and must be reinforced with curriculum documents that provide tools to support the common language, meetings with the campus administrators that support the implementation of the curriculum documents, and purposeful district-wide professional development to support teachers as they work to make the curriculum accessible to our young mathematicians on a daily basis. When we journey together, grow together, and develop our collective expertise regarding what is best for our young mathematicians, we see the impact of our work through the mathematizing of our district.

Developing a Common Language: Curriculum Documents

Two of the four most critical questions that we need to ask ourselves, as defined by the work of professional learning communities (PLC), are, "What is it we expect our students to learn?" and "How will we know when they have learned it?" (DuFour, DuFour, Eaker, Many, Mattos, 2016) When we are able to collectively answer these questions and ensure that we have a common understanding of our end goal, then we are able to identify the "what" it is that our students need to learn and the "how" of what we need to do to make it happen. Asking these two critical questions is important, but equipping ourselves with the tools that provide these answers is even more critical.

One of the first steps we took on this journey was redefining district documents called "Standard Clarifications" that included information such as the standard, possible vocabulary that is embedded in the standard, and textbook pages that could be used to teach the standard. We began to add components that would provide teachers with the tools necessary to answer the first two critical questions of a PLC. At that time we had 35 campuses and approximately 1,100 teachers, and we had to have tools that could be shared across the campus in order to support the many team conversations for which it was not logistically possible to be present. Our Standard Clarification documents began with critical components such as the language of the standards (in both English and Spanish), the core vocabulary that was either explicitly stated in the standard or implied by the standard (in both English and Spanish), and the prerequisite standards that reflected the prior knowledge students must have as well as the standards to which the grade level standards would build (see Figure 2.1). These pieces were critical in ensuring that teachers understood where the concepts/skills fell in light of a vertically aligned curriculum as well as the academic language that students needed to utilize in order to develop understanding of the standard.

Another critical aspect that was provided in the clarification documents were "instructional clarifications." These clarifications included examples of what the standard looks like and sounds like when it is being explored in the classroom. These examples included questions that could be asked to engage students in the concepts or skills, images of how the concepts or skills could be taught with manipulatives, and "must knows" that reflect common misunderstandings or misapplications of the standard (see Figure 2.2). Our goal in creating these components of the documents was to ensure that

Figure 2.1 Portion of Standard Clarification

Mathematics TEKS (English)	**3.2 Number and Operations** **3.2D Reporting Category 1 (Numerical Representations and Relationships)** - Readiness Standard *The student applies mathematical process standards to represent and compare whole numbers and understand relationships related to place value.* • 3.2D Compare and order whole numbers up to 100,000 and represent comparisons using the symbols >, <, or =.
Mathematics TEKS (Spanish)	• 3.2D Compare y ordene números enteros hasta el 100,000 y represente comparaciones utilizando los símbolos >, < o =.
Process Standards	**Mathematical Process Standards** *The student uses mathematical processes to acquire and demonstrate mathematical understanding.* (1A) Apply mathematics to problems arising in everyday life, society, and the workplace. (1B) Use a problem-solving model that incorporates analyzing given information, formulating a plan or strategy, determining a solution, justifying the solution, and evaluating the problem-solving process and the reasonableness of the solution. (1C) Select tools, including real objects, manipulatives, paper and pencil, and technology as appropriate, and techniques, including mental math, estimation, and number sense as appropriate, to solve problems. (1D) Communicate mathematical ideas, reasoning, and their implications using multiple representations, including symbols, diagrams, graphs, and language as appropriate. (1E) Create and use representations to organize, record, and communicate mathematical ideas. (1F) Analyze mathematical relationships to connect and communicate mathematical ideas. (1G) Display, explain, and justify mathematical ideas and arguments using precise mathematical language in written or oral communication.
Possible Core Vocabulary	compare (comparar), order (ordenar), digit (digito), comparison symbols (símbolos de comparación), equal to (es igual a) (=), less than (es menor que) (<), greater than (es mayor que) (>), least to greatest (menor a mayor), greatest to least (mayor a menor), place value (valor de posición)

Vertical Alignment		
Prior Grade Level: Grade 2	**Current Grade Level: Grade 3**	**Next Grade Level: Grade 4**
2.2D Use place value to compare and order whole numbers up to 1,200 using comparative language, numbers, and symbols >, <, or =.	3.2D Compare and order whole numbers up to 100,000 and represent comparisons using the symbols >, <, or =.	4.2C Compare and order whole numbers to 1,000,000,000 and represent comparisons using the symbols >, <, or =. 4.2F Compare and order decimals using concrete and visual models to the hundredths.

Instructional Clarifications
• Use tools such as number lines and place value charts to compare and order whole numbers. • Use vocabulary and symbols such as "less than", "<", "greater than", ">", "equal to", "=", "least to greatest", or "greatest to least" to describe the comparison of whole numbers. • Numbers may be presented within a table of data. • Students might be asked to use comparison symbols to compare a sequence of three numbers (ex. 1,749 > 1,700 > 1,695). • Students might be asked to list numbers in order from greatest to least/least to greatest or list categories/labels that represent numbers in order from greatest to least/least to greatest.

© Pasadena Independent School District 2017

Figure 2.2 Example of Instructional Clarifications

• **Use "make 10 and some more" to determine the solution to story problems with +/- 7,8,9.**

Addition: Joda has 4 counters in her left pocket and 9 counters in her right pocket. How many counters does Joda have in all?

Step 1: Create sets	Step 2: Make 10 and Some More

Possible Answer: 4+9 is the same as (1+3)+9 or (1+9)+3. 4 and 9 is the same as 10 and 3. 4+9 =13.

Subtraction: Joda had 17 counters and gave 9 counters to her math partner. How many counters does Joda have left?

Step 1: Create set to represent the subtrahend.	Step 2: Build Up to 10 and More to determine the difference.

Possible Answer: 9 + 1 + 7 = 17. 9 and 8 more equals 17. 17-9=8

© Pasadena Independent School District 2017

teachers and teacher teams had a resource that outlined the "what" of what we should be teaching and the "how" of what we should be teaching.

Also during these first years of development we added other critical tools including possible anchor charts that could be used to support instruction as well as possible graphic organizers that could be used to capture key concepts in students' interactive journals. At the time, there was not a wealth of resources that provided standards-based examples of anchor charts or paper folds for our standards, so we relied on the images captured through internet searches and efforts made by curriculum writers to create examples that we could include in our Standard Clarification documents. In fact, we started with a very limited number of anchor chart examples and soon reached out to the campuses to have teachers share examples from their classroom. With time, we've acquired a healthy number of examples from our teachers' classrooms and have been able to utilize examples from online resources such as Pinterest. Because there was a limited number of paper fold examples available through online resources, we utilized curriculum writers to create examples and included pictures of the examples in the Standard Clarification documents (see Figure 2.3 and Figure 2.4).

Our first steps to provide tools to support common knowledge regarding "What is it we expect our students to learn?" and "How will we know when they have learned it?" took shape and provided teachers with tools that outline the academic language for the standards (in English and Spanish), the prerequisite skills from which students would build on to develop their grade level knowledge, and examples of what standards-based instruction would look like in the classroom. We utilized the documents during professional development, encouraged teachers to utilize the documents during team planning, and always directed teachers to the documents in order to answer common questions about the standard.

Figure 2.3 Example of Graphic Organizers

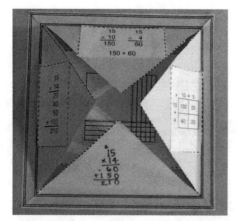

© *Pasadena Independent School District 2017*

Figure 2.4 Example of Anchor Charts

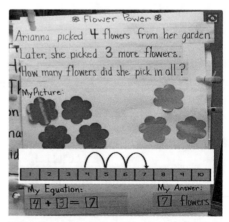

© *Pasadena Independent School District 2017*

With time we've added other components to the Standard Clarification documents in order to create a "one stop shop" to support team planning conversations. We've added components such as sample assessment items to support conversations about "the end in mind" (see Figure 2.5 and Figure 2.6), the items from our state assessments that reflect the depth and complexity of the standards, possible formative assessment strategies that would fit seamlessly into instruction while providing teachers with formative data on their students' understanding of mathematical concepts (see Figure 2.7), possible academic language strategies to promote students' use of academic language, possible graphic organizers that could be used to outline key concepts or examples aligned to the standards (see Figure 2.8), mini-lessons that support our students' transition from Spanish to English, question prompts and sentence starters that encourage student discourse in the classroom (see Figure 2.9), and workstations that could be used during various components of Math Workshop (see Figure 2.10).

The addition of these components has taken place over time. We've made the additions as a team of two district specialists and have also sought support through the curriculum writing efforts of our district math coaches and teacher leaders from our classrooms. The documents are robust, and while we sometimes hear that the amount of information can be overwhelming, we think that the resource provides numerous tools to support both new and veteran teachers as well as teacher teams with the tools necessary to answer the critical PLC questions during team planning conversations. Also, with a district that has grown to have 36 elementary campuses, it is critical to provide tools that support teachers and their varying levels

Figure 2.5 and Figure 2.6 Example of Assessment Items

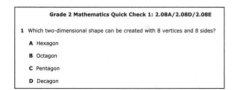

Figure 2.7 Example of Formative Assessment Strategy

Possible Formative Assessment Strategy

Assessment Probe: Strategies for Multiplication

Directions:
- Prompt students to complete a problem-solving task.
- Prompt students to examine examples of how other students solved the problem correctly.
- Prompt students to circle the process/strategy that best matches their own and response to the questions.

Example:

What's Your Multiplication Strategy?
Circle the strategy that most closely shows how you solved the problem.
There are six classrooms in the fifth-grade pod at Miller Middle School. There are 27 desks in each classroom. What is the greatest number of students that can sit at desks in the fifth-grade pod?

Examples from Other Students	Do the other three methods that you did not circle make sense mathematically? Why or why not?
Norma's Method 27×6=◆ 25×6=150 2×6=12 150+12=162	
Blanca's Method 27×6=◆ 20×6=120 7×6=42 120+42=162	
Enemencio's Method 4 27 × 6 162	
Deshaun's Method 30×6=180 3×6=18 180-18=162	

Figure 2.8 Example of Graphic Organizers

Two-Dimensional Shapes

Circle	Triangle	Rectangle	Square (a special rectangle)	Rhombus	Hexagon

Attributes

Figure 2.9 Example of Question Prompts and Sentence Starters

Resources to Promote Student Discourse: Content Question Stems & Sentence Frames/Starters
Sentence frames are a scaffold to help students respond to questions using grade level academic vocabulary. Once students are able to respond appropriately, the sentence frames may be taken away or modified to prompt students to use multiple language structures.

1. How many hundreds, tens, and ones compose the number _____?
- The number _____ is composed of _____ hundreds, _____ tens, and _____ ones.
2. How could you represent the number _____ in expanded form/word form/standard form?
- The number _____ can be represented in expanded/standard/written form as _____.
3. Which set of concrete objects represents the number _____? Why?
- The set of concrete of objects that represents the number _____ is _____ because _____.
4. Describe the value of _____ in the number _____.
- The value of the _____ in the number _____ is _____.
5. What is one way to represent _____ using expanded form?
- One way to represent _____ using expanded form is _____.
6. What is the value of the underlined digit in the number _____?
- The value of the underlined digit in the number ____ is _____.
7. What happens to the value of the number _____ when you decompose one hundreds flat into tens rods?
- When a one hundreds flat is decomposed into ten rods the value of the number _____ _____.
8. What is the relationship between ones and tens?
- The relationship between ones and tens is _____.
9. How does the position of a digit in a number affect its value?
- The position of a digit in a number affects its value by _____.
10. What place value patterns do you see as you compose and decompose numbers?
- When I compose and decompose numbers a place value pattern I see is _____.

1. ¿Cuántas unidades de millar, centenas, decenas y unidades componen el número _____?
- El número _____ está compuesto de _____ unidades de millar, _____centenas y _____ unidades.
2. ¿Cómo se puede representar el número _____en forma desarrollada/escrita/estándar?
- El número _____ se puede representar en forma desarrollada/escrita/estándar como _____.
3. ¿Cuál conjunto de objetos concretos representa el número _____? ¿Por qué?
- El conjunto de objetos concretos que representa el número _____ es _____ porque _____.
4. Describe el valor del _____ en el número _____.
- El valor del _____ en el número _____ es _____.
5. ¿Cuál es una manera de representar _____ usando forma desarrollada?
- Una manera de representar _____ en forma desarrollada es _____.
6. ¿Cuál es el valor del dígito subrayado en el número ____?
- El valor del dígito subrayado en el número _____ es _____.
7. ¿Qué le ocurre al valor del número _____ cuando descompones un bloque de cien a barras de diez?
- Cuando un plano de cien se descompone a diez barras de diez el valor del número _____ _____.
8. ¿Cuál es la relación entre unidades y decenas?
- La relación entre unidades y decenas es _____.
9. ¿De qué manera afecta la posición de un dígito en un número el valor del número?
- La posición de un dígito en un número afecta el valor de un número porque _____.
10. ¿Cuáles patrones de valor de posición puedes ver cuando compones y descompones números?
- Cuando descompongo y compongo números un patrón de valor de posición que yo puede ver es _____.

Figure 2.10 Example of Workstations

Decimal Card Match

(Teacher directions)

Student Expectation

4.2A Interpret the value of each place-value position as 10 times the position to the right and as one-tenth the value of the place to its left. (RC1: Supporting)
4.2B Represent the value of the digit in whole numbers through 1,000,000,000 and decimals to the hundredths using expanded notation and numerals. (RC1: Readiness)

Description

Materials Needed

- Decimal Cards (included)*
- Expanded Form Cards (included)*
- Expanded Notation Cards (included)*
- Recording Sheet (included)

*Teacher Note: It is suggested that the Decimal Cards, Expanded Form Cards, and Expanded Notation Cards be printed on different colors of paper.

Directions

- Draw a Decimal Card.
- Use the Expanded Form Cards to represent the value of each digit with numbers.
- Record the expanded form of the decimal on the recording sheet.
- Use the Expanded Notation Cards to represent the value of each digit with expanded notation.
- Record the expanded notation of the decimal on the recording sheet.

Decimal Card Match

(Student directions)

Materials:

- Decimal Cards
- Expanded Form Cards
- Expanded Notation Cards
- Recording Sheet

Directions:

- Draw a Decimal Card.
- Use the Expanded Form Cards to represent the value of each digit with numbers.
- Record the expanded form of the decimal on the recording sheet.
- Use the Expanded Notation Cards to represent the value of each digit with expanded notation.
- Record the expanded notation of the decimal on the recording sheet.

Decimal Card Match

Decimal Cards	Decimal Cards
1.24	1.04
2.55	2.98
3.67	3.02
4.93	4.29
5.19	5.09
6.04	6.89
7.39	4.21
8.95	8.04
9.65	9.37

Decimal Card Match

Expanded Notation Cards	Expanded Notation Cards	Expanded Notation Cards
(1 × 1)	(1 × 0.1)	(1 × 0.01)
(2 × 1)	(2 × 0.1)	(2 × 0.01)
(3 × 1)	(3 × 0.1)	(3 × 0.01)
(4 × 1)	(4 × 0.1)	(4 × 0.01)
(5 × 1)	(5 × 0.1)	(5 × 0.01)
(6 × 1)	(6 × 0.1)	(6 × 0.01)
(7 × 1)	(7 × 0.1)	(7 × 0.01)
(8 × 1)	(8 × 0.1)	(8 × 0.01)
(9 × 1)	(9 × 0.1)	(9 × 0.01)

Decimal Card Match

Expanded Notation Cards	Expanded Notation Cards	Expanded Notation Cards
(1 × 1)	$(1 \times \frac{1}{10})$	$(1 \times \frac{1}{100})$
(2 × 1)	$(2 \times \frac{1}{10})$	$(2 \times \frac{1}{100})$
(3 × 1)	$(3 \times \frac{1}{10})$	$(3 \times \frac{1}{100})$
(4 × 1)	$(4 \times \frac{1}{10})$	$(4 \times \frac{1}{100})$
(5 × 1)	$(5 \times \frac{1}{10})$	$(5 \times \frac{1}{100})$
(6 × 1)	$(6 \times \frac{1}{10})$	$(6 \times \frac{1}{100})$
(7 × 1)	$(7 \times \frac{1}{10})$	$(7 \times \frac{1}{100})$
(8 × 1)	$(8 \times \frac{1}{10})$	$(8 \times \frac{1}{100})$
(9 × 1)	$(9 \times \frac{1}{10})$	$(9 \times \frac{1}{100})$

Decimal Card Match

Expanded Form Cards	Expanded Form Cards	Expanded Form Cards
1	0.1	0.01
2	0.2	0.02
3	0.3	0.03
4	0.4	0.04
5	0.5	0.05
6	0.6	0.06
7	0.7	0.07
8	0.8	0.08
9	0.9	0.09

of knowledge about the math standards as well as the sometime varying level of comfort with the standards and/or the teaching of mathematics.

An important note is that these documents have evolved over time and have evolved based on feedback provided through formal and informal conversations with staff members as well as based on needs that we have surmised through campus conversations. While time sometimes poses a challenge to creating thorough resources to support teachers' development of content knowledge, it is imperative that resources such as these are created so that teams within a campus, across a campus, and across a district have a common starting point for ensuring that we facilitate standards-based instruction with our students. We now see campus math coaches making spiral-bound notebooks of the documents for use during team meetings, teachers referencing the documents during team planning, and administrators using the documents to frame the background for an upcoming classroom observation or a conference with a teacher.

The documents, sometimes referenced by teachers as their "Math Bible," have become a critical tool for team planning conversations and have been critical in supporting our efforts to develop a common language about what mathematics instruction should look like and sound like. While the documents have evolved over time, the documents started with basic components pulled from the standards and an empty document created on a computer.

> The Standard Clarification documents have supported me as a mathematics teacher by providing a "complete package" resource to plan and deliver my instruction to my students. The academic vocabulary both in English and Spanish, the instructional clarifications that explain the standard in a more detailed manner, and the vertical alignment information are just a few components from the document that guide my planning efforts. Other components that guide my instruction are the "TEKS Clarifications," which provide me with a possible outline of my lesson, as well as the strategies and mini-lessons for introducing English academic language to my bilingual students.
>
> Grade 3 Bilingual Teacher

> The Standard Clarification documents that the district provides its educators are a powerful tool! These documents support my instruction with a comprehensive "bird's-eye view" of what I need for any concept that I'm covering in my instruction. The documents provide me with a list of resources such as student materials, English Language Development instruction, vertical alignment, and question stems. Most importantly, the documents support me with instructional strategies that I can apply in my lessons. Having the district's support with the Standard Clarification documents allows

me to work smarter, not harder, when planning rigorous instruction for my students.

Grade 3 Bilingual Teacher

I use the Standard Clarification documents on a daily basis. The documents provide us with a variety of resources and tools to use during mathematics instruction. The vertical alignment section allows us, as teachers, to see what the students should have learned in the previous grade level as well as what the expectation will look like in the next grade level. The documents also provide examples of how to teach the student expectation as well as important academic vocabulary and released test questions. By utilizing the Standard Clarification, we are able to plan and get a clear picture of where our students are expected to be with the expectation.

Grade 3 Teacher

Developing a Common Language: Meetings With Campus Administrators

As we worked to provide our classroom teachers and campus coaches with the tools necessary to facilitate standards-aligned, engaging instruction, we also worked to equip our campus administrators with the conversation points and tools to support the implementation of our curriculum. Through district-designated meeting dates with our campus administrators, we first embarked on conversations related to content and then added conversations related to Math Workshop.

Our content-rich conversations including conversations focused on "hot topics" in mathematics instruction such as fact fluency as well as the exploration of strategies and tools that could be used to teach the student expectations. These topics were simultaneously being explored in our "Focus" professional development sessions with teachers, which are described later in this chapter. One of the "hot topics" that we explored early on focused on the strategies to support the development of fact fluency. We explored three core strategies for addition and subtraction facts such as counting-on/counting-back, making ten and more, and doubles/ near doubles (see Figure 2.11). Our conversations included an exploration of the tools that could be used (number paths, double ten frames, doubles mats) as well as visual organizers that demonstrated how one or two of these core strategies allowed students to determine the sum of most facts.

We examined strategies that could be used to "change up" the traditional routines of test review and encourage students to justify their thinking and share their responses with peers. One strategy we explored was

Figure 2.11 Instructional Leadership Conversations Fact Fluency

Developing Fluency with Addition/Subtraction Facts

Addition Facts

+	0	1	2	3	4	5	6	7	8	9
0	0	1	2	3	4	5	6	7	8	9
1	1	2	3	4	5	6	7	8	9	10
2	2	3	4	5	6	7	8	9	10	11
3	3	4	5	6	7	8	9	10	11	12
4	4	5	6	7	8	9	10	11	12	13
5	5	6	7	8	9	10	11	12	13	14
6	6	7	8	9	10	11	12	13	14	15
7	7	8	9	10	11	12	13	14	15	16
8	8	9	10	11	12	13	14	15	16	17
9	9	10	11	12	13	14	15	16	17	18

 Mathematics

© *Pasadena Independent School District* 2017

called, "What is the best worst answer?" (see Figure 2.12). We modeled how to use this strategy using sample items from our state assessment. We examined an item and then asked the administrators to share their responses to the following prompts.

- What is the worst answer? Why?
- What is the best incorrect answer? Why?
- What is the correct answer? Why?

We also explored engaging ways for students to review previously taught concepts, as opposed to repetitive practice in a question/answer worksheet type format. One tool we explored was an activity called "Bell Ringer Bunco" where students begin class by rolling a number cube (1, 2, or 3 times based on the teacher's preference) and completing the task assigned to the number from the number cube (see Figure 2.13 and Figure 2.14).

We incorporated these various strategies into our conversations, in addition to the exploration of content-specific, hands-on, engaging resources that promote understanding of concepts, not just the practice of concepts. Our goal was to provide examples of activities and strategies that represented the type of instruction that should be occurring in our classrooms and allow us to better answer the question, "What should our classrooms look like and sound like?"

Figure 2.12 Instructional Leadership Conversations: Strategies for Review of Assessment Items

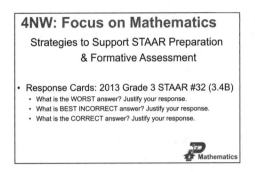

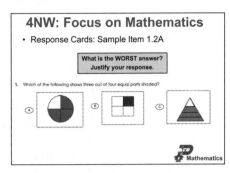

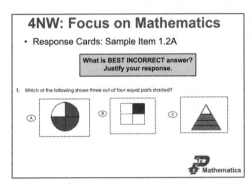

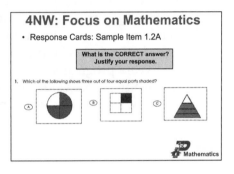

Figure 2.13 and Figure 2.14 Instructional Leadership Conversations: Bell Ringer Bunco

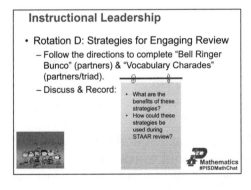

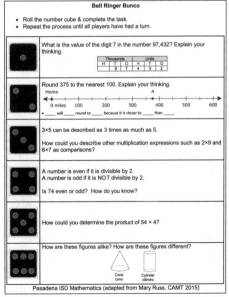

Our conversations focused on Math Workshop paralleled the conversations that were occurring during our district-wide book studies, which are described later in this chapter. When our budget allowed, we provided campus administrators with individual copies of resources to support our conversations such as Dr. Newton's *Guided Math in Action*.

During our meetings, we would examine sections of chapters and spend time debriefing the chapter's content through collaborative table and whole group conversations (see Figure 2.15). One of our early conversations included addressing the critical question, "What beliefs do we need to have about students and learning math?," as we needed to address our own perceptions about mathematics compared to the perceptions we wanted to share with our students (see Figure 2.16). We used the time together to "jigsaw" key points from a chapter, allowing the content to be divided among team members with each team member reading his/her section and then sharing the key points with his/her colleagues.

As the years progressed, we continued devoting a portion of our time together to reading from valuable resources such as Dr. Newton's *Math Workshop in Action*, which allowed key terms and language to become commonplace

Figure 2.15 and Figure 2.16 Instructional Leadership Conversations: *Guided Math in Action*

© *Pasadena Independent School District 2017*

in our conversations about mathematics (see Figure 2.17 and Figure 2.18). Our language about Math Workshop, guided math, and workstations was aligning across our 36 campuses and our "look fors" during mathematics instruction were becoming clearer through our collaborative conversations.

With time we've begun to add additional resources into our conversations, most recently being NCTM's *Principles to Actions* (see Figure 2.19). Our conversations about Math Workshop haven't been put aside, but because of our purposeful and continued discussions over several years, we now had a common language about Math Workshop and we're ready to expand our toolboxes with common language about other critical components of mathematics instruction.

Figure 2.17 and Figure 2.18 Instructional Leadership Conversations: *Math Workshop in Action*

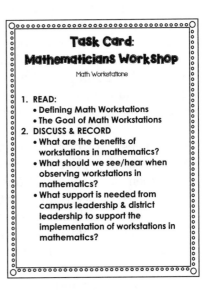

Instructional Leadership

- Rotation A: *Math Workshop in Action*
  - Divide/Jigsaw & Read "Guided Math Groups"
  - Debrief the key ideas from your section
  - Discuss & Record:
    - What are two key points that resonate with your table group?

Mathematics
#PISDMathChat

Task Card:
Mathematicians Workshop
Math Workstations

1. **READ:**
   - Defining Math Workstations
   - The Goal of Math Workstations
2. **DISCUSS & RECORD**
   - What are the benefits of workstations in mathematics?
   - What should we see/hear when observing workstations in mathematics?
   - What support is needed from campus leadership & district leadership to support the implementation of workstations in mathematics?

© *Pasadena Independent School District 2017*

Figure 2.19 Instructional Leadership Conversations: NCTM *Principles to Action*

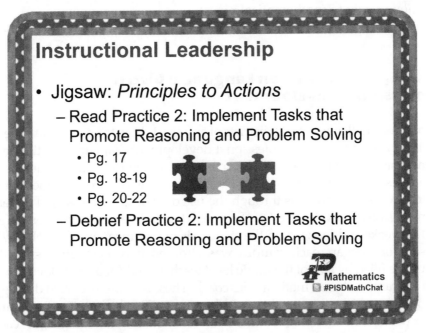

Instructional Leadership

- Jigsaw: *Principles to Actions*
  - Read Practice 2: Implement Tasks that Promote Reasoning and Problem Solving
    - Pg. 17
    - Pg. 18-19
    - Pg. 20-22
  - Debrief Practice 2: Implement Tasks that Promote Reasoning and Problem Solving

Mathematics
#PISDMathChat

© *Pasadena Independent School District 2017*

It is not uncommon to come across elementary campuses where the campus administrators, campus coaches, and classroom teachers have a large repertoire of strategies related to reading instruction and a common belief that all students should be successful readers while having a smaller repertoire of strategies related to mathematics and a sometimes diminished belief that all students can be successful mathematicians. In our district, these patterns were not uncommon either. We had to be purposeful in changing mindsets about what mathematics instruction should look like and sound like and providing opportunities for all stakeholders to develop a common language regarding mathematics instruction in order to support the implementation of the mathematics curriculum.

> As a result of our conversations during our Instructional Leadership meetings, I've been more focused during walkthroughs on the mathematical conversations taking place in the classroom. Since the work we've been doing with Dr. Newton, our math conversations have been much more focused on the process rather than the answer. Students are able to intelligently discuss multiple ways to solve problems. It's less about the answer and more about divergent thinking.
>
> The conversations have helped me as an administrator because I gain a deeper understanding of what "high quality" math instruction looks like. After our conversations, I'm able to compare my new vision of "high quality" math instruction to what is going on at my school. I can focus on what next steps we need to take to help us move closer to mathematical nirvana.
>
> Campus Administrator

Developing a Common Language: District Professional Development

A common challenge among districts of any size is how to ensure that all teachers have access to timely professional development that supports the implementation of the standards in the scope and sequence. With 35 elementary campuses and over 1,100 elementary teachers, this challenge is one that our district worked to address through the use of "Focus" professional development sessions. These "Focus" professional development sessions were offered each 9-weeks and focused on the standards in the upcoming 9-weeks. When these efforts began, each campus was afforded two registration spots that would be filled by two of the grade level teachers and/or a grade level teacher and the campus-based mathematics coach. These sessions occurred during the school day, which warranted the need for up to 70 substitute teachers amidst other possible needs for substitutes based on district meetings and/or teacher absences. Each participant was provided with electronic access to the handout materials, as well as the PowerPoint that was used to facilitate the session.

The goal was that each team of attendees would take the materials explored during the professional development session and share the instructional strategies and materials with the teachers on their team at their home campus. This "trainer of trainer" approach was created to include all teachers in the conversations, as it was not possible to provide all 200+ grade level teachers with a substitute for the sessions' conversations. To address the circumstances that would arise such as a campus having zero participants due to an unexpected teacher illness, a campus event such as a field trip, or a substitute's cancelation, attempts were made to repeat the sessions on Saturdays and to record audio files of the conversations to share with teachers.

With time and due to the need to address constraints related to available monies to provide substitutes and the desire to ensure that all teachers had firsthand opportunities to engage in the professional development conversations, a new structure was created for the "Focus" professional development sessions. Dates for professional development were added to the district's calendar and the "Focus" professional development sessions moved from during the school day to the district professional development dates. This change would allow every teacher to attend each 9-week's "Focus" session. The efforts were only possible with the assistance of our campus-based mathematics coaches. To meet these needs, we utilize ten of our campus-based coaches as "Master Trainers" (see Figure 2.20) to work

Figure 2.20 Team of Master Trainers

© *Pasadena Independent School District 2017*

in teams of two to prepare the upcoming 9-weeks "Focus" professional development for one of five grade levels: Kindergarten—Grade 4.

Our 36 campuses are divided into six groups with six campuses in each group (mostly by location), and each campus coach is assigned a grade level for which they will facilitate the "Focus" sessions for the current school year (see Figure 2.21). The ten "Master Trainers" prepare and facilitate a "trainer

Figure 2.21 Focus Professional Development: Campus Groups

2016-2017 Elementary Mathematics
Campus Assignments: Focus PD

Gardens: Kindergarten McMasters: Grade 1 LF Smith: Grade 2 Young: Grade 3 Williams: Grade 3 Morales: Grade 4	Richey: Kindergarten South Houston: Grade 1 Bailey: Grade 2 Pearl Hall: Grade 3 Red Bluff: Grade 3 Sparks: Grade 4	Parks: Kindergarten Kruse: Grade 1 Jessup: Grade 2 Pomeroy: Grade 3 South Shaver: Grade 4 Hancock: Grade 4
Turner: Kindergarten Frazier: Grade 1 Moore: Grade 2 Teague: Grade 2 Laura Bush: Grade 3 South Belt: Grade 4	Stuchbery: Kindergarten Jensen: Grade 1 Golden Acres: Grade 2 Meador: Grade 2 Atkinson: Grade 3 Genoa: Grade 4	Garfield: Kindergarten Burnett: Grade 1 Fisher: Grade 1 Mae Smythe: Grade 2 Freeman: Grade 3 Matthys: Grade 4

© *Pasadena Independent School District 2017*

of trainer" "Focus" session and support the remaining math coaches with their preparation for the upcoming session.

With the opportunity to have every one of our mathematics teachers participating in a common professional development experience, we've explored critical components of a Math Workshop environment as well as topics that are timely to current mathematics education research.

We utilize conversations at the start of the school year to revisit the purpose and components of Math Workshop, often using resources such as Dr. Nicki Newton's *Math Workshop in Action* to spur team conversations about using the start of the school year to establish classrooms as communities of learners (see Figure 2.22, Figure 2.23, and Figure 2.24).

We explore multiple ideas, strategies, and resources to support purposeful math routines that set the tone for the mathematics classroom.

The morning routine we establish sets the tone for the day.

Guided Math, Laney Sammons, p. 67

Examples of these math routines resources have included Estimation 180 (www.estimation180.com/; see Figure 2.25), SPLAT! (www.stevewyborney.

Figure 2.22 Focus Professional Development: Math Workshop Conversations

1NW Focus PD

- Goal: Create a Community of Learners
  - "In a numeracy-rich classroom culture, children are taught to be respectful, to honor everyone's thinking, and to encourage each other. They respect the risk-taking challenge. They feel that they are all on the same team, so they can ask each other questions, challenge each other's ideas, share their thinking, and defend their thoughts. The place that provides this sense of belonging is the math workshop." *(Guided Math in Action, pg. 17)*

1NW Focus PD

- Goal: Create a Community of Learners
  - View: With Math I Can
    https://www.amazon.com/gp/withmathican
  - Read: *Math Workshop in Action* (Newton)

1NW Focus PD

- Goal: Create a Community of Learners
  - Examine "Mathematicians Workshop Checklist - Environment"
  - Examine "1st 20 Days of Guided Math"

1NW Focus PD

- Goal: Create a Community of Learners
  - Campus Anchor Chart
    - What are the key characteristics of a community of learners in mathematics?
    - What would a visitor to a community of learners in mathematics see? hear?
    - What "next steps" are needed to establish communities of learners in our grade level?
  - Debrief: Next Steps

© *Pasadena Independent School District 2017*

com/?p=893; see Figure 2.26), and Which One Doesn't Belong? (http://wodb.ca/; see Figure 2.27).

We model the use of graphic organizers to organize thoughts and capture key ideas from conversations (see Figure 2.28).

We utilize video clips from our teachers' classrooms to allow teachers to see what components of Math Workshop look like across the grade levels and in both bilingual and non-bilingual classrooms (see Figure 2.29).

We use "end in mind planning" to examine sample assessment items for the upcoming standards and answer two of the four critical PLC questions, "What do we expect our students to know?" and "How will we know when they've learned it?" (see Figure 2.30).

We model the use of workstations to explore instructional activities that could be used during various components of Math Workshop (see Figure 2.31 and Figure 2.32).

We incorporate conversations that focus on the recently released research from Jo Boaler (see Figure 2.33 and Figure 2.34).

With each year of these new efforts, we've been intentional in the grade level assigned to each mathematics coach (see Figure 2.35). If a campus coach facilitated the Grade 3 "Focus" sessions during the first year, then the campus coach was likely assigned to facilitate the Kindergarten or Grade 1

Figure 2.23 Focus Professional Development: Math Workshop Reading Task

Math Workshop: A Community of Learners

Building a community of learners takes time. It is much more intensive than a traditional math classroom (see Figure 1.22). It is well worth the investment at the beginning of the year so that your students can thrive throughout the year. Your students must learn the importance of persevering through problem solving. They have to learn how to communicate with each other using math words. They need time to speak, listen, process, record, and learn. They need to learn how to model their thinking and show what they are talking about by using the tools appropriate to their grade. They also need to learn to "double, double check" their thinking and their work. Both national standards (CCSS, 2010) and state standards are promoting these processes and practices so that students know math deeply, and own it. A community of mathematical learners expects to have to explain, listen, question, justify, verify, expand upon, critique, model, defend, and show what they know. In order to scaffold this type of environment, you should use talk structures and language stems that promote listening intensely to the conversation at hand. The norm in your class should promote "intellectual risk taking" so that your students develop "mathematical argumentation, intellectual autonomy and mathematical power" (Hunter & Anthony, 2011).

Key Points
- Great mathematicians live in a respectful community
- Great mathematicians work together throughout workshop
- Great mathematicians persevere in problem solving
- Great mathematicians share their thinking and use math words
- Great mathematicians listen to each other and question each other
- Great mathematicians use tools
- Great mathematicians model their thinking and double check their work

---

Community

A group of people sharing the same space and following the same rules.

We are a community of mathematicians!

As a **community of mathematicians,** we need to:

Share our thinking.
Model our thinking.
Ask each other questions.
Prove what we are doing is correct!
Justify our thinking with examples.
Help each other.
Use our toolkits.
Make helpful comments to each other.

In Our Classroom

We respect each other.
We listen to each other.
We apologize.
We forgive.
We persist.
We help each other.
We encourage each other.
We laugh.
We get along well.
We are all good friends.

From *Math Workshop in Action* (Newton, 2016) pg. 1, 2, 16, 19

© *Pasadena Independent School District 2017*

"Focus" session the next year. Likewise, if a campus coach facilitated the Grade 1 "Focus" sessions during the first year, then the campus coach was likely assigned to facilitate the Grade 3 or Grade 4 "Focus" session the next year. These intentional efforts are based on the goal of building the vertical knowledge of each campus coach, allowing him/her to further deepen their knowledge of each grade level's standards and resources. While working with the standards in a grade level for which the campus coach did not have any teaching experience could be unsettling, our campus coaches have embraced the opportunity to grow and now anticipate shifting efforts between primary and intermediate grade levels.

Figure 2.24 Focus Professional Development: Math Workshop Checklist - Environment

Pasadena ISD: Mathematician's Workshop Checklist: Environment

	Observed	Not Observed	Comments
Whole Group Instruction			
There is a well-defined, clutter free area for large group instruction.			
Whole group area is being used for whole group instruction.			
Guided Math/Small Group Instruction			
There is a well-defined, clutter free area for small group instruction.			
Small group materials (including student records) are organized and at reach.			
There is a clear view from the small group table of the whole classroom, including all work stations.			
Small group area is being used for small group instruction.			
Work Stations			
Work Stations are accessible, clearly labeled, organized, and clutter free.			
Work Stations are being used to support instruction • Preview: Upcoming SE(s) • Spiral Review: Problem Solving & Operations • Spiral Review: Vocabulary • Spiral Review: Preview (SEs) • Number Sense (K-1) or Fact Fluency (2-4) • Technology			
Work Stations reflect the differentiated needs of students.			
Independent Work			
Independent work area is conducive to independent learning and teacher/student conferences.			
Independent work area is conducive to cooperative learning and student/peer conferences.			
Students have access to needed supplies (paper, pencils, etc.).			
Math Toolkits (Tools & Templates)			
Math tools (manipulatives) are accessible, clearly labeled, organized, and clutter free.			
Math tools (manipulatives) are being used to support instruction (preview, review,remediate,extend/enrich).			
Math tools (manipulatives) reflect the differentiated needs of students.			
Math templates are accessible, clearly labeled, organized, and clutter free.			
Math templates are being used to support instruction (preview, review,remediate,extend/enrich).			
Math templates reflect the differentiated needs of students.			
Wall Space			
Anchor charts are displayed, created with student input, and reflect the SEs currently being taught.			
Content word walls/word banks reflect grade level vocabulary and academic language.			
Student work is displayed and reflects the SEs currently being taught.			

© *Pasadena Independent School District 2017*

Figure 2.25, Figure 2.26 and Figure 2.27 Focus Professional Development: Math Routines

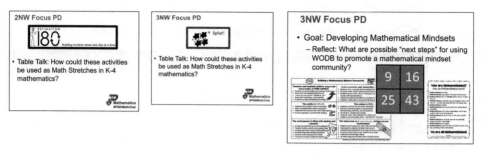

© *Pasadena Independent School District 2017*

Figure 2.28 Focus Professional Development: Graphic Organizers

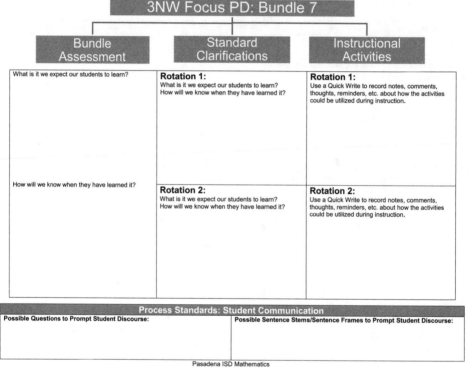

© *Pasadena Independent School District 2017*

Figure 2.29 Focus Professional Development: Classroom Videos

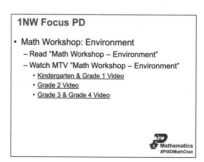

© *Pasadena Independent School District 2017*

Figure 2.30 Focus Professional Development: End in Mind Planning

1NW Focus PD

- The End in Mind: Bundles 1 & 2

PLC 1 "What is it we expect students to learn?"

PLC 2 "How will we know when they have learned it?"

    – Work in partners to examine the …

        • Bundles 1 & 2 Assessments

        • Bundles 1 & 2 Quick Checks

    (arrow: Divide & Conquer with an Elbow Partner)

    – Debrief as a campus team

    – Record responses in the graphic organizer

    – Large Group Debrief: Bundles 1 & 2

Mathematics
#PISDMathChat

Figure 2.31 Focus Professional Development: Task Card

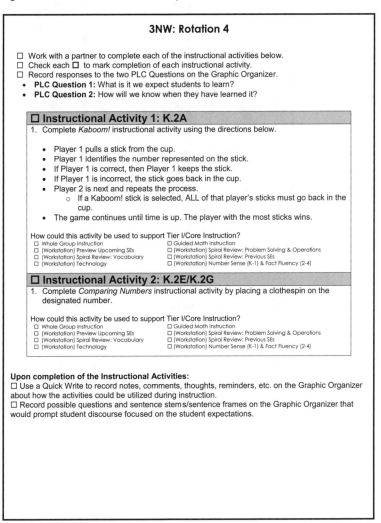

3NW: Rotation 4

☐ Work with a partner to complete each of the instructional activities below.
☐ Check each ☐ to mark completion of each instructional activity.
☐ Record responses to the two PLC Questions on the Graphic Organizer.
- **PLC Question 1:** What is it we expect students to learn?
- **PLC Question 2:** How will we know when they have learned it?

☐ Instructional Activity 1: K.2A

1. Complete *Kaboom!* instructional activity using the directions below.

- Player 1 pulls a stick from the cup.
- Player 1 identifies the number represented on the stick.
- If Player 1 is correct, then Player 1 keeps the stick.
- If Player 1 is incorrect, the stick goes back in the cup.
- Player 2 is next and repeats the process.
  - If a Kaboom! stick is selected, ALL of that player's sticks must go back in the cup.
- The game continues until time is up. The player with the most sticks wins.

How could this activity be used to support Tier I/Core Instruction?

☐ Whole Group Instruction	☐ Guided Math Instruction
☐ (Workstation) Preview Upcoming SEs	☐ (Workstation) Spiral Review: Problem Solving & Operations
☐ (Workstation) Spiral Review: Vocabulary	☐ (Workstation) Spiral Review: Previous SEs
☐ (Workstation) Technology	☐ (Workstation) Number Sense (K-1) & Fact Fluency (2-4)

☐ Instructional Activity 2: K.2E/K.2G

1. Complete *Comparing Numbers* instructional activity by placing a clothespin on the designated number.

How could this activity be used to support Tier I/Core Instruction?

☐ Whole Group Instruction	☐ Guided Math Instruction
☐ (Workstation) Preview Upcoming SEs	☐ (Workstation) Spiral Review: Problem Solving & Operations
☐ (Workstation) Spiral Review: Vocabulary	☐ (Workstation) Spiral Review: Previous SEs
☐ (Workstation) Technology	☐ (Workstation) Number Sense (K-1) & Fact Fluency (2-4)

Upon completion of the Instructional Activities:
☐ Use a Quick Write to record notes, comments, thoughts, reminders, etc. on the Graphic Organizer about how the activities could be utilized during instruction.
☐ Record possible questions and sentence stems/sentence frames on the Graphic Organizer that would prompt student discourse focused on the student expectations.

Figure 2.32 Focus Professional Development: Instructional Activity

Kaboom!

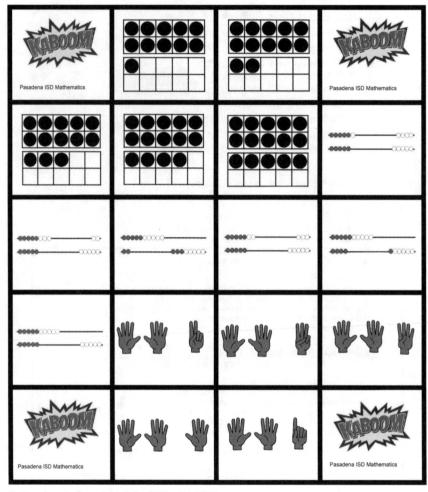

Figure 2.33 and Figure 2.34 Focus Professional Development Resources from Jo Boaler

2NW Focus PD

- Goal: Create a Math Workshop Community
  - Read: *Math Workshop in Action* (Newton)
  - View: How You Can Be Good at Math
    - https://youtu.be/saZrEGfGVlY
  - Examine: How do Mathematicians work?

The full length video can be found here: https://www.youtube.com/watch?v=3icoSeGgQtY

 Mathematics
#PISDMathChat

3NW Focus PD

- Revisit: Mathematical Mindsets
  - Watch "Maths: Everyone Can"
  - Read "When You Believe in Your Students They Do Better" (Jo Boaler)
  - Partner Debrief: What does this mean for our classrooms and our team planning conversations?

Mathematics
#PISDMathChat

Figure 2.35 Focus Professional Development: Grade Level Assignments

2017-2018 Focus PD Clusters (K-4 Mathematics)

Goals:
- Attend to Location/Proximity
- Balance Expertise/Experiences within each Cluster of MPFs
- Build Vertical Knowledge/Capacity of MPFs

Campus	Mathematics Peer Facilitator(s)	2015-2016	2016-2017	2017-2018
Group A				
Matthys	M. Banda	2	4	K
Bailey*	L. Roberts[MT]	3	2	1
Golden Acres	M. Esparza	NA	2	1
Fisher	D. Cruz[MT]	4	1	2
LF Smith	R. Guzman	4	2	3
South Houston	S. Contreras	3	1	4
Group B				
Bush	J. Kennedy	NA	3	K
Frazier*	A. Oquin	3	1	K
South Belt	R. Sanders	K	4	1
Atkinson	R. Whittaker	K	3	2
Moore	B. Mullen	1	2	3
Meador	C. Daumas[MT]	3	2	4
Group C				
Genoa	V. Rodriguez-August[MT]	1	4	K
Young	C. Pace[MT]	4	3	1
Stuchbery	S. Woodruff	4	K	2
Burnett	L. Baumann[MT]	2	1	3
Teague*	S. Hall	K	2	4
Turner	S. Brown	3	K	4
Group D				
Hancock	J. Ochoa	NA	4	K
Pearl Hall	R. Tice	K	3	1
Freeman*	P. Jordon	1	3	2
Jensen	B. Melendez	NA	1	2
Garfield	J. Saenz	4	K	3
Jessup	M. Rayford	1	2	4
Group E				
Pomeroy	P. Infante[MT]	1	3	K
Sparks	T. Lazenby	2	4	1
Mae Smythe	P. Fonseca	NA	NA	2
Parks*	A. Head	NA	NA	2
Gardens	N. Jimenez[MT]	2	K	3
McMasters	C. Lopez	K	1	4
Group F				
Williams	M. Watson	NA	3	K
Red Bluff	M. Gonzalez	NA	NA	1
Morales*	B. Martinez	NA	NA	1
South Shaver	A. Chavez[MT]	K	4	2
Kruse	J. Teague & J. Herrera	4	1	3
Richey	M. Breaux[MT]	2	K	4

*Host Campus for teams of Co-Facilitators

Master Trainers[MT]	Kindergarten	P. Infante	V. Rodriguez-August
	Grade 1	C. Pace	L. Roberts
	Grade 2	A. Chavez	D. Cruz
	Grade 3	N. Jimenez	L. Baumann
	Grade 4	M. Breaux	C. Daumas

© *Pasadena Independent School District 2017*

Facilitating professional development with multiple grade levels spanning the primary and intermediate grades has supported me in my growth as a math coach. When my district began these efforts, I was a bit apprehensive because I did not feel as though I had enough knowledge and experience to facilitate professional development in the primary grades. Through preparing for the professional development sessions in the primary grades, I have learned to provide better support for the primary teachers at my campus.

Mathematics Peer Facilitator

The opportunities to facilitate professional development for multiple grade levels have affected me in a positive way. As a mathematics coach, I embrace the growth mindset of learning as much as I can about each grade level in order to better support our teachers in our district. The preparation for each professional development session gives me a deeper understanding of the curriculum for the different grade levels.

Mathematics Peer Facilitator

As an instructional coach, I believe sometimes we feel more comfortable coaching grade levels where we have had the most experience. When I learned I would be delivering the focus training for a grade level outside of my "comfort zone," I was very apprehensive at first because I didn't feel I knew the grade level curriculum as well as I did others and I wanted to guide the teachers in the right direction. Having to prepare for the training and really dive into the instruction and activities each nine-weeks really helped me grow as an instructional coach because it pushed me to really understand the depth and complexity of that grade level curriculum whereas before I had not taken that extra step forward on my own. During our focus professional development sessions, everyone is definitely learning and growing together!

Mathematics Peer Facilitator

The most valuable aspect of serving as a Master Trainer has been the detailed planning that goes into the preparation for a three-hour training. As a result, I have become more organized and disciplined with time management.

Mathematics Peer Facilitator

The original structure of our "Focus" professional development allowed our campus coaches to attend sessions for multiple grade levels, providing opportunities for our campus coaches to develop their vertical knowledge of the standards and instructional resources. The new structure of our "Focus" professional development allows every teacher to participate in the conversations, though it prevents our campus coaches from attending sessions for multiple grade levels as they are now facilitating the conversations. With that in mind, we set aside 1 hour during the next monthly meeting with our campus

Figure 2.36 Focus Professional Development, Vertical Conversations

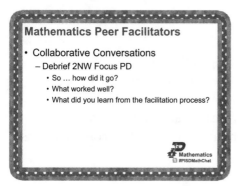

© *Pasadena Independent School District 2017*

coaches to allow the vertical teams of coaches to meet and debrief the sessions as well as share two key instructional activities from their grade level session (see Figure 2.36). These conversations encourage collaborative efforts among the team and allow the campus coaches the opportunity to explore "the best of the best" from each grade level's conversations.

The feedback from these efforts has been positive, as all teachers are now exposed to the "end in mind" conversations about the upcoming standards as well as the exploration of district-provided resources that will support the implementation of the standards.

> I really enjoyed having all of our team at the focus, so that everyone could hear the information at the same time. We were able to speak with teachers from different schools to get different ideas of how they teach certain TEKS.
>
> Grade 2 Teacher

> I think this plan, the whole team attending the focus, is the best plan. We were able to discuss it later since we all attended, having shared the experience.
>
> Grade 2 Teacher

Mathematics is its own language. Learning a new language involves knowing how to speak the language, read the language, write using the language, and understand the spoken language. Learning a new language takes time. Teaching mathematics requires developing a common understanding of mathematical terms and how the terms are used in order to plan effective, standards-based instruction. In order to develop a common language about mathematics and mathematics instruction, purposeful efforts must be made to equip all stakeholders with tools and experiences that develop proficiency with the language.

Lessons Learned

- Change takes time. Systemic change takes time.
- Building a common language occurs through products and processes.
- Having shared knowledge is critical to any change process.
- Focus professional development and collaborative conversations on core components.
- Revisit core components on a continual basis and over time.

Getting Started Checklist

- Articulate the vision and goals for mathematics instruction and mathematics classrooms.
- Determine the needs to support the implementation of the vision and goals.
- Devise an action plan that uses products such as curriculum documents and processes such as district-wide professional development that support the development of a common language.
- Commit to the process and to the time it will take to facilitate change.

Key Points

- Change takes time.
- Develop a common language.
- Build shared knowledge.
- Focus on core components and consistent conversations.
- Persistence is key.
- Learn together.

Summary

Change takes time, though when it comes to our students there is no time to waste when considering how we ensure that mathematics is accessible to our students. With that in mind, we must be intentional and purposeful with the structures we advocate for, the resources we provide, and the professional learning opportunities we facilitate. We must build shared knowledge so that we have a common language and understanding regarding what mathematics instruction should look like and sound like. We must keep critical conversations at the forefront of all discussions so that common, core messages are reinforced and expectations are clear and consistent. Mathematicians learn and grow together; therefore, it is imperative that we provide products and processes to support these efforts.

Reflective Questions

- Do the curriculum documents being used in your district provide adequate resources to help teachers accurately determine what students should know and be able to do? If not, what resources are needed to support teachers with these efforts?
- Do the professional development opportunities being facilitated in your district support teachers in their efforts to build shared, common knowledge about what mathematics instruction should look like and sound like? If not, what are the missing opportunities and how can you make arrangements to facilitate these learning opportunities?

Resources

- *Guided Math* (Laney Sammons)
- *Guided Math in Action* (Nicki Newton)
- *Math Workshop in Action* (Nicki Newton)
- *Math Running Records in Action* (Nicki Newton)
- *Mathematical Mindsets* (Jo Boaler)
- *Learning by Doing* (DuFour, DuFour, Eaker, Many, Mattos)
- CCSS (Common Core State Standards)
- TEKS (Texas Essential Knowledge and Skills)
- *Learning to "friendly argue" in a community of mathematical inquiry* (Roberta Hunter & Glenda Anthony)

3

Mathematizing Your District

Building on Shared Knowledge

Janet Nuzzie is the district instructional specialist for kindergarten through fourth grade mathematics in Pasadena ISD (TX). Her school district has over 55,000 students with 78% of the students being economically disadvantaged. The student population is 83% Hispanic, 8% African American, 6% White, and 3% Asian. Janet has over 23 years of experience in education which includes serving seven years at the district level as an instructional specialist for elementary mathematics, nine years at the regional level as an education specialist for elementary mathematics, and seven years at the classroom level as a fourth-grade teacher. Her synergistic efforts include serving as the president of TASM (an organization of mathematics supervisors in Texas), serving as vice-president (elementary) of TCTM (an organization of mathematics teachers in Texas), serving on numerous mathematics committees at the state and national level, and presenting over 90 mathematics conference sessions at the regional, state, and national level. (Connect with Janet on Twitter: @janetdnuzzie)

Introduction

> *Mathematicians learn and grow together.*
>
> —Janet Nuzzie

Lifelong learners. It's what we want all of our students to become. We want to see our students recognize the value of learning, the power of individual and collective growth, the satisfaction from overcoming challenges, and the awareness that all of these outcomes are the result of choosing growth over remaining stagnant. The same goals hold true for us as educators. We must be lifelong learners. We must recognize the value of learning more about effective mathematics instruction, the power that individual and collective growth can make when working to meet the diverse needs of OUR young mathematicians, the satisfaction that comes from developing a sense of efficacy in our students about their mathematical knowledge and abilities in mathematics, and the impact that our actions that model lifelong learning have on our students. The text that follows shares the journey our district has made . . . a journey to provide opportunities for all of our educators to be lifelong learners about mathematics and mathematics education and share their knowledge with others.

Building on Shared Knowledge: Book Studies

Mathematicians learn and grow together. This phrase has been used over the course of the past few years as we've highlighted the work occurring at our campuses. The phrase is very intentional because it draws attention to the fact that mathematicians are always learning and growing, and just like our students, we need to always be learning and growing as educators of mathematics. The phrase also draws attention to the fact that mathematicians learn together, and just like our students, we need to make efforts to learn together with our colleagues on our grade level teams, across grade level teams at our campuses, and across campuses in a district. One person cannot know everything, but together we can build a shared knowledge that will help us work as a team in meeting the individualized and unique needs of each student.

To provide opportunities for the teachers, coaches, and administrators within our district to build our individual and collective expertise regarding best practices for our students in mathematics, we had to be intentional with the professional development that we offered. In addition to numerous after-school professional development offerings, we began the facilitation of district-wide book studies in order to build common knowledge and a common language about mathematics instruction (see Figure 3.1).

One of the first book studies we facilitated was focused on Laney Sammons' resource, *Guided Math*, a resource that had been shared at a regional meeting that several of our campus administrators had attended. The campus administrators returned buzzing about this new term "guided math" and wanted our teachers to start doing "guided math," though the term

Figure 3.1 Details of District-Wide Book Studies

From Mathematics Class to ... Mathematician's Workshop

- Book Studies: "Trainer of Trainer" Model
  - One-hour sessions after-school
  - Representatives from each campus are invited
  - Each participant receives a copy of the book
  - Reading assignments are to be completed before each session
  - PPT/Handouts are provided for campus turnaround conversations

© *Pasadena Independent School District 2017*

was new to most folks within the district. We had an interest in learning more about mathematics instruction and a tool to support the efforts, and together these two pieces led us to our first district-wide book study. We encouraged our 35 campuses to register a vertical team of three to participate in the study: a teacher from Grades K–2, a teacher from Grades 3–4, and the campus coach. Each participant was provided a personal copy of the resource and any additional or leftover spaces were given to teachers on a waiting list. We met after school eight times over the course of the school year with each meeting being from 3:45–4:45.

Participants were expected to complete a reading assignment before the start of each session, as these reading assignments were the basis of the book study conversations. During our after-school meetings, each participant was provided with some sort of a note taker with prompts or tasks to complete as a campus team (see Figure 3.2). The goal was for each campus team to reflect on the content of what was read, discuss reflections and questions together as a team, determine key points from each chapter, and use the answers from the team conversations to facilitate campus turn-around conversations. In this first book study, we sent a document to the participants before each meeting

Figure 3.2 Recording Sheet from *Guided Math* Book Study

<u>**Guided Math for the Mathematics Classroom – Week 3 Reflections (Individual)**</u>
11.27.12 Orozco 101ABCD 3:45-4:45

1. "The morning routine we establish sets the tone for the day." (pg 67) – What are your thoughts on this quote (as it relates to the start of your mathematics class/instruction) and what kind of tone is set by the morning/starting routines in your mathematics classroom?

2. What are 3-5 resources/tools commonly used in your classroom/at your campus to start each mathematics class? How do these compare to the different types of "math stretches" (data collection and analysis, number of the day, what's next, how was math used, makes me think of) described in pg. 69-85?

Resources/Tools Commonly Used to Start Each Math Class	How are these similar to/different from "math stretches" to start each math class?

3. How do the "Problems of the Day" described in pg. 100-101 compare to the "Problems of the Day" used in your classroom/campus classrooms? What are the strengths of the sample POTD listed on pg. 101?

© *Pasadena Independent School District 2017*

with questions that needed to be answered individually before the upcoming meeting. These questions and the participants' individual responses would serve as a catalyst for team conversations during the book study meeting.

During our first meeting, we asked each campus to put dot stickers next to the top three areas for growth or topics that presented challenges for our current practices. The feedback was captured in the pictures below (see Figure 3.3) and represents that we were in fact heading in the right direction, as we had areas of identified needs and many commonalities among the areas.

The goal of the book study was not only for the book study participants to learn and grow together; the goal was for the book study participants to

Figure 3.3 Example of Dot Sticker Data

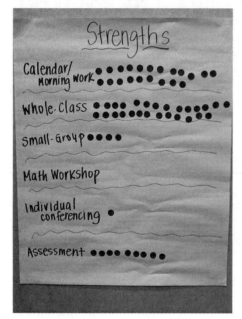
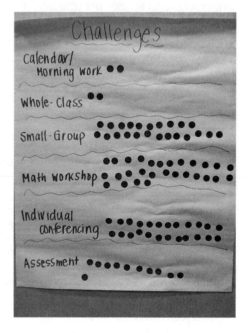

take what was learned and share the information back at their home campuses. With a district our size, the only way for a common message to be shared is to provide tools and structures for the conversations and encourage administrative support of the conversations during campus meetings.

With that in mind, a PowerPoint was used to facilitate each session's conversations and after each session, a PowerPoint was provided to each participant for use during campus turn-around conversations (see Figure 3.4). The goal was for the participants to take the notes from a chapter's discussion and enter the team's key points or takeaways into the presentation for campus conversations. With the varying backgrounds of so many teachers, we relied on the teacher teams to draw out the points that were critical to the learning but even more so, critical to the needs of their campus.

Figure 3.4 Examples of Book Study Slides (Team Conversations and Campus Turn-Around Conversations)

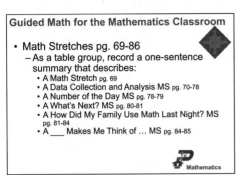
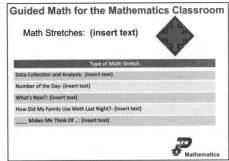

© *Pasadena Independent School District 2017*

We utilized these team conversations and the turn-around conversations that we encouraged at each campus to start building our shared knowledge about this term "guided math" that was new to so many of us. Because of these efforts, we started to develop a common language about mathematics instruction across grade levels and across campuses and started reframing what we hoped to see and hear in our mathematics classrooms.

> The book study gave me an opportunity to explore deeper into how Math Workshop would benefit the students in my classroom. It helped me build an environment where I could start implementing ideas of Math Workshop, like having a designated whole group area, small group area, and meaningful workstations.
>
> Grade 3 Teacher

It would be wonderful if we could say that every campus participated in the book study, that every participating campus facilitated turn-around conversations, that the message was communicated to all 1,100 of our elementary mathematics teachers, and that we were all able to start the next school year facilitating guided math like we had read in our resource. Yes, this would have been wonderful. But, just as we know that the needs of each student vary and that students learn in different ways and at a different pace from each other, it became evident that there were many parallels to professional learning.

Just because we had "taught it" didn't mean that everyone "got it," and we had to use our anecdotal data and formative assessment data to determine that we needed to take additional steps to build common knowledge and a common language about mathematics instruction across the campuses. While we continued to provide professional development sessions after school and during the summer, it became evident that we needed to be intentional in continuing our book study efforts and use resources provided by knowledgeable experts in the field to guide our conversations. And so the next book study began.

The next school year we offered a district-wide book study focused on a resource recommended by other colleagues in the field, *Math Misconceptions* by Honi J. Bamberger and Karen Schultz-Ferrell. Again, we advocated for a vertical team of teachers to attend from each campus: a teacher from Grades K–2 and a teacher from Grades 3–4. Again, we provided copies of the resource to each participant, along with the accompanying grade level book, and communicated the reading assignments and classroom activities that needed to be completed before each book study meeting (see Figure 3.5).

This book study presented numerous opportunities for the vertical teams to interact with content from other grade levels and collectively explore the reasons behind common misconceptions that students have about mathematics concepts and/or skills. We provided the PowerPoint from each session to the book study participants, though we didn't place a huge emphasis on campus turn-around conversations. There were many "a-ha" moments focused on the "what" of our student expectations, though it became evident that we still needed to develop our common language and common vocabulary regarding the "how" we needed to structure mathematics instruction to meet the depth and complexity of our student expectations. We made arrangements to facilitate a district-wide book study again the next year, though returning to the focus on guided math.

Our third district-wide book study focused on Dr. Nicki Newton's resource, *Guided Math in Action*. Again we encouraged each campus to participate by registering a vertical team of participants: a teacher from Grades K–2, a teacher from Grades 3–4, and the mathematics coach. We met for 1 hour after school eight times over the course of the school year. Participants were expected to read an assigned chapter before each meeting, and we would frame our conversations around the content of each chapter. Sometimes we used recording sheets to capture important points from a chapter (see Figure 3.6), and other times we relied on prompts to guide campus conversations (see Figure 3.7). As with earlier book studies, we provided each participant with the PowerPoint used to facilitate the book study conversation and encouraged campus turn-around conversations focused on key points from the chapter (see Figure 3.8). We were adding to our earlier knowledge about guided math and using the lessons learned to better delineate how we should structure the various components in a Math Workshop environment.

> Participating in a book study focusing on Nicki Newton's Guided Math in Action helped me in my growth as a teacher and coach with regards to how to facilitate meaningful small group math instruction where students are able to verbalize their misconceptions in a safe environment. The book study further supported my development in learning how to support mathematics instruction through a Math Workshop model by giving real-world examples of what a successful math environment embodies. Facilitating turn-around conversations at my campus supported the implementation of Math Workshop

Figure 3.5 Example Agenda from *Math Misconceptions* Book Study

Pasadena ISD, Grades Kindergarten – Grade 4 Mathematics
2013-2014 Math Misconceptions Book Study

Date	Reading Assignment (to be read before date)	Classroom Assignment (to be completed before the next date)
09.25.13	Due: 09.25 Grades K-2 & Grades 3-4 • Foreword v-vii • Introduction xi-xiv • Chapter 1 pg. 1-20 (Number and Addition/Subtraction)	Due: 10.23 Kindergarten • Back & Forth pg. 4-5 Grade 1 • Use Dominoes to Solve Story Problems pg. 7 Grade 2 • Make 100 pg. 14-15 Due: 10.23 Grade 3 • There's More Than One Way to Add! pg. 13 Grade 4 • Count Up & Back to Get Sums and Differences pg. 12 • There's More Than One Way to Add! pg. 13
10.23.13	Due: 10.23 Grades K-2: • Chapter 1 pg. 34-40 (Understanding Fractions) • Chapter 4 pg. 108-121 (Reading an Analog Clock & Determining the Value of Coins) Grades 3-4 • Chapter 1 pg. 20-34 (Multiplication & Division) • Chapter 1 pg. 43-48 (Decimals)	Due: 11.20 Kindergarten • Fair Shares or Equal Parts pg. 26 Grade 1 • Fair Shares pg. 27 • Complete the Clock pg. 86 Grade 2 • How Many in a Dollar? pg. 93 • 10 Dimes pg. 94 Due: 11.20 Grade 3 • Count Up & Back to Get Sums and Differences pg. 12 • Different Ways to Multiply (2×1) pg. 24 Grade 4 • Racing to 4! pg. 41 (*two 0-9 spinners)
11.20.13	Due: 11.20 Grades K-2 & Grades 3-4: • Chapter 2 pg. 49-77 (Algebra)	Due: 01.22 Kindergarten • Representations of 5 pg. 59 Grade 1 • How Many Toes? pg. 58 Grade 2 • Mystery Number Squares pg. 46 • The Mystery of the Missing Words pg. 53 Due: 01.22 Grades 3-4 • Algebra Challenge pg. 57 • Math Equations pg. 60
01.22.14	Due: 01.22 Grades K-2 & Grades 3-4: • Chapter 3 pg. 78-88, 95-107 (Geometry)	Due: 02.19 Kindergarten • Draw What You Saw pg. 82 • What to Do Bullet 3 & 5 pg. 64 Grade 1 • Try, Try Again! pg. 83 • What to Do Bullet 3 & 5 pg. 64 Grade 2 • Using a Geoboard to Create Polygons pg. 63 • What to Do Bullet 3 & 5 pg. 64 Due: 02.19 Grades 3-4 • Categorizing Quadrilaterals pg. 67 • Logical Reasoning with Nonsense Figures pg. 69 • View and Build pg. 88
02.19.14	Due: 02.19 Grades K-2: • Chapter 4 pg. 121-127 (Measurement Units) • Chapter 5 pg. 137-142 (Sorting & Classifying) Due: 02.19 Grades 3-4 • Chapter 4 pg. 121-127 (Measurement Units) • Chapter 4 pg. 127-136 (Area & Perimeter & Conversions)	Due: 03.19 Kindergarten – Grade 2 • "What to Do" Bullet 1 pg. 95 • Sorting Storybooks pg. 113-114 Due: 03.19 Grade 3 • Area and Perimeter in My World pg. 105 Grade 4 • Figuring Out Different Ways to Show Liquid Measure pg. 107
03.19.14	Due: 03.19 Grades K-2 & Grades 3-4: • Chapter 5 pg. 142-147, 152-158 (Displays of Data & Analyzing Data) • Chapter 6 pg. 164-171 (Assessment)	Due: Personal Learning Kindergarten – Grade 4 • Open-Ended Questioning • Diagnostic Interviews

Figure 3.6 Example of Note Taker from *Guided Math in Action* Book Study

Guided Math in Action
Chapter 2: Guided Math in a Numerate Environment

Elements of a Math Workshop	What & Why
Calendar/Morning Routines _____	What: Why:
Daily Word Problem/ Vocabulary Review _____	What: Why:
Whole-Class Mini-Lesson _____	What: Why:
Rotations/Student Math Centers _____	What: Why:
Share _____	What: Why:

Figure 3.7 Example of Discussion Prompts from *Guided Math in Action* Book Study

Guided Math in Action

- ## What are your thoughts regarding these quotes from Chapter 4?
  - "...when a teachers tries to teach something to the entire class at the same time, chances are, one-third of the kids already know it; one-third will get it; and the remaining third won't. So two-thirds of the children are wasting their time." pg. 41
  - "By the end of every week, the teacher should have connected with every student in some form or another, possibly through small-group work, conferencing, or math interviews." pg. 41

 Mathematics

© Pasadena Independent School District 2017

Figure 3.8 Examples of Book Study Slides (Team Conversations and Campus Turn-Around Conversations)

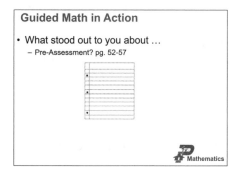

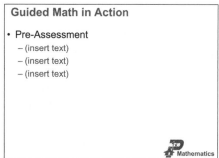

© Pasadena Independent School District 2017

because educators were more open to taking a new approach to creating a math-rich environment and also became interested in reading Dr. Newton's *Guided Math in Action* for themselves.

Grade 1 Teacher

The book study allowed me to so see examples of how Math Workshop can be designed to support guided math. It also made me realize how important using guided math is, in order to meet the needs of all my students. Participating in the book study taught me different ways to group my students and the importance on making those groups flexible in order to get the full benefit for my students. It also taught me how to arrange my Math Workshop to support teaching using guided math on a daily basis. I was able to meet with my team each week to discuss what I had learned during the book study. It allowed us to work together as a team to design our math schedule to support teaching using guided math. We worked together to form groups and also developed activities to use as stations to review skills based on the student's needs.

Grade 4 Teacher

When I first started teaching, math was taught in a very traditional setting. The teacher stood in front of the class, introduced the lesson, and the expectations were the same for everyone. Students transferred their learning during independent practice hoping everyone "got it" and we all moved on. This was the one size fits all model. Later, a book study "Guided Math" began at my campus and it was then that we understood the importance of teaching math in small groups. Small group teaching allows us teachers the opportunity to differentiate the instruction and target skills at students' individual needs. Likewise, it empowers students to build self-confidence and take risks on their learning. Guided Math is the structured math that both teacher and student can learn and benefit best from.

Grade 3 Teacher

Our fourth district-wide book focused on Dr. Nicki Newton's resource *Math Workshop in Action* (see Figure 3.9). We encouraged all of our campuses to participate and we encouraged registration as a vertical team: a teacher from Grades K–2, a teacher from Grades 3–4, and the mathematics coach. We met six times after school for an hour. We provided various tools to support campus turn-around conversations including a copy of the resource, graphic organizers, card sorts (see Figure 3.10), and the PowerPoint used to facilitate the book study conversations.

This book study helped me gain a better understanding of what the Math Workshop should look like from start to finish. This book study also helped me teach my students Math Workshop guidelines and expectations. Together, we created an anchor chart about what Math Workshop looks like, sounds like, the student's job, and teacher's job. By creating this anchor chart together, the students took ownership and gained a deeper understanding of the Math Workshop, guidelines and expectations. It was also a great reference tool for students while they were in workstations.

Grade 2 Teacher

Our fifth district-wide book study focused on Dr. Nicki Newton's resource *Math Running Records in Action*. We encouraged all of our campuses to participate, though we only offered one registration per campus as we wanted to focus these book study conversations with teachers in Grades

Figure 3.9 Example Agenda from *Math Workshop in Action* Book Study

Trainer of Trainers
Math Workshop in Action

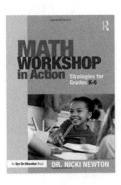

09.23.15 Book Study Week 1
Due: Chapter 1

10.21.15 Book Study Week 2
Due: Chapters 2 & 3

11.18.15 Book Study Week 3
Due: Chapters 4 & 5

01.13.16 Book Study Week 4
Due: Chapter 6

02.10.16 Book Study Week 5
Due: Chapters 7 & 8

03.09.16 Book Study Week 6
Due: Chapter 9

Figure 3.10 Example Card Sort from *Math Workshop in Action* Book Study

Math Workshop in Action

Traditional Classroom	Math Workshop Classroom

Everybody talks, the teacher encourages students to comment on the mathematical thinking of others (child to child talk; teacher to child talk; child to teacher to child talk)

Varied teaching formats: direct instruction, videos, interactive lectures, discussion, small groups

Text is one of many resources; texts could even be main resource, but other supplementary resources are pulled in to address the different needs, learning styles, and interests of all the students; some schools use teacher-created curricula rather than a standard textbook

Focus is on sense-making, differentiation, student-driven, standards-oriented fidelity to the developmental process of learning math

© *Pasadena Independent School District 2017*

2–4. We met five times after school for an hour, and our topics included an overview of running records and the tools and resources to support administering running records with the four operations: addition, subtraction, multiplication, and division. We provided various tools to support campus turn-around conversations including a copy of the resource, graphic organizers, and the PowerPoint used to facilitate the book study conversations. We increased our communication regarding our expectations for campus turn-around conversations by emailing the time frames during which we encouraged timely turn-around conversations (see Figure 3.11).

We were in our fourth year of encouraging the use of Twitter to share what mathematics conversations looked like at the campuses, and we started to see more and more tweets regarding the campus turn-around conversations (see Figure 3.12, Figure 3.13, and Figure 3.14). We retweeted each tweet (see Figure 3.15 and Figure 3.16) and posted each tweet on our Facebook page and made sure to include Dr. Newton in the text.

> This study enabled me to apply running records in my classroom and has made me aware of a student's understanding of number sense or lack of number sense. Additionally, I have been able to facilitate campus trainings to promote and encourage number sense in teachers classrooms.
>
> Grade 4 Teacher

Figure 3.11 Example of Campus Communication Regarding Book Studies

Janet Nuzzie

From:	Janet Nuzzie
Sent:	Thursday, January 26, 2017 10:45 AM
To:	_Elementary Principals; _Elementary Assistant Principals
Cc:	Toni Lopez; Scott Harrell; Cindy Garcia
Subject:	Follow-Up: Session 4 (Math Running Records in Action)

Good Morning, Campus Administrators!

We had a great afternoon of collaborative learning at yesterday's Session 4 of the *Math Running Records in Action* book study focused on multiplication running records!

As a follow-up to these conversations, we are encouraging all participants (see the list below) to request 10-15 minutes of a campus meeting to share the "key points" from Chapters 9-11 with all teachers (particularly Grades 2-4 Mathematics Teachers) so that we can develop shared knowledge across the campuses this year about a possible district-wide initiative next year. We appreciate your support in carving out some time between now and 02.21.17 for these folks to share their findings with your campus mathematics teachers. Each participant has access to a PPT, draft running record, and foldable to facilitate these efforts ... so the needed tools have been provided!

We enjoyed seeing pictures of these conversations in action! We've seen pictures from at least 7 campus' conversations thus far ... and we hope to hear about these efforts at all of the campuses! We hope that you will join the efforts in sharing what the mathematics conversations at your campus look like! (Tweet a picture with the hashtag #PISDMathChat!)

Figure 3.12, Figure 3.13, and Figure 3.14 Tweets from Campus Turn-Around Conversations

Figure 3.15 and Figure 3.16 Re-Tweets from Campus Turn-Around Conversations

PISD Mathematics
@PISDMathematics

#Mathematicians learn and grow together ... and learn about running records in #mathematics! (Hancock ES) #PISDMathChat @drnickimath

Jackie Ochoa @JmochoaOchoa
Presenting math running records in action!! Finally! #pisdmathchat

5:36 PM - 8 Dec 2016

PISD Mathematics
@PISDMathematics

#Mathematicians learn & grow together ... and learn about running records in #mathematics! (Turner ES) #PISDMathChat @drnickimath

Sharon Brown @skbrown3906
Learning & Growing together. Math running records - addition and subtraction. #PISDMATHCHAT #dmickinewton

5:24 PM - 12 Jan 2017

I learned how to complete and administer math running records. I also learned how to take the information and align specific differentiated material for my students. I learned that I can learn more in depth where my students are and how I can further their learning by starting with basic facts. It still shocks me to see how much a math running record can tell so much on how your students use strategies to answer questions. It's a great tool to have and use to make your instruction more beneficial!

Grade 4 Teacher

Our sixth district-wide book study that we offered was Jo Boaler's *Mathematical Mindsets*. We facilitated this book study during the summer months (see Figure 3.17) through a Twitter slow chat and offered the book study to a limited number of participants.

Each participant was provided with a copy of the resource and expected to read one chapter each week over the course of the 9-weeks. Two to three prompts that were related to the assigned chapter were tweeted every Monday morning, and participants were expected to respond to the two to three prompts as well as respond to the tweets of at least two other colleagues each week during the book study (see Figure 3.18 and Figure 3.19).

Facilitating a book study on Jo Boaler's *Mathematical Mindsets* led to several discussions in which a shift in teachers' thinking about their approach to teaching mathematics at our campus was evident. Her research-based strategies for teaching mathematics facilitate a love for learning math versus a dread of it, for students as well as teachers.

Mathematics Peer Facilitator

Participating in the *Mathematical Mindsets* book study gave me a platform to share my thoughts and excitement about math. The mathematical thoughts and ideas of others are tinged with their varied experiences; they're an open door for a rich narrative about long-held practices and beliefs and how those compare to what studies say about math ability. As a math coach it has planted the seed that everyone can learn math which is helpful and inspirational when I'm working with students who have struggled with math for years because they have come to believe that they cannot learn math.

Mathematics Peer Facilitator

The flexibility of being able to interact with other colleagues from any location and at any time during the day was a definite advantage of facilitating a book study in this manner. The short, reflective prompts also made the weekly time commitment manageable.

During these consecutive years of encouraging participation from vertical teams of teachers in district-wide book studies and encouraging

Figure 3.17 Example Agenda from *Mathematical Mindsets* Twitter Chat Book Study

PISD Twitter Slow Chat #PISDMathChat

Reading Assignments

• 06.05–06.11: Chapter 1	• 07.10–07.16: Chapter 6
• 06.12–06.18: Chapter 2	• 07.17–07.23: Chapter 7
• 06.19–06.25: Chapter 3	• 07.24–07.30: Chapter 8
• 06.26–07.02: Chapter 4	• 07.31–08.06: Chapter 9
• 07.03–07.09: Chapter 5	

What is a Twitter Slow Chat?

- A Twitter slow chat is a week-long chat (Monday-Sunday) focused on a specific topic/task. A slow chat book study happens online but does not require the participants to be online at a specific or specified time. Rather, those participating can share ideas and respond to others' thoughts when it is conducive to them or as time allows within their schedules during the time window specified. The goal is to encourage dialogue, allow for meaningful conversations to gradually emerge, and maximize community participation.
- We will use the Twitter hashtag #PISDMathChat to share and follow the comments of others. Once you log into Twitter, search for hashtag #PISDMathChat. Be sure to include this hashtag when you post your ideas, thoughts, comments or responses, so others can follow along and find your comments easily. Click here for a short video on how to use hashtags on twitter if needed.
- Course credit (9 CPE hours) will be granted upon completion of each week's tasks within the designated timeframes.
  - Read the assigned chapter of Mathematical Mindsets
  - Tweet responses to the questions posted on the Monday of each week
  - Respond to at least 2-3 tweets from other participants in order to share ideas/network about the content

Book Study Participants:

M. Breaux	S. Brown
S. Benavides	N. Smith
K. Jernigan	S. Redwine
J. Wedgeworth	S. Grounds
B. Martinez	C. Garcia
C. Daumas	J. Nuzzie

Figure 3.18 and Figure 3.19 Samples Slide from *Mathematical Mindsets* Twitter Chat Book Study

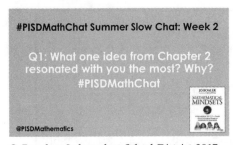

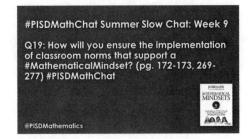

© *Pasadena Independent School District 2017*

campus turn-around conversations, we started to see and hear a shift in the language being used to describe how mathematics instruction should be structured and what mathematics instruction should look like and sound like. The terms "math workshop" and "guided math" were being used to guide conversations and frame conversations during team planning. We were hearing of more and more teachers beginning instruction with a routine such as a number talk or a math stretch rather than test-formatted questions. The journey had been a long one, with over 5 years of conversations focused on the same topic of Math Workshop, but the conversations about mathematics and the mindset about mathematics instruction was changing. As noted in *The Math Coach Field Guide*:

- "Change takes time."
- "We should always have a plan, but know that it is subject to change."
- "Persistence is important."

To build a common language about mathematics, we have to be persistent in our efforts (see Figure 3.20). Not only are we working to equip teachers with the language needed for everyday instruction, we are also working to change mindsets about what mathematics should look like and sound like. We must constantly remind ourselves that mathematics instruction is not about us as teachers and our experiences or preferences; it is about our students and the steps we need to take to make mathematics accessible to them.

Building on Shared Knowledge: Social Media

While working to build a common language about mathematics standards and mathematics instruction, we've also been working to encourage our teachers to look beyond the walls of their own classrooms and the classrooms on their campuses to the classrooms of teachers within our district and around the world. We started using social media sites such as Facebook

Figure 3.20 Progression of District-Wide Efforts Over Six Years

From Mathematics Class to Mathematician's Workshop

Our Journey

2011-2012	2012-2013	2013-2014	2014-2015	2015-2016	2016-2017	Next Steps
• CBA Round Tables • TEKS Talks • "Just in Time" Professional Development	• Book Study: Guided Math • TOT: Redefining the Math Block • Components of Math Workshop Checklist: Environment • 1st 12 Days of Math Workshop • Anchor Charts • Foldables • After-School PD: Various Topics	• Book Study: Math Misconceptions • 1st 20 Days of Math Workshop • Article: Advantages of Math Workshop Implementation Goals • After-School PD: Work Station Ideas	• Book Study: Guided Math in Action • Article: The Tools of Classroom Talk • After-School PD: Work Station Ideas • Calendar of Number Talks • Calendar of Math Stretches	• Book Study: Math Workshop in Action • Lesson Plan Template • Checklist: Math Routines • Academic Language Strategies • Formative Assessment Strategies • Communication Questions Posters • After-School PD: Content Strands Bilingual Mini-Lessons • Thinking Maps™	• Book Study: Running Records in Action • Components of Math Workshop (refined) • Who are Mathematicians? • Talk Moves & Communication Questions Bookmarks • Article: Building a Community of Learners • Article: Traditional Classrooms vs. Math Workshop Classrooms • After-School PD: Implementing Math Workshop • "I Can" Statements • Content Questions & Sentence Frames/Starters	• Math Toolkits • Running Records to Support Fact Fluency • Student Self-Assessment • Word Walls with Visual

© *Pasadena Independent School District 2017*

Figure 3.21, Figure 3.22, and Figure 3.23 Pasadena ISD Facebook and Twitter Accounts

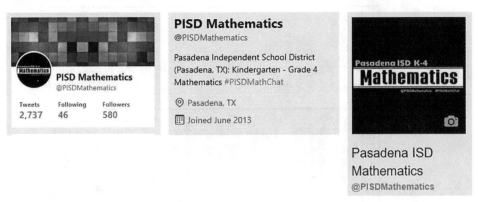

and Twitter (see Figure 3.21, Figure 3.22, and Figure 3.23) to showcase the work of our teachers with pictures from classrooms that showcase instructional resources such as anchor charts, interactive journals, graphic organizers, and workstations. We emphasized the need to be a connected educator and develop a PLN, professional learning network (see Figure 3.24).

We began this work by identifying a hashtag that was unique to our district, #PISDMathChat, and tweeting pictures from professional development sessions and campus visits (see Figure 3.25, Figure 3.26, Figure 3.27, Figure 3.28, Figure 3.29, Figure 3.30, Figure 3.31).

Figure 3.24 The Connected Educator

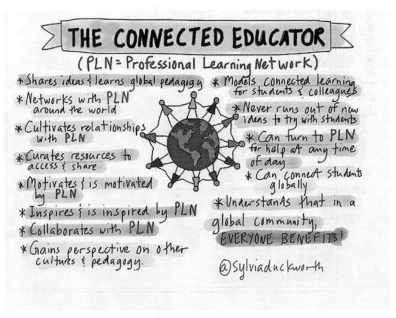

Figure 3.25 Our First Tweet

PISD Mathematics
@PISDMathematics

Exploring "Building Block Cards" - provide core vocabulary (brick) - students create the sentence (mortar).

Figure 3.26, Figure 3.27, Figure 3.28, Figure 3.29, Figure 3.30, Figure 3.31 Examples of Our First Tweets

While Twitter is a commonly used venue for collaborating with colleagues in education from all reaches of the earth, it took a while for the efforts to take off in our district. Though we were constantly encouraging our mathematics coaches and teachers to use Twitter to share what mathematics instruction looked like in their classroom, the vast majority (if not the entire majority) of the tweets using the hashtag #PISDMathChat were those being tweeted from our own account. We started incorporating "Talk and Tweets" into our meetings with our mathematics coaches and campus administrators, as we wanted to encourage the use of Twitter to connect with others and promote our conversations about mathematics (see Figure 3.32 and Figure 3.33).

Figure 3.32 and Figure 3.33 Samples Slides from "Talk and Tweets" with Campus Administrators and Campus Coaches

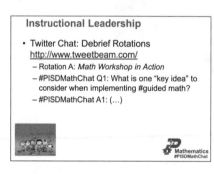

© *Pasadena Independent School District 2017*

With time, we have increased the number of mathematics coaches and mathematics teachers posting tweets that reflect the mathematics happening at their campuses and including pictures that reflect components of Math Workshop, campus professional development conversations, classroom tools such as anchor charts and student interactive journals, and efforts that reflect the mathematizing of their campus (see Figure 3.34, Figure 3.35, Figure 3.36, Figure 3.37, Figure 3.38, Figure 3.39).

We now have teachers connecting through tweets and sharing ideas and resources across campuses. We have teachers sharing tools being created to support mathematics instruction, such as differentiated workstations and word walls that spotlight academic language (see Figure 3.40).

While it is now common to find several tweets with the hashtag #PISDMathChat being posted each week, these collaborative efforts were a long time in the making. It took promoting an effort that seemed to be so easily and commonly used in many other districts and by many other mathematics educators consistently over time, while also modeling how its use can be beneficial to the work of our district for these additional efforts to take root

Figure 3.34, Figure 3.35, Figure 3.36, Figure 3.37, Figure 3.38, Figure 3.39 Sample Tweets Using the Hashtag #PISDMathChat

Mindy Cantu
@mindytrinidad

Following

Modeling to students how to find missing numbers on a number line. #PisdMathChat #We_Pride

4:56 PM · 6 Oct 2017

Daniela Cruz
@dcruz139

Following

Mrs. Meza conducted a mathematics class for parents--modeled 2nd grade math expectations. #pisdmathchat #fisheres

Cristi Pace
@CristiPace61

Following

Young Elementary 2nd graders are creating 2-D shapes! We ♥ Math! #pisdmathchat

6:30 PM · 6 Feb 2018

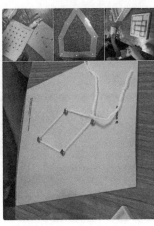

samantha
@Scortez7176

Following

Working on making anchor charts more meaningful by having student input. #pisdmathchat

3:49 PM · 16 Nov 2017

Jessica Garza
@JessicaCGarza

Following

Output & Input -interactive journal Ss generated word problems & solved using multiple strategies. #PISDMathChat

11:19 AM · 2 Nov 2017

Vanessa Gil
@vgil1010

Following

#pisdmathchat I love that our hallways are filling up with math talk and thinking 😊 all the time. Laura Bush Elementary Rocks!

11:37 AM · 18 Jan 2018

Figure 3.40 Sample Tweets Using the Hashtag #PISDMathChat

Mackenzie Watson
@MackenzieW7911

Following ∨

Thank you Ms. Galaviz for allowing us to learn & grow from you! Your math workshop is on point! #pisdmathchat @JessicaGalavizG

5:05 PM - 11 Oct 2017

and grow. Just like mathematicians have to be persistent in their efforts, we must be persistent in our own efforts.

Since I began tweeting the work of teachers on my campus, teachers have started reaching out to me more and more than ever are inviting me into their classrooms to see the creative, fun, and engaging ways they are teaching mathematics. I think it is important for the teachers to see that their work is being acknowledged and even more importantly appreciated and shared by others. Twitter has also grown my professional learning network (PLN) as an instructional coach. I have been able to attend free webinars on coaching strategies, implement mathematics activities and resources that I have seen others share from their classrooms, and I have built stronger connections with other instructional coaches within our district team.

Mathematics Peer Facilitator

By utilizing Twitter, I have been able to connect with other teachers and learn new ideas and techniques to implement in my classroom. I have grown professionally by observing and applying tweets from other educators in my district and from the education community on Twitter. Twitter has been a great resource for me to use, learn, and grow from. I enjoy sharing the learning that is going on in my classroom as well as connecting and learning from other educators.

Grade 2 Teacher

Building on Shared Knowledge: Opportunities for Teacher Leaders

During the 2016–2017 school year we offered an application-based Emerging Leaders in Mathematics Education Collaborative to provide emerging teacher leaders with an opportunity to develop their skill sets as leaders in mathematics. The application included questions such as:

- What would visitors to your classroom observe if they visited your classroom over the course of several days during mathematics instruction? Please provide a brief description.
- What is your understanding of a professional learning community? What experience(s) do you have as a member of a professional learning community? Please provide a brief description.
- What professional reading/piece of professional literature has been the most influential to your work as a mathematics educator? Why? Please provide a brief description.

We accepted 16 applicants during our first year including 13 teacher leaders and three first-year mathematics coaches. We met a total of 11 times after school for 1 hour 15 minutes (one session was canceled due to a change in my own calendar). We framed our conversations around four main components: *The Math Coach Field Guide* (Math Solutions), vertical alignment of standards, resources made available through social media, and sharing our expertise through presentations at a regional conference. Participants were assigned chapters of *The Math Coach Field Guide* to read between meetings, and each meeting included reading and reflecting on one of the guiding principles about being a mathematics coach (see Figure 3.41).

Figure 3.41 Sample Notes Page to Debrief *The Math Coach Field Guide*

The Math Coach Field Guide

Chapter 1
Being a Successful Math Coach: Ten Guiding Principles

Principle 3:
Begin by Working with Teachers Who Are Interested, Curious, or Open to Change About a Different Way to Teach Math

Key Points:	What Can I Apply Now?

Principle 4:
Recognize That Change in Instruction Happens Primarily When Support Relates to Teachers' Specific Classroom Instructional Needs

Key Points:	What Can I Apply Now?

pageborders.org

© *Pasadena Independent School District 2017*

We emphasized that it doesn't take a title to establish yourself as a leader, rather we become leaders when we immerse ourselves into research-based mathematics instruction and pull other teachers into and along with the conversations. We explored the vertical alignment of concepts such as addition/subtraction, fractions, and geometry through sorting activities focused on standards, assessment items, and instructional activities.

Figure 3.42 Samples Slide from Vertical Alignment Activities (Standards)

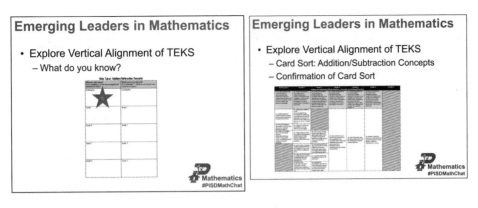

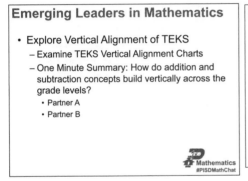

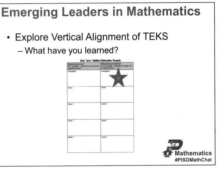

Vertical Alignment: Standards

During this activity, members first recorded the main addition and subtraction concepts/skills that they thought students would learn at each grade level. Then the members examined cards with various standards and recorded the grade level from which they thought each standard came and then verified their thinking using a vertical alignment standards chart (see Figure 3.42, Figure 3.43, and Figure 3.44).

Vertical Alignment: Assessment Items

During this activity, members first recorded the main fraction concepts/skills that they thought students would learn at each grade level. Then the members examined assessment items that reflected various standards, recorded the grade level from which they thought each standard came, and then verified their thinking using a vertical alignment standards chart (see Figure 3.45, Figure 3.46, Figure 3.47, and Figure 3.48).

Figure 3.43 and Figure 3.44 Sample Note Taker and Card Sort from Vertical Alignment Activity (Standards)

Note Taker: Addition/Subtraction Concepts

What do you know? PLC Question 1: What do we expect our students to learn?	What have you learned? PLC Question 1: What do we expect our students to learn?
Kindergarten	Kindergarten
Grade 1	Grade 1
Grade 2	Grade 2
Grade 3	Grade 3
Grade 4	Grade 4

TEKS Card Sort: Addition/Subtraction

Model the action of joining to represent addition and the action of separating to represent subtraction.	Add up to four two-digit numbers and subtract two-digit numbers using mental strategies and algorithms based on knowledge of place value and properties of operations.
Solve word problems using objects and drawings to find sums up to 10 and differences within 10.	Solve one-step and multi-step word problems involving addition and subtraction within 1,000 using a variety of strategies based on place value, including algorithm.
Explain the strategies used to solve problems involving adding and subtracting within 10 using spoken words, concrete and pictorial models, and number sentences.	Solve with fluency one-step and two-step problems involving addition and subtraction within 1,000 using strategies based on place value, properties of operations, and the relationship between addition and subtraction.
Use objects and pictorial models to solve word problems involving joining, separating, and comparing sets within 20 and unknowns as any one of the terms in the problem such as 2 + 4 = [ ]; 3 + [ ] = 7; and 5 = [ ] – 3.	Add and subtract whole numbers and decimals to the hundredths place using the standard algorithm.
Explain strategies used to solve addition and subtraction problems up to 20 using spoken words, objects, pictorial models, and number sentences.	Estimate to determine solutions to mathematical and real-world problems involving addition, subtraction, multiplication, or division.

Figure 3.45 Samples Slide from Vertical Alignment Activities (Assessment)

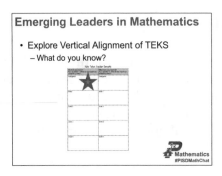

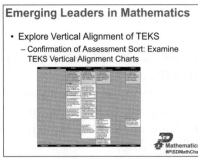

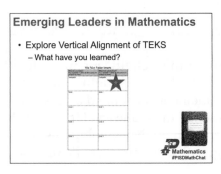

Figure 3.46, Figure 3.47, and Figure 3.48 Sample Note Taker and Assessment Items from Vertical Alignment Activity (Assessment)

Note Taker: Fraction Concepts

What do you know? PLC Question 1: What do we expect our students to learn?	What have you learned? PLC Question 1: What do we expect our students to learn?
Kindergarten	Kindergarten
Grade 1	Grade 1
Grade 2	Grade 2
Grade 3	Grade 3
Grade 4	Grade 4

1 Which statement correctly compares two fractions?

A $\dfrac{2}{6} > \dfrac{6}{10}$

B $\dfrac{2}{6} = \dfrac{6}{10}$

C $\dfrac{5}{8} < \dfrac{5}{10}$

D $\dfrac{5}{8} > \dfrac{5}{10}$

1 Below is a model of a two-dimensional rhombus.

Which answer choice describes the parts that compose the rhombus shown above?

A The rhombus is composed of five equal parts.

B The rhombus is composed of two equal parts.

C The rhombus is composed of two unequal parts.

The goal of these vertical alignment activities was to encourage the members to look beyond their current grade levels and consider what the standards look like not only in other grade levels but also when examined vertically. These efforts were made so that the teacher leaders would gain a broader perspective of the mathematics happening in other grade levels and begin establishing a working knowledge of the standards for when one might transition into a leadership role supporting multiple grade levels of mathematics teachers.

We utilized resources made available through social media to encourage growth among the participants. We provided each member with an #ObserveMe sign (per the work of Robert Kaplinsky; see Figure 3.49) and encouraged each member to tweet a picture with the sign and solicit feedback from campus colleagues regarding the instruction in their classrooms (see Figures 3.50, 3.51, 3.52). We emphasized that leaders must be willing to open up their classrooms and share the expertise that sets them apart from other educators, while also modeling an interest in continual improvement using feedback from peers.

Figure 3.49 Examples of #ObserveMe Challenge Task Cards

Figure 3.50, Figure 3.51, and Figure 3.52 Examples of #ObserveMe Challenge Tweets

We had a cadre of 16 teachers and coaches that were making steps on a daily basis to grow, and we had to find a way for the participants to share their growing knowledge with the other teachers at their home campus and pull those teachers into the conversations. With that in mind, one of the last assignments for the participants to complete was to facilitate one of the tasks from our meetings at their home campus (see Figure 3.53). The choices included:

- Vertical Alignment (Addition/Subtraction Standards)
- The Connected Educator
- Vertical Alignment (Multiplication/Division Standards)

Figure 3.53 Examples of Individual Project Choices

EMERGING LEADERS IN MATHEMATICS EDUCATION COLLABORATIVE

REFLECTION & APPLICATION PROJECT: DUE 05.16.17

Project A: Vertical Alignment of Addition/Subtraction TEKS (10.04.16)
Explore the vertical alignment of the +/- SEs through the "card sort" activity and use the TEKS Vertical Alignment Charts to verify vertical alignment. Facilitate reflective conversations that discuss how the concepts build vertically and how individual teachers can support these efforts.

Project B: The Connected Educator (10.04.16)
Explore the importance of developing a PLN and describe the steps you've taken to establish your PLN. Share resources and ideas that you have gleaned from Twitter and how the use of social media has allowed you to connect with other educators. Share examples of your tweets to validate the reflections. Recruit at least 5 teachers from your campus to join Twitter, follow the people/organizations followed by PISD, and use #PISDMathChat to share ideas from their classrooms.

Project C: Vertical Alignment of Multiplication/Division TEKS (10.25.16)
Explore the vertical alignment of the ×/÷ SEs through the "activity sort" and use the TEKS Vertical Alignment Charts to verify vertical alignment. Facilitate reflective conversations that discuss how the concepts build vertically and how individual teachers can support these efforts.

Project D: Vertical Alignment of Fraction TEKS (01.17.17)
Explore the vertical alignment of the fraction SEs through the "assessment sort" activity and use the TEKS Vertical Alignment Charts to verify vertical alignment. Facilitate reflective conversations that discuss how the concepts build vertically and how individual teachers can support these efforts.

Project E: The Math Bulletin Board (MCFG Chapter 2)
Create a Math Bulletin Board and facilitate the progression of activities outlined in Chapter 2: describe the project to teacher teams, ask what the teacher teams might hope to learn, facilitate examination of student work, collect student work samples from each grade level, facilitate examination of student work ("meet standard" or "needs more instruction") with each grade level, meet with teams to examine the bulletin board and discuss "What do you notice?" and the take-aways from examining student work from across the grade levels.

Project F: #ObserveMe
Explore the importance of peer observations/feedback and describe the steps you've taken to encourage peer observations/feedback in your classroom. Recruit at least five teachers from your campus (various grade levels) to join the #ObserveMe challenge (with pictures posted on Twitter #ObserveMe #PISDMathChat) and ensure that each of the teachers observes each other and provides feedback related to mathematics instruction.

Project G: Personal Choice
Choose a project of your choice and confirm your plan with Janet Nuzzie.

For each project, be prepared (with artifacts such as pictures from meetings, chart paper with team notes from meetings, etc.) to share and discuss the following items:
- Which project did you choose and why?
- How did you approach the project?
- How did you facilitate the project and "what happened"?
- What did you learn from facilitating the project?
- What are some of your next steps to continue promoting mathematics at your campus?

© *Pasadena Independent School District 2017*

- Vertical Alignment (Fraction Standards)
- The Math Bulletin Board
- #ObserveMe
- Personal Choice

Participants were provided with the blackline masters used during the meeting for their campus turn-around conversations. At our final meeting, we celebrated our growth from the year with a 5-minute presentation by each participant of the project facilitated at their home campus and the lessons learned from the project. Other district leaders including our Deputy Superintendent of Academic Achievement, an Associate Superintendent for Campus Development, and an Executive Director in Curriculum and Instruction were invited to join us for the presentations and celebrations (see Figure 3.54 and Figure 3.55).

Figure 3.54 and Figure 3.55 Final Meeting: 2016-2017 Emerging Leaders in Mathematics Education Collaborative

The collaborative provided teacher leaders with opportunities such as networking with other teacher leaders, developing vertical knowledge of the standards, exploring the attributes of an effective mathematics coach, and sharing their expertise by presenting a session at a regional conference. In providing a more in-depth professional development opportunity to interested teacher leaders, we continued to build upon our efforts to mathematize our school district by building shared knowledge about mathematics and mathematics instruction. Mathematicians learn and grow together!

The opportunity to participate in ELMEC has definitely made an impact in my current and future professional career. It was a great experience, filled with a prodigious amount of valuable information. What I enjoyed the most was the opportunity for colleagues to collaborate and discuss vertical alignment. I definitely have a better understanding of how mathematics is interconnected and will make an impact in all aspects for students.

2016–2017 ELMEC Member

ELMEC helped me grow as a leader because it pushed me to make time for the "wants." Being a new Math PF there are SO many initiatives and goals I had for this campus, but it is impossible to do it all. Being in ELMEC allowed me to at least focus on one or two small changes for the teachers/students at my campus. I also learned about coaching and building relationships with my teachers, which I truly felt impacted the effectiveness I had as a coach in my first year.

2016–2017 ELMEC Member

Participating in the "Emerging Leaders in Mathematics Education Collaborative" provided a great opportunity to come out of my comfort zone and expand my horizon. I was able to conduct a professional development in Region 4 ESC, collaborate with my colleagues in professional growth, develop knowledge of coaching skills, and we learned about the TEKS K-4. I will continue to collaborate with my colleagues to continuously improve our mathematics instruction. I will follow up on #ObserveMe challenge and work with my administrators to provide coverage for those teachers who participate.

2016–2017 ELMEC Member

Building on Shared Knowledge: Campus Spotlights From Campus Coaches

The facilitation of our district curriculum is supported by the efforts of our Mathematics Peer Facilitators, the campus coaches who support the day to day implementation of our curriculum across the grade levels. These campus coaches wear many hats and support district-curriculum initiatives as well as campus initiatives. With 36 campuses that share common needs as well as diverse and unique needs, it goes without saying that the work of each campus coach looks similar in many aspects, but different in others. Our campus coaches support anywhere from 18 mathematics teachers to 45 mathematics teachers depending on the size of their campus, which means that the support can look very different at each campus based on the collective and individual needs of the teachers. Through discussions during team meetings or during campus visits to mathematics classrooms, it became apparent that our coaches were making phenomenal efforts to promote mathematics at the campus level and support the implementation of the mathematics curriculum. When we noticed an efficient or unique way that mathematics was being promoted by the campus coach, we would ask him/her to share a "campus spotlight" during a monthly meeting. The spotlight was intended to be brief, no more than 5 minutes, and to share the specific actions or tasks that the campus coach was using to promote mathematics (see Figure 3.56, Figure 3.57, and Figure 3.58). The notion that mathematicians learn and grow together extended beyond the classroom to this team of campus leaders as well. During the first year of these conversations, we learned about efforts such as:

Figure 3.56 How the mathematics instructional block was being structured (Genoa Elementary)

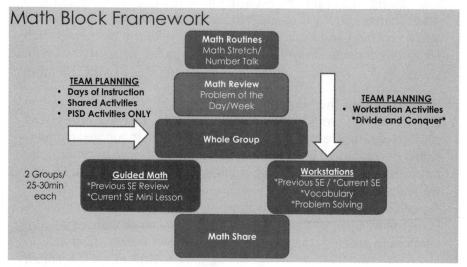

© *Pasadena Independent School District 2017*

Figure 3.57 How data walls were being used for team discussions and planning (Young Elementary)

© *Pasadena Independent School District 2017*

Figure 3.58 How tools were being created to support classroom visits and data discussions (Bailey Elementary)

Teacher: _____
Date: _____

Mathematics Walk-through Form

Student Expectation(s):		
Math Routine ☐ Math Stretch ☐ Number Talk ☐ Fact Fluency ☐ Other:	Notes:	

Math Instruction: Whole Group
  ☐ Use of manipulatives
  ☐ Modeling
  ☐ Guided/shared practice
  ☐ Visuals (video or anchor chart)
  ☐ Academic vocabulary
	Notes:	

Math Instruction: Guided Math		

Group 1
  ☐ Use of manipulatives
  ☐ Higher level questions
  ☐ Students actively doing math
Notes:
		Group 2
		  ☐ Use of manipulatives
		  ☐ Higher level questions
		  ☐ Students actively doing math
		Notes:

Group 3
  ☐ Use of manipulatives
  ☐ Higher level questions
  ☐ Students actively doing math
Notes:
		Group 4
		  ☐ Use of manipulatives
		  ☐ Higher level questions
		  ☐ Students actively doing math
		Notes:

Math Instruction: Work Stations		

☐ Fact fluency
  ☐ Computer (DreamBox, TTM)
  ☐ Preview of upcoming concept
  ☐ Review of previously taught concept
  ☐ Problem Solving
  ☐ Vocabulary
  ☐ Independent work
  ☐ Marcy Cook
	Notes:	

Math Share Time		
Notes:		

*The use of Whole Group Instruction, Small Group Instruction, and Work Stations might vary based on the differentiated needs of students.

© *Pasadena Independent School District 2017*

The team of campus coaches appreciated the opportunity to learn about how mathematics instruction was being supported at other campuses, and the knowledge gleaned from colleagues spurred additional networking conversations as well as shared efforts across the campuses. Because these conversations resulted from seeing these efforts at play during campus visits, we knew that we were only catching a glimpse of the powerful work being facilitated by our campus coaches. With that in mind, we sought a structure to hear from all 36 of the campus coaches over the course of the year during our monthly meetings.

When the next school year rolled around, we assigned a date for each campus coach to prepare and share a 5-minute "Campus Spotlight" to share about the mathematics happening at their campus (see Figure 3.59). The task was left open-ended so that campus coaches could share about any effort related to mathematics. Over the course of the school year we heard about how campus coaches were facilitating efforts such as after-school book studies, family math nights, creating tools to support team planning, facilitating team data meetings, starting math committees with a vertical team of teachers, mathematizing their campus, and creating opportunities for teachers to spotlight their work with other teachers (see Figure 3.60, Figure 3.61, and Figure 3.62). The amount of work happening to support mathematics was amazing, and now our math coaches were sharing their work with others and providing ideas from which other ideas were spurred or replicated at their own campus.

One of the efforts shared during the Campus Spotlight conversations included Mariana Breaux's "Mathematician of the Month" (see Chapter 6; see Figure 3.63). These efforts were unique to Mariana's campus and inspired many conversations about recognizing our students as mathematicians. The "Mathematician of the Month" efforts have since been replicated at several of our other campuses (see Figure 3.64).

Figure 3.59 Sample Schedule of Campus Spotlights

2016-2017 MPF Meeting Campus Spotlight

Date	Campus	Campus	Campus	Campus	Campus	Campus
09.30.16 (2NW TOT)	M. Rayford (Jessup)	S. Benavides (Parks)	S. Contreras (South Houston)			
10.21.16	R. Whittaker (Atkinson)	P. Jordon (Freeman)	R. Tice (Pearl Hall)	J. Kennedy (Bush)	C. Daumas (Meador)	R. Sanders (South Belt)
11.11.16	L. Roberts (Bailey)	C. Pace (Young)	M. Esparza (Golden Acres)	J. Teague (Kruse)	K. Calaway (Red Bluff)	A. Chavez (South Shaver)
12.02.16 (3NW TOT)	J. Saenz (Garfield)	J. Ochoa (Hancock)	B. Mullen (Moore)			
01.20.17	M. Breaux (Richey)	D. Cruz (Fisher)	A. Pena (Mae Smythe)	C. Lopez (McMasters)	P. Infante (Pomeroy)	S. Hall (Teague)
02.10.17 (4NW TOT)	A. Oquin (Frazier)	B. Melendez (Jensen)	C. Washburn (Morales)	M. Banda (Matthys)	T. Vance (Sparks)	S. Woodruff (Stuchbery)
03.03.17	V. Rodriguez-August (Genoa)	L. Baumann (Burnett)	N. Jimenez (Gardens)	R. Guzman (LF Smith)	S. Brown (Turner)	M. Watson (Williams)
05.12.17	Celebrations!					

© *Pasadena Independent School District 2017*

Figure 3.60 Sample Slide from Campus Spotlight (Meador Elementary)

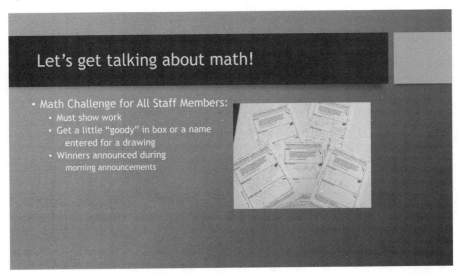

Figure 3.61 Sample Slide from Campus Spotlight (Kruse Elementary)

These opportunities to purposefully and intentionally share how the implementation of our mathematics curriculum was being supported by our campus coaches has been critical to our efforts to mathematize our district. As we have shared earlier, mathematicians learn and grow together,

Figure 3.62 Sample Slide from Campus Spotlight (Pomeroy Elementary)

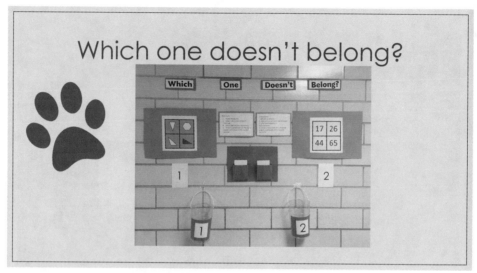

Figure 3.63 Sample Slide from Mariana Breauxs Mathematician of the Month

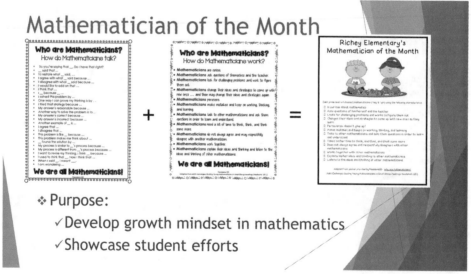

and it is only through collaborative efforts that we will continue to build shared knowledge and a shared enthusiasm about mathematics.

The sharing of Campus Spotlights has opened the doors to 36 campuses across our district. I love hearing how others are implementing their PIE (Planned Intervention and Enrichment) time and what

Figure 3.64 Replicating Mathematician of the Month at Another Campus

 **Martha Banda**
@MiBanda17

  ⌄

The Mathematician of the Month, # of the
day and Countdown to 100th Day Wall-done!
Next:pictures for Mathematicians at Work
#PISDmathchat

11:17 AM - 24 Oct 2017

resources they are currently finding successes with. Seeing other
MPF's Campus Spotlights makes me want to go back to my school and
work even harder to "mathematize" my building for our students!

Mathematics Peer Facilitator

The Campus Spotlights provide me with many ideas ranging from
teacher support to student achievement. These spotlights also allow
me to network with fellow Mathematics Peer Facilitators, grab ideas
from their tool box, and troubleshoot areas of concern. The sharing
of Campus Spotlights validates the efforts and successes of our
math teachers, and it also allows me to reflect on our mathematical
growth. I have started many activities across our campus because of
the conversations such as the Mathematician of the Month, which
in turn has also prompted and encouraged several grade levels to
implement their own Mathematician of the Month.

Mathematics Peer Facilitator

Lessons Learned

- Change takes time. Systemic change takes time.
- Building on shared knowledge creates lifelong learners.
- Social media can support cross-campus collaboration.
- Opportunities for growth need to be provided on a continual basis.
- Teachers learn from other teachers. Coaches learn from other coaches.

Getting Started Checklist

- Articulate the vision and goals for mathematics instruction and mathematics classrooms.
- Determine the needs to support the implementation of the vision and goals.
- Devise an action plan that uses products such as curriculum documents and processes such as book studies and learning opportunities that support the building of shared knowledge.
- Commit to the process and to the time it will take to facilitate change.

Key Points

- Change takes time.
- Develop lifelong learners.
- Use social media.
- Persistence is key.
- Learn together.

Summary

Change takes time. Changing mindsets about mathematics instruction takes time. Developing a common language about mathematics takes time. Building shared knowledge about mathematics instruction takes time. Building on shared knowledge takes time. Promoting the use of social media to encourage cross-campus collaborative efforts focused on mathematics takes time. Creating opportunities for emerging teacher leaders to further develop their skills as leaders in the mathematics classroom takes time. Making time for mathematics coaches to share "what's working" at their campuses takes time. Mathematizing a district does not happen overnight. It requires purposeful, continual efforts to bring core conversations to the forefront over and over again. And over and over again. Persistence is key. Patience is critical. The cause is worthy. Mathematicians learn and grow together!

Reflective Questions

- Do the professional development opportunities being facilitated in your district support teachers in their efforts to build shared, common knowledge about what mathematics instruction should look like and sound like? If not, what are the missing opportunities and how can you make arrangements to facilitate these learning opportunities?
- How could social media be used to promote the work being facilitated by teachers in your district and to promote personal learning networks?
- What professional development opportunities are being provided to build the capacity of current campus leaders and provide learning opportunities for emerging teacher leaders?

Resources

- *The Math Coach Field Guide* (Carolyn Felux and Paula Snowdy)
- *Guided Math* (Laney Sammons)
- *Guided Math in Action* (Nicki Newton)
- *Math Workshop in Action* (Nicki Newton)
- *Math Running Records in Action* (Nicki Newton)
- *Mathematical Mindsets* (Jo Boaler)
- *Learning by Doing* (DuFour, DuFour, Eaker, Many, Mattos)

4

Mathematizing Your Staff

Lara Roberts has been a mathematics instructional coach at an elementary school in Pasadena, Texas for eight years. The campus contains about 700 students in grades pre-kindergarten to fourth grade with 95% being identified as low socio-economic status. Lara has been in education for 19 years. She spent 11 years as a third- and fourth-grade teacher in the same district. Lara has written mathematics curriculum to support efforts with assessment, instructional activities, and professional development at the district level. She has facilitated professional development at the campus and district level while also serving as a Master Trainer for district-wide mathematics professional development. She has presented at numerous regional and state mathematics conferences and written an article published in a statewide professional publication. (Connect with Lara on Twitter: @LaraRobMath)

Jacquelyn Kennedy has been a mathematics instructional coach for two years at an elementary school in Pasadena, TX that serves students in pre-kindergarten through fourth grade. 87% of the students on the campus qualify for free and reduced lunch. Prior to being an instructional coach, Jacquelyn taught third-grade for 3 years. She taught in both self-contained and departmentalized settings, teaching only mathematics in the departmentalized setting. Jacquelyn has presented mathematics professional development sessions at the campus and district level, presented numerous sessions at regional and state mathematics conferences, and written an article published in a statewide professional publication for mathematics. Jacquelyn has helped write curriculum for the district's elementary mathematics program as well as for Connect, a computer-based individualized learning platform in fourth-grade mathematics. (Connect with Jaquelyn on Twitter: @jackenn27)

Introduction

As you walk around your campus, what do the conversations between teachers portray about the attitudes and feelings toward mathematics at your school? So often, we hear children say, "I don't like math," and this feeling does not necessarily go away just because we have grown into adults who teach math.

On the first day of my new career as a mathematics coach, I (Jacquelyn) was meeting with teams of teachers as they planned their math instruction for their students. One teacher was very open to share his feelings toward math saying, "I hate math!" I was not shocked at his statement, and I was glad he was open with his feelings, but I felt sad. How can we share a love for mathematics with our students if we don't love mathematics ourselves?

At that moment, I knew my response could be crucial in changing this teacher's perception of mathematics for both him and his students. I answered, "I love math, and I cannot wait to help you feel the same." I started thinking about where this negative perception might come from. It seems to be that many teachers say that mathematics was a subject they did not understand well as a child, that mathematics was a subject in which they never felt "successful," and that the thought of mathematics elicits a negative response. With that in mind, it became my goal to build every teacher's knowledge of mathematics and to grow a love for mathematics among the faculty at my school. How do you build your teachers' knowledge of mathematics? How do you spread a love for mathematics with your teachers? How do you build mathematical capacity among your teachers so they are confident with their teaching skills? What does the knowledge you share and the professional development you provide say about your attitude towards mathematics? In this chapter, we will explore ways to mathematize your staff in order to share the love of math with your teachers and ultimately your students.

Share a Love of Mathematics: Math All-Stars

When I (Lara) began working at my campus, the teachers used incentives to encourage students to be active readers. When students earned a certain number of reading points, they won a prize. I wanted something similar to be done for mathematics, and that is how Math All-Stars came to be.

I started the Math All-Stars initiative by finding challenging problems that would be appropriate for students in each grade level. Our district purchased a resource called Math Exemplars (www.exemplars.com), and I began examining this resource to see what challenging problems could be utilized to support these efforts. I was very selective with the problems I chose. I wanted problems that had multiple solutions, multiple steps, and multiple entry points so that the questions would be accessible to all students (see Figure 4.1). Next, I posted the problems on a bulletin board that would be visible to all of the grade levels on my campus. I also emailed a copy of the problems to every teacher so that the problem could be displayed in their classrooms. As students submitted correct answers to the problems, I wrote the student's name and the student's teacher's name on a star to display on the bulletin board (see Figure 4.2). In the beginning only a few teachers participated in the problem-solving effort; however, as

Figure 4.1 Example of a Math All-Star Problem

Exemplars

Second Grade

Birthday Gift Shopping

You have 13 cents to spend at the store on gifts for your friend's birthday. Show by writing and/or drawing what you would choose to buy from the product list if you spent all 13 cents. (See the product list below for items.)

Can you show more than one way? Write number sentences that show your answer(s).

Compras de regalo de cumpleaños

Tienes 13 centavos para gastar en la tienda de regalos para el cumpleaños de un amigo. Muestra escribiendo o dibujando qué escogerías para comprar de la lista de productos si gastas en total los 13 centavos.

¿Puedes mostrar más de una manera? Escribe oraciones numéricas para mostrar tus respuestas.

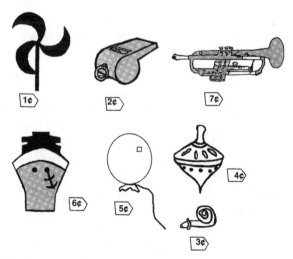

Birthday Gift Shopping

Figure 4.2 Student Stars for Math All-Star Board

more stars were posted on the bulletin board, the excitement began to grow. To make submitting an answer even more accessible, teachers allowed students to work in groups or partners to solve the problem. At the end of the month, I took the stars down and attached a bracelet that said "All-Star Student" to each star before it was returned to the student or teacher.

> I like to do the math problem because it challenges me. The math is hard, but that is what makes it fun!
>
> Grade 4 Student

When I began the Math All-Stars, I only included challenges for the students. As excitement over the initiative grew and the challenges became more popular, I added a challenge for the teachers. I went online and found different math puzzles and problems that could be used to challenge the teachers. I tried to choose challenges that would not be too time consuming but would be fun for the teachers to complete. When the teachers emailed me their answers, I added their star to the bulletin board and gave them candy at the end of the month (see Figure 4.3).

The entire campus looks forward to the new challenge each month, and the teachers feel a sense of pride when they get their star put up on the bulletin board. I have heard students and teachers discussing the solutions and challenges they faced as they attempted to answer the problem. A third-grade teacher said, "Math All-Stars has taught my students to be independent thinkers and to persevere when faced with unfamiliar problems." I even have students stop me in the hallway to submit answers to the challenge they worked on overnight. I think the success of the Math All-Stars is evident by the amount of excitement created when the newest problems are posted and the fact that throughout the year, the number of stars on the bulletin board grows (see Figure 4.4).

Figure 4.3 End of the Month Incentives for Teachers and Students

© *Pasadena Independent School District 2017*

Figure 4.4 The Math All-Star Board

© *Pasadena Independent School District 2017*

Share a Love of Mathematics: Celebrations

When I (Jacquelyn) began my coaching journey, I was new to the campus. Most teachers at my school were not excited about mathematics and I had the impression that accomplishments in mathematics had not been celebrated like they should be. Along with trying to improve the overall attitude of the staff toward mathematics, I needed to build relationships with the teachers so that they would have buy-in to celebrate mathematics along with me. I thought one of the best ways to share my love of mathematics was to show each teacher my appreciation for their mathematics efforts, both big and small, so I began celebrating mathematics anyway I could.

I began making instructional rounds so that I could make notes regarding the mathematics instruction that was occurring in our classrooms. I started writing simple "warm fuzzies" to teachers to point out the great instruction I saw happening in their classrooms. A warm fuzzy is a simple note expressing appreciation for the hard work being done by teachers (see Figure 4.5). In Jim Knight's book *The Impact Cycle*, he describes the importance of building trust with teachers. "We have found that coaches who do not demonstrate warmth, even when they possess expertise that could be extremely helpful for teachers, struggle to even get the coaching process started" (Knight, 2018, p. 74). Shortly after I wrote my first couple notes, teachers were talking. Teachers would ask each other whether or not they received a note. Teachers were excited to share their notes, and when I walked back into classrooms weeks later, their notes were posted near their desk or at their small group table. Teachers valued my words of appreciation and I felt teachers knew that when I entered their classroom, I always had a 100% positive intent to encourage and coach.

> Those notes are motivation to continue, to keep on doing what you are doing even when the going gets tough.
>
> Grade 4 Teacher

> Our school days are jam packed with teaching, paperwork, conferences, meetings, and so on. So when my math coach uploads a picture of my classroom on Twitter, leaves me a little note on my desk after she comes in to observe me, or sends an appreciated email, it makes me feel appreciated that my hard work doesn't go unnoticed. #itsthelittlethings
>
> Grade 2 Teacher

I found it was equally important to share celebrations with teachers, campus administrators, and district administrators via email (see Figure 4.6 and Figure 4.7). I shared about our teachers' efforts to develop and implement hands-on, engaging workstations for our students. I shared about our

Figure 4.5 Example of a "Warm Fuzzy"

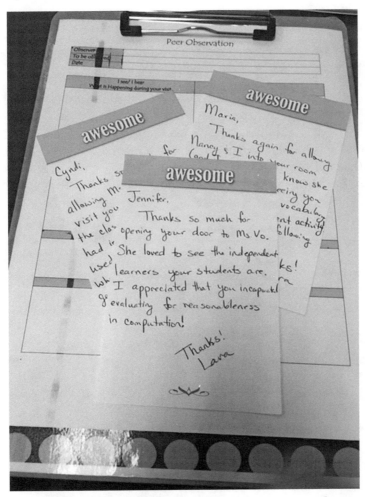

Figure 4.6 Example of a Celebratory Email

Good afternoon!

I had the chance to visit many of your classrooms this afternoon during your math block, I just wanted to say THANK YOU! I was so impressed and excited to see how engaged your kids were in their math stations/whole group/small group etc.

Some highlights...just to name a few:

- Turn and Talk Math Conversations
- Singing/Dancing
- EnVision Videos
- Lonestar Math
- Academic Vocabulary: **partition (AMAZING!)**, more than, less than, equal to, heavier, whole, fractions, halves, fourths, etc. WOW!
- Small Group Teaching
- Brain Breaks
- Positive reinforcement
- Formative assessment
- Real-world examples

And the list goes on...

I appreciate you making instruction of math a fun experience for our kids! You make the difference!

Figure 4.7 Example of a Math Celebration

© *Pasadena Independent School District 2017*

teachers' efforts to encourage students to complete lessons in our district's personalized-learning platform. I shared about our teachers' efforts to plan collaboratively, beginning with the end in mind. I encouraged teachers to connect with each other and share the effective teaching strategies I had seen in their classrooms. I made it a point to thank teachers for attending professional development sessions on their own time, acknowledging their commitment to their students and to their personal growth as educators.

I also found that social media was a fast and easy way to share mathematical celebrations with teachers, administrators, district personnel, parents, and the surrounding community. Every "like," "favorite," and "retweet" sparked a light in our teachers because others outside of our campus were noticing their work and were interested in the work they were doing. In addition, our teachers' willingness to reach out and invite people into their

Figures 4.8, 4.9, 4.10, 4.11 Examples of Tweets

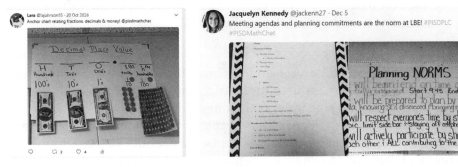

classrooms increased when they knew their efforts were appreciated. I also utilized our district's "Tweet About It Tuesday!" to share the work of our teachers with others and to share the work of other teachers in our district with the teachers at my campus (see Figures 4.8, 4.9, 4.10, and 4.11).

> Being recognized as a teacher through Twitter was the experience I needed to feel a bit more motivated. When what you're doing everyday gets recognized in a novel and special way, it gives you the extra push to keep going in a job that often does not give much recognition or appreciation.
>
> Grade 3 Teacher

When my work is shared with others it makes me feel motivated to
be the best that I can be and I know I am able to make an impact on
our students, so they too can be their best!

Grade 4 Teacher

It has been powerful to see and celebrate the amazing instruction happening on our campus, around our district, and around the world. There is
always something to celebrate! Find something to celebrate such as classrooms where teachers use songs and music to further develop students
understanding of mathematical concepts, classrooms that are immersed
in mathematics, classrooms where students lead conversations and justify
their thinking, classrooms where teachers work collaboratively as they plan
instruction and write assessments to track student achievement, classrooms
where students practice mathematics skills through engaging workstations,
and classrooms where small group instruction is targeted for each student
ensuring success for all students and then celebrate it!

Build Capacity: Professional Development

In order to mathematize a staff, it is important to find people who love mathematics and are willing to help lead the way in transforming the campus.
Through seeking out opportunities to share celebrations regarding the work of
teachers in their classrooms, you might notice teachers who are ready and open
to learn more about mathematics instruction. To build the capacity of these interested teachers, encourage and support their attendance of professional development sessions that focus on campus or district initiatives with mathematics.

These sessions might occur in your district, in your region, or around
the state. These sessions provide opportunities for teams of teachers to
delve deeper into the student expectations and the level of rigor anticipated on state assessments. The sessions also provide opportunities for
teams of teachers to do mathematics together such as sampling workstation
activities, vocabulary activities, and assessment items (see Figure 4.12). As a
result, great conversations can occur about instructional strategies that can
be used to develop grade level proficiency in our students.

Region 4 (Education Service Center) math training was awesome,
I went away with rigorous stations that aligned with low perform-
ing math SE's.

Grade 4 Teacher

Attending CAMT was such a rewarding experience. A highlight for me
was being able to attend a break-out session about Marcy Cook Tiles . . .
actually taught by Marcy Cook herself! Getting that firsthand information helped me to use those tools more effectively with my students.

Grade 3 Teacher

Figure 4.12 Professional Development: Regional Service Center

When an instructional coach attends professional development sessions alongside their teachers, it shows a united front and strengthens the idea that we are working together to help our students. It demonstrates leadership of the coach but also allows for a teacher and coach to build a personal connection along with their professional relationship. I am beyond grateful to have a coach to bounce ideas off of and to guide me throughout my math teaching.

Grade 1 Teacher

Attending professional development with my peer facilitator is a great way to learn from her, collaborate, and figure out which strategies can effectively be used to provide engagement into the classroom to promote student success.

Grade 2 Teacher

It was very meaningful that you took part in the workshops with us. You lead by example in demonstrating that we are all life long learners. It also helped reinforce the fact that you are here to help us grow as educators, so that we may be of even greater help to our students! Thank you for all you do to help and support our school family!

Grade 3 Teacher

Summer conferences are another great opportunity for building up a team of passionate math teachers. Attending professional development during the summer can sometimes be more feasible (and less stressful) than during the school year. Regardless of whether the professional development occurs during the school year or the summer, we try as often as possible to attend the sessions with our teachers. By attending the session together, we build stronger connections (both professional and personal) as a unified team and hold each other accountable for implementing what we have learned.

Every 3 years a statewide mathematics conference is held in our city. When it was time for the conference to be held in our area, I (Lara) asked a teacher from each grade level to attend the conference with me and our principal paid for each team member's registration. At that time we were just starting to implement the Math Workshop model in our classrooms. I asked the teachers to attend sessions that focused on that initiative. I needed teachers on my campus to be well versed in Math Workshop and to have the knowledge base and skill set to put it into practice. Attending the conference as a team was a perfect way to form a group of math leaders on my campus because they felt they learned enough about Math Workshop to be confident about implementing it (see Figure 4.13). During

Figure 4.13 Statewide Mathematics Conference

© *Pasadena Independent School District 2017*

the following school year the team met periodically and discussed the ideas they got from the conference that made an impact on their teaching. The focused efforts to cultivate this leadership team helped me the following school year. As teachers had questions about different parts of Math Workshop, I could direct them to the mathematics leader on their grade level. The teachers appreciated seeing firsthand how it worked for their grade level.

Find a need on your campus within the area of mathematics and find professional development opportunities that are geared towards that need. When teachers see a need for the professional development and they know they will have colleagues in attendance with whom they can discuss successes and failures, they will be more invested in the day of learning and can build upon one another's ideas when given opportunities to collaborate during a session. Because there is limited time during the school day for teachers to meet in vertical teams, attending a professional development session together provides the opportunity to have vertical discussions about content and pedagogical practice. Attending staff development with your teachers helps you to build relationships with teachers centered around mathematics and build mathematical leaders on your campus.

Build Capacity: Host a Book Study

A great way to build knowledge about research-based strategies for teaching mathematics is with a book study. The book study could be an optional professional development opportunity or a required campus-wide opportunity. The chapters of the book could be divided among the months of school year and discussed on a regular basis, perhaps during a faculty meeting. The book study conversations could be facilitated at the campus, off-site at a location such as a restaurant or coffee shop, or even through social media. The goal is to find a schedule that is "doable" and a location that will be "risk-free" so that as many teachers as possible will join in on the collaborative efforts.

After a year of implementing guided math on my campus, my principal allowed me to purchase *Math Workshop in Action* by Dr. Nicki Newton for all of our classroom teachers. The book had nine chapters, so we met once a month and discussed the content of one chapter and how the ideas within the chapter could impact our classrooms (see Figure 4.14). Usually these meetings happened during our after-school faculty meetings, but there were a few times where I (Lara) was able to meet with each grade level during their conference time to discuss the chapter. When we were able to meet as a grade level team, we were able to tailor the conversations to best meet the needs of the grade level. We discussed how activities in the book such as the math warm-ups, exit tickets, or fluency energizers could be used or adapted to meet the needs of our classrooms (see Figure 4.15).

Figure 4.14 *Math Workshop in Action:* Book Study Plan

Math Workshop in Action

Book Study Plan

Month	Chapter-topics
September	1-3- Managing math workshop
October	4- Opening (Part 1) Math starters and daily routines
November	5- Opening (Part 2) Mini-lessons
January	6- Workstations
February	7- Guided Math Groups
March	8- Share
April	9- Assessments

© Pasadena Independent School District 2017

After each chapter, the campus administrative team conducted classroom visits and we shared how the content learned during the book study was being implemented across the grade levels.

Another option is a small group books study. My administrator purchased five copies of *Mathematical Mindsets* by Jo Boaler. I was able to find

Figure 4.15 *Math Workshop in Action:* Book Study Activity

Fluency Energizers (Pg. 55)

	Summary of the activity	Grade Level Applications
Half it!/Double It!		
Number Line it!		
True or False		
What doesn't belong?		
I was walking down the street...		

© *Pasadena Independent School District 2017*

five classroom teachers interested in the content of the book. Our group consisted of a pre-Kindergarten teacher, a Kindergarten teacher, a third-grade teacher, a technology teacher, and a special education teacher. We met once a month at a restaurant off campus to discuss the book. Four times a year we presented what we learned at a faculty meeting (see Figure 4.16). Meeting off campus made it more casual and fun, but the content of the book stayed the focus. The conversations about how each teacher saw the content of the book working with their students were very powerful. The longevity of the book study kept all of us engaged but not overwhelmed with the reading. Knowing we would need to present it to the faculty helped to keep us on task during our meetings. These meetings also helped us to develop personal relationships beyond the school walls.

A book study ensures that all teachers are learning the same information about mathematics instruction but allows teachers to implement it in the way that works best for their students and themselves. A book study sends the message that this is important information but acknowledges that everyone can use the information in different ways based on their needs. The discussion about the book is an integral part because as each participant reads, they form their own ideas about the content. Through the discussion, teachers learn from each other and can see the content in a different way.

Reading *Mathematical Mindsets* by Jo Boaler through a book study has changed the way I question my students. I am less concerned about the right answer and more interested in how they solved it.

Special Education Teacher

Figure 4.16 *Mathematical Mindsets* Book Study

© *Pasadena Independent School District 2017*

Build Capacity: Peer Observations

To further build the capacity of your mathematics teachers, encourage the campus administrators to implement peer observations. Peer observations are short observations of classroom instruction by a teacher of another teacher. They allow teachers to experience one of the best forms of professional development—learning from each other! On my campus we utilized peer observations when we began the implementation of balanced literacy. The peer observations were so successful and well-received that we now do them every year and focus on different areas of teaching both reading and math.

About 2 years after our district began the implementation of a Math Workshop model, I (Lara) felt the teachers were ready to participate in peer observations focused on the components of Math Workshop. During the first year, the observations lasted 15–20 minutes and I attended the peer observation with the teacher. We have utilized various structures during the past 2 years such as facilitating peer observations in the same grade level, in other grade levels, and allowing the teachers to choose which teacher they wanted to observe.

We encourage the teacher who will be observed to create a reflection form for the observing teacher to complete in order to provide feedback on instruction and allow both teachers to reflect on the experience. We have focused on components of Math Workshop such as the implementation

Figure 4.17 Sample Form for Peer Observations

Teacher Observed: _____   Date: _____

Observation Reflection

As you reflect on the peer observation, use the following prompts to guide your reflection.

- What are THREE take-aways/"Ah-Ha's" that you received from the observation?

- What are TWO things you are still wondering about/want clarification on?

- What is ONE thing you plan to implement immediately into your classroom?

© *Pasadena Independent School District 2017*

of whole group instruction, guided math instruction, and workstations. Teachers may want to observe how teachers organize their workstations, how students rotate among workstations, how teachers organize their classroom space, etc. You will find that the teachers being observed will make the extra effort to highlight the component being observed.

Because observing everything in a classroom can be overwhelming, a good strategy is the "3, 2, 1 Observation." With this form, the observer records three takeaways from the teaching they observe, two questions they have regarding what was taught, and one goal to immediately implement into their own classroom (see Figure 4.17). The responses should never be evaluative of the teacher who is being observed, as the purpose of peer observations is for both teachers to learn from each other and support each other's growth with instruction.

Figure 4.18 #ObserveMe Challenge

© *Pasadena Independent School District 2017*

Both the teacher being observed and the teacher facilitating the observation benefit from this experience. Teachers being observed are able to ask questions about their teaching and gain feedback to enhance their effectiveness and add tools to their teacher toolbox. Teachers who are observing are able to reflect on their own practice as they observe another's teaching practices. These observations lead to great collaborative conversations among the teachers and in our situation, the math coach. By attending the observations, I found more opportunities to develop coaching relationships.

If the teachers at your campus aren't ready for formally scheduled peer observations, you can spark teacher interest by asking them to join the #ObserveMe movement started by Robert Kaplinsky. Teachers will show their willingness to be observed by posting a sign that says #ObserveMe and a short list of instructional efforts for which they would like feedback (see Figure 4.18). The #ObserveMe challenge can lead to great conversations about math instruction and possibly create an interest in scheduling peer observations.

Build Capacity: Math Committee

Another way to build capacity among your teachers is to implement a math committee. The purpose of the math committee will depend on the needs of your campus. When starting a math committee at my campus, I (Jacquelyn) first asked for volunteers. Then I chose one to two representatives from each grade level. If your campus has classes with different languages of instruction, you might want a representative from each type of classroom. At the same time, be selective with your committee members. It can be difficult to make decisions with too many members.

As a committee, set a goal for the year that all members can stick to and achieve. One goal our committee set was to create a platform to help parents learn about content in order to better assist their children at home with homework or in areas of struggle. We wanted to deepen the understanding of mathematics and strategies to learn mathematics among our community members. In order to achieve this goal our committee members committed to creating short video snippets of them teaching difficult concepts that we anticipated to be a challenge for our students. Mathematics looks very different than it did when most parents learned mathematics in school, hence why we are calling the video selections "Learn Like a Kid!"

It is important to establish the frequency of the committee meetings, the norms for the committee meetings, and the topics that will be discussed during the meetings. Math Committees could meet on a monthly basis and discuss topics such as vertical alignment, a campus-wide problem solving protocol, the organization of campus mathematics events, building a mathematics environment on the campus, and so much more.

Below is a sample agenda that could be used to facilitate an initial Math Committee meeting (see Figure 4.19).

I have found it very beneficial for the committee members to leave every meeting with clear action steps. This lends to natural accountability among our committee. I also make sure to follow up our meetings with an

Figure 4.19 Sample Math Committee Agenda

Laura Bush Math Committee 2017-2018 Agenda
5.10.17

Today's Meeting:

- Set Norms
- Take care of logistics: time, meeting place, dates, etc.
- Campus Mission
- Campus Strengths
- Campus Concerns
- Mathematics Community: What is our vision?
- Goals for next year!

1. When will we meet and how often?

2. What is our mission as LBE Math Committee?

3. What are my responsibilities as a member of the math committee?

4. What do we love that we are already doing?

5. What concerns do we currently have for our campus mathematics?

6. What are action steps for next year (spring and fall goal)?

© *Pasadena Independent School District 2017*

email that includes reminders of due dates, tasks to be completed, etc. The time together has been worthwhile, as evidenced by the feedback provided by one of the committee members.

> By beginning a math committee teachers were able to "vertically align the curriculum throughout the grade levels so students are going to the next grade level with the skills to succeed in mathematics."
>
> Grade 4 Teacher

Build Capacity: Research in Mathematics Education

One way to get staff members talking about mathematics is to let them know what is new in mathematics education and mathematics research. As I (Lara) participate in professional development sessions, read blogs, or read professional magazines, I often find an article that addresses campus

Figure 4.20 Math Research Bulletin Board

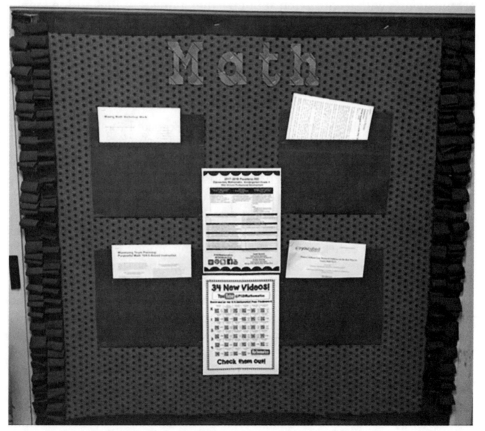

initiatives that I wish my faculty could read. I always struggled with how to share this information, as teachers do not want to go to a faculty meeting so that they can read an article.

With that in mind, I began placing the articles in the teachers' lounge. I wasn't sure how many teachers would read the articles. One day as I was walking down the hall, a teacher stopped me to tell me how much she enjoyed the article and that she wanted to discuss some ideas for how she could make some changes in her classroom. Right then I knew that if it helped one teacher, it was worth it. Through the years, my approach has changed. Instead of just placing articles in the teachers' lounge, I now use a bulletin board to post several articles (see Figure 4.20). I also send an email with the articles attached in case teachers would rather read at home. I have also included information on the bulletin board about professional development being held in our district or the surrounding areas.

The National Council of Teachers of Mathematics (NCTM), youcubed. org, and educationworld.com are some of the sources I have used for articles. I frequently refer to *Math Coach's Corner*, a great blog with many articles, activities, and resources for teachers and instructional coaches. Another blog with great information is *Teaching to Inspire*. *Teaching to Inspire* features posts with information about partner game activities, guided math resources, whole group instruction, exit slips in the upper elementary grades, and so much more!

Build Capacity: Teacher Spotlights

As a mathematics instructional coach, we are expected to share about our coaching efforts and the mathematics instruction happening on our campus. These efforts that encourage the growth of mathematics initiatives throughout our district are shared through "Campus Spotlights," which are 5-minute presentations facilitated during our monthly meetings as a team of math coaches. After our first couple of meetings, I (Jacquelyn) thought about how powerful a similar approach could be with teachers on my campus and I was inspired to facilitate this same method of sharing among the teachers.

I always hear teachers asking each other questions such as "What do you do in your classroom?," "What does Math Workshop look like in your classroom?," "How do you teach . . .?" What better way for teachers to find out than through "Teacher Spotlights?" Teacher spotlights are a great way to get a quick glimpse into someone else's teaching perspective. Because I am expected to host one faculty meeting every month or two, this became the time to allow teachers to share resources, instructional strategies, and updates from professional development sessions with their peers. These efforts exemplify how coaches are not the only people on campus with great ideas to share.

Jim Knight, in his book *The Impact Cycle*, discusses how the most effective instructional coaches do not prescribe teachers effective strategies. "A coach's role is to help them [teachers] unpack what they already know" (Knight, 2018, p. 10). Encouraging teachers to share what someone else has found valuable in their classroom builds confidence and opens lines of communication among grade levels and between teachers on campus. "Teachers get a deeper understanding of teaching strategies when they see them modeled" (Knight, 2018, p. 128). As you observe great instruction happening in the classroom, ask these teachers if you can help them facilitate a mini-professional development session (10 minutes) to share their expertise with others.

Teachers may be hesitant at first, but with a coach by their side, it will feel less intimidating. I have also found that by keeping the session short, teachers are more willing to share. A fourth-grade teacher shared it was "interesting to see all the different ways a concept can be taught . . . nice knowing that you're able to show other teachers another hands-on way to teach math that can take place of a boring worksheet."

Some topics that teachers have chosen to share about include how to keep anecdotal notes during guided math instruction, how to promote the

Figure 4.21 Teacher Spotlights

© *Pasadena Independent School District 2017*

use of manipulatives to teach subtraction in the upper grades, and how to use strip diagrams to visualize word problems (see Figures 4.21 and 4.22). Teacher spotlights serve as a great outlet for teachers to share what they have learned at conferences and other professional development sessions. I was so proud watching my teachers share the great instructional strategies being used in their classrooms!

Figure 4.22 Teacher Spotlights Agenda

Teacher Spotlight Faculty Meeting Note Taker
3.30.17

Kennedy Kahoot It! Training Tuesday April 18th 3:35–4:30	Guerra Educational Galaxy • Targeted TEKS questions for K–4 (Writing, Math, Reading) • Free Basic account for teachers • Add students account • All subjects, one grade level
Hubert/Wedgeworth Subtraction Strategies	Vega Harris County Strip Diagram Training Anecdotal Notes
Contreras/Breed Guided Math & Fact Fluency Fluency Games (Dr. Newton) ▪ I love math! ▪ Give me 5! Give me 10!	Math News...Coming Up: ▪ Mathematizing Our Campus ▪ Math Committee (pending grade level decisions) ▪ Dive into Data Faculty Meeting 4/6 ▪ Math Fact Carnival Spreadsheets ○ Due May 2nd ▪ #ObserveMe!

Figure 4.22 (Continued)

Teacher Spotlight Websites & Resources
3.30.17

Kahoot It! https://create.kahoot.it/account/register/	[QR code]
Educational Galaxy www.EducationGalaxy.com	[QR code]
Subtraction Work Mat File Folder	Email
Miss. Giraffe-Fact Fluency Resource	
Dr. Newton Pinterest www.pinterest.com/drnicki7	[QR code]
Dr. Newton Running Record Documents https://guidedmath.wordpress.com/math-running-records-videos/	[QR code]
Harris County Strip Diagram Handout	Email
Things to Remember (Everything from this PD will be emailed to you as well.)	

Lessons Learned

- Start small. Any new initiative can quickly become overwhelming, so start small. Set one goal for the year or maybe one per semester if you are feeling ambitious. By starting small, you can narrow your focus and stay true to the goal that was set. When trying to facilitate too many projects at once, implementation can become difficult and the project is less likely to be effective. It is important to follow up with teachers throughout the implementation of a new teaching strategy to ensure success. Once a goal is set and the initiative is in place, the next year will be easier to facilitate and the next mathematical mission can be tackled.

- Willingness is key. Find teachers who are open to learning more about mathematics instruction and are willing to jump on board with you. Once these teachers have experienced the benefits of these efforts, they will share the work with others and the love for mathematics will spread quickly. Change is hard, but once the other teachers see that the efforts are meaningful and are positively affecting others, they will soon want to become involved.
- Get creative! Pave a way for mathematics that is creative and unique! Make mathematics fun and allow your love for mathematics and professional development opportunities to reflect these endless possibilities!

Getting Started Checklist

- As you evaluate your campus for the overall attitude felt about mathematics among your staff, find areas where you can let your mathematical excitement shine. Share your love for mathematics with teachers and students by implementing a campus incentive program centered on mathematics. This can be done using Math All-Stars or other mathematical bulletin boards that allow the entire campus to get in on the fun of problem solving in mathematics.
- As you visit classrooms, snap a photo of the awesome work being done, and then share these photos along with a short description with your administrative team via email. Some examples could be a small group lesson on fractions, a workstation on number concepts, an anchor chart that gets to the depth of the standard, and many more. Be sure to include the teachers on this email, so they can see that their hard work is being shared, noticed, and appreciated.
- As you discover areas where teachers need more support, work to build their capacity. In order to do this, identify teachers on campus who have a strength in the area of need and ask them to work with you to facilitate professional development for the other teachers on your campus. Implement a book study on a mathematics topic that could benefit a majority of teachers on your

campus. The professional development could be done through a face-to-face training or could even be implemented using a Twitter slow chat. This could allow more teachers to participate in these efforts.

- Build teacher capacity by facilitating peer observations. Ask teachers to choose specific components of their teaching they want feedback on and bring other teachers to observe and provide feedback. This is a great way to build teacher capacity in both the teaching observing and the teacher being observed.
- Create a collaborative team devoted to building the capacity of your campus by starting a math committee! Start small and work to build the knowledge of committee members so they can share their new knowledge with others. Select a focus area for the year, which could include conversations focused on vertical alignment, community outreach involving mathematics, or tackling a concept that teachers struggle with campus-wide.
- As you come across articles about mathematics education, find a way to share them with the faculty. Think about putting the articles in the teachers' lounge or some other place where teachers gather. Select articles that are short and easy to read. Articles should support the campus goals for mathematics instruction.

Key Points

- Share your love of mathematics.
- Celebrate mathematical efforts.
- Facilitate professional development.
- Host a book study.
- Encourage peer observations.
- Initiate a math committee.
- Share research about mathematics.

Summary

Mathematizing your staff begins with you loving mathematics. Observe teachers and other staff members on your campus, then reflect about your campus' mathematical atmosphere, how do those surrounding you feel about mathematics? The attitude exhibited about mathematics affects everyone—students, teachers, and administration. To begin the process of mathematizing your campus you must share your love for mathematics. This is done by celebrating teachers' efforts toward mathematics instruction and success and by building teacher capacity. In order to build teacher capacity, facilitate professional development, host a book study, encourage teachers to observe one another, build a mathematical community through a campus mathematics committee, and always implement new strategies and practices based on research that supports these efforts. By starting small and working diligently you can create an environment that is flourishing with mathematized leaders.

Reflective Questions

1. What inspired your love for mathematics? How can you use this to inspire the staff at your campus?
2. As you read about building capacity, did certain staff members come to mind? How will you encourage them to lead the way for other teachers?
3. Considering the current mathematical needs at your campus, what would be the best way to address these needs? How could you include teacher leaders at your school in the solution? Is there a book, article, or program that would help address the need?
4. How can campus administrators contribute to your campus vision of mathematizing your staff?

Resources

- *Math Workshop in Action* (Dr. Nicki Newton)
- *Math Running Records in Action* (Dr. Nicki Newton)
- *Mathematical Mindsets* (Jo Boaler)
- *The Math Coach Field Guide* (Marilyn Burns)
- *The Impact Cycle* (Jim Knight)
- NCTM (National Council for Teachers of Mathematics, www.NCTM.org)
- Jo Boaler's Mathematical Mindset Resources www.youcubed.org
- Education World (www.educationworld.com)
- Math Coach's Corner (www.mathcoachscorner.com/)
- Teaching to Inspire (https://teachingtoinspire.com/)
- Robert Kaplinsky (http://robertkaplinsky.com/observeme/)

5

Mathematizing Your Campus

Mariana Breaux has been a mathematics instructional coach for three years at an elementary school in Pasadena, TX that serves students pre-kindergarten through fourth grade. 95% of students on the campus qualify for free and reduced lunch. Prior to being an instructional coach, Mariana taught first-grade for three years and third-grade for two years. She has written mathematics curriculum to support district efforts focused on student discourse, engaging instructional activities, and purposeful review for state assessments. Mariana has presented mathematics professional development sessions at the campus and district level while also serving as a Master Trainer for district-wide professional development. She has also presented at numerous regional and state mathematics conferences and at Dr. Nicki's Guided Math Boot Camp in San Antonio. (Connect with Mariana on Twitter: @MarianaBreaux)

Introduction

The journey to mathematize my campus began as I embarked on a new position as Kindergarten-Grade 4 Mathematics Peer Facilitator at a new campus. During that same year our team of Mathematics Peer Facilitators began a book study using Dr. Nicki Newton's book *Math Workshop in Action*. As I read through the first couple of chapters of the book, the following quotes really resonated with me.

> A glance around the room tells you how important math is. . .
> —Dr. Nicki Newton (*Math Workshop in Action*, p. 21)

> What do your walls say about the importance of math in your class?
> —Dr. Nicki Newton (*Math Workshop in Action*, p. 22)

Reading those quotes forced me to ask myself the tough question, "What did the walls at my new campus say about the importance of mathematics in our campus?" As I looked around the walls on my campus, I saw very little evidence of mathematics. As I visited classrooms, I began to notice that mathematics materials and displays took a back seat to language arts. I started to listen to the conversations happening around me and learned that prior to my arrival, the campus' focus had been on building the teachers' capacity with Reader's Workshop. I quickly assessed that most teachers on my campus felt much more comfortable with language arts, were more focused on language arts than mathematics, and were not *yet* comfortable with the components of Math Workshop such as guided math and math workstations. I was able to share my observations with the administration team on my campus and that my goal was to mathematize our campus and allow the walls to tell a different story. The administrators were very supportive and encouraged me to get started.

Facts Around the Campus: Flashcards

As I embarked on the journey to mathematize my campus, I decided to start with something easy to manage and a topic always of interest to teachers: math facts. I began by implementing two fact-related projects: making fact flashcards available in campus hallways and creating videos of facts to display around the campus. I decided to make flashcards available in high-traffic areas such as the restrooms in each grade level POD. Typically when teachers take their students for restroom breaks, the students are allowed to take a book to read as they wait for the rest of their classmates. I wanted to provide students with an opportunity to practice math facts. I made an effort to be strategic and align the flashcards to the district's Scope and Sequence (see Figure 5.1) so that whatever flashcards were available were focused on the strategies students had covered in class (examples of addition/subtraction strategies: counting-on/counting-back, making ten and more, building up to ten/down through ten, doubles/near doubles).

I didn't have to look very long in our storage closets before I found many boxes of flashcards that aligned to the addition, subtraction, multiplication, and division standards (see Figure 5.2).

I decided to begin the implementation of "facts around the campus" with multiplication in Grades 3–4. When I began to place the flashcards around the campus it was around the time where the Scope and Sequence indicated that both the third- and fourth-grade students would have been exposed to different strategies to solve multiplication facts and were now moving on to using those facts to solve for division. Fortunately, I was able to find some flashcards that focused on multiplication and division fact families (see Figure 5.3).

Once I found the cards to use, I printed a "Math Fact Corner" sign (see Figure 5.4), punched a hole in each flashcard, grouped the flashcards using a binder clip, and hung the binder clip using an adhesive hook.

Once the cards were set up in the third- and fourth-grade PODs, I placed flashcards near the restroom next to the cafeteria. Because the restroom is a high-traffic area on our campus that students from five different grade

Figure 5.1 Example from Scope and Sequence Document

2017-2018 Pasadena ISD Scope & Sequence: Year at a Glance Grade 1 Mathematics (REVISED)

	Bundle 1:	Bundle 2:	
1NW: Bundles 1-2	**Bundle 1:** Subitize (0-10), Compose 10, & Addition/Subtraction (Strategies) 09.12-09.22 8 Days of Instruction + 1 Day Common Formative Assessment 1.2A: 2 days (0-10) 1.3C/1.5E: 4 days 1.3D/1.3E/1.5E: 2 days Strategy: Count-on/Count-back (+/- 0,1,2,3) (Number Paths) Ongoing 1.5A: Count Forward and Backward 1-20	**Bundle 2:** Addition/Subtraction (Word Problems), Compose/Decompose Numbers (0-20), More/Less Concepts (0-20), & Compare/Order Numbers (0-20) 09.25-10.13 12 Days of Instruction + 1 Day Common Formative Assessment 1.5D/1.3F/1.5E: 2 days Word Problems: Count-on/Count-back (+/- 0,1,2,3) (Number Paths) Results Unknown 1.2B/1.2C/1.3A/1.5E/1.5B: 4 days (0-20) 1.2D/1.5C: 2 days (0-20) 1.2E/1.2G: 2 days (0-20) 1.2F: 2 days (0-20) Ongoing 1.5A: Count Forward and Backward 1-20	CBA Testing Window: No 1NW CBA

	Bundle 3:	Bundle 4:	Bundle 5:	
2NW: Bundles 3-5	**Bundle 3:** Compose/Decompose Numbers (0-40), More/Less Concepts (0-40), Compare/Order Numbers (0-40), & Geometry (2-D Shapes) 10.16-11.03 14 Days of Instruction + 1 Day Common Formative Assessment 1.2B/1.2C/1.3A/1.5E/1.5B: 5 days (0-40) 1.2D/1.5C: 2 days (0-40) 1.2E/1.2G: 2 days (0-40) 1.2F: 2 days (0-40) 1.6A/1.6B/1.6D: 3 days Ongoing 1.5A: Count Forward and Backward 1-40	**Bundle 4:** Geometry (2-D Shapes & 3-D Solids), Addition/Subtraction (Strategies & Word Problems), & Coins (Values & Relationships) 11.06-12.01 14 Days of Instruction + 1 Day Common Formative Assessment 1.6C/1.6F: 2 days 1.6E/1.6B: 3 days 1.3D/1.3E/1.5E: 2 days Strategy: Make 10 and More & Build Up/Back Down through 10 (+/-7,8,9) (Double Ten Frames) 1.5D/1.3F/1.5E: 2 days Word Problems: Make 10 and More & Build Up/Back Down through 10 (+/-7,8,9) (Double Ten Frames) Results Unknown 1.4A/1.4B: 5 days Identify coins by value (2 days) Describe relationships among coins (3 days) Ongoing 1.5A: Count Forward and Backward 1-40	**Bundle 5:** Addition/Subtraction (Strategies & Word Problems) 12.04-12.15 9 Days of Instruction + 1 Day Common Formative Assessment 1.3D/1.3E/1.5E: 2 days Strategy: Doubles/Near Doubles (Doubles Mats) 1.5D/1.3F/1.5E: 2 days Word Problems: Doubles/Near Doubles (Doubles Mats); Results Unknown 1.5D/1.3F/1.3B/1.5E: 5 days Word Problems: Mixed Strategies (Number Paths, Double Ten Frames, Doubles Mats) Various Unknowns Ongoing 1.5A: Count Forward and Backward 1-40	CBA Testing Window: 12.18-12.20

Figure 5.2 Boxes of Flashcards Found In Storage Room

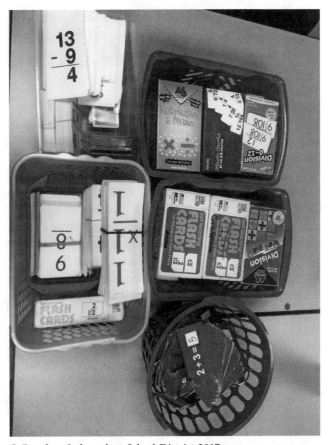

Figure 5.3 Examples of Cards Displayed in 3rd and 4th Grade POD

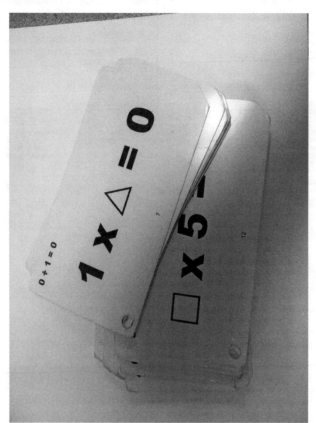

levels utilize on a daily basis, it was difficult to differentiate the flashcards for every grade level. I decided to place addition and subtraction flashcards there. Every teacher who uses these flashcards has a different system for using the cards. Some teachers allow students to work in pairs, others lead the activity by flashing a card to their entire class and allowing students to respond chorally. One of our teachers decided to have her students bring their personal sets of cards and her restroom managers were responsible for carrying them to and from the restroom (see Figure 5.5).

By the time the 2016–2017 school year came to a close, there were some things I knew I needed to re-think. The first thing I wanted to do was to support all of the grade levels with flashcards that aligned with the strategies outlined in their Scope and Sequence documents. Fortunately, when we came back in August 2017, our district introduced a new resource: Pasadena ISD's Number Sense and Fact Fluency Plan (see Figure 5.6).

This new resource outlined the progression of facts to be explored during each nine-weeks (by grade level) and provided scaffolded flashcards

Figure 5.4 4th Grade "Math Fact Corner" Sign and Cards

(see Figure 5.7) to support the strategies identified for each 9-week period. The scaffolded flashcards included images of the facts with the tools specified in the Scope and Sequence.

The second thing I wanted to do was update the system I used to display the flashcards, as the system I was using was not the most efficient system. One of the problems with the initial system was that by the end of the school year, the hooks I used to hang the flashcards were falling off the walls. Taking that issue into consideration and also considering the newly created Fact Fluency Plan, I made some changes. I set up a Fact Fluency Corner next to every restroom in the Kindergarten–fourth grade PODs. I updated the poster with the directions (see Figure 5.8) and displayed the documents outlining each grade level's Fact Fluency Plan for the

Figure 5.5 1st Graders Practicing with Addition Flashcards

Figure 5.6 Pasadena ISD's Fact Fluency Plan

Pasadena ISD Number Sense & Fact Fluency Plan

	1NW	2NW	3NW	4NW
Kindergarten	**Number Concepts 0-5** • Five Frame Cards (0-5) • Rekenrek Cards (0-5) • Counting Fingers Cards (0-5) • Dot Plate Cards (1-5)	**Number Concepts 6-10** • Ten Frame Cards (6-10) • Rekenrek Cards (6-10) • Counting Fingers Cards (6-10) • Dot Plate Cards (6-10)	**Number Concepts 11-15** • Double Ten Frame Cards (11-15) • Rekenrek Cards (11-15)	**Number Concepts 16-20** • Double Ten Frame Cards (16-20) • Rekenrek Cards (16-20)
Grade 1	**Number Concepts 0-20** • Double Ten Frame Cards (0-20) • Rekenrek Cards (0-20)	**Addition/Subtraction Concepts** • Count-on (+ 0,1,2,3) on Number Path Cards • Count-back (- 0,1,2,3) on Number Path Cards	**Addition/Subtraction Concepts** • Make 10 and More (+7,8,9) on Double Ten Frame Cards • Build Up/Back Down Through Ten (-7,8,9) on Double Ten Frame Cards	**Addition/Subtraction Concepts** • Doubles on Doubles Mat Cards • Near Doubles on Doubles Mat Cards
Grade 2	**Addition/Subtraction Facts** • Count-on (+ 0,1,2,3) on Number Path Cards • Count-back (- 0,1,2,3) on Number Path Cards • Doubles on Doubles Mat Cards	**Addition/Subtraction Facts** • Make 10 and More (+7,8,9) on Double Ten Frame Cards • Build Up/Back Down Through Ten (-7,8,9) on Double Ten Frame Cards • Near Doubles on Doubles Mat Cards	**Addition/Subtraction Facts** • Facts By Strategy	**Addition/Subtraction Facts** • Mixed Facts
	August/September • Teacher: BOY Running Record (+/-) & Supports		**December/January** • Teacher: MOY Running Record (+/-) & Supports	**May** • Teacher: EOY Running Record (+/-) & Supports

*Differentiate tools/cards according to individual student needs

> "Fluency is not a simple idea. Being fluent means that students are able to choose flexibly among methods and strategies to solve contextual and mathematical problems, they understand and are able to explain their approaches, and they are able to produce accurate answers efficiently. Fluency builds from initial exploration and discussions of number concepts to using informal reasoning strategies based on meanings and properties of the operations to the eventual use of general methods as tools in solving problems."
> NCTM *Principles to Actions* (2014, pg. 42)

Figure 5.7 Pasadena ISD's Fact Fluency Flashcards

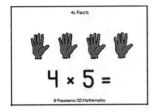

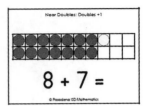

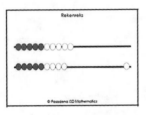
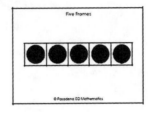

Figure 5.8 Kindergarten Fact Fluency Corner

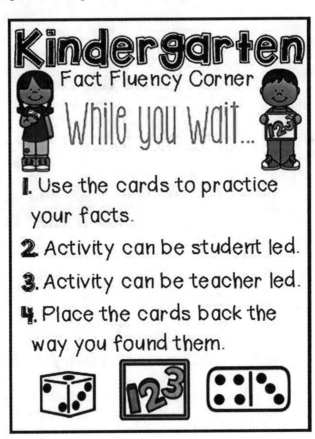

Figure 5.9 Fact Fluency Plan Posted in Kindergarten POD

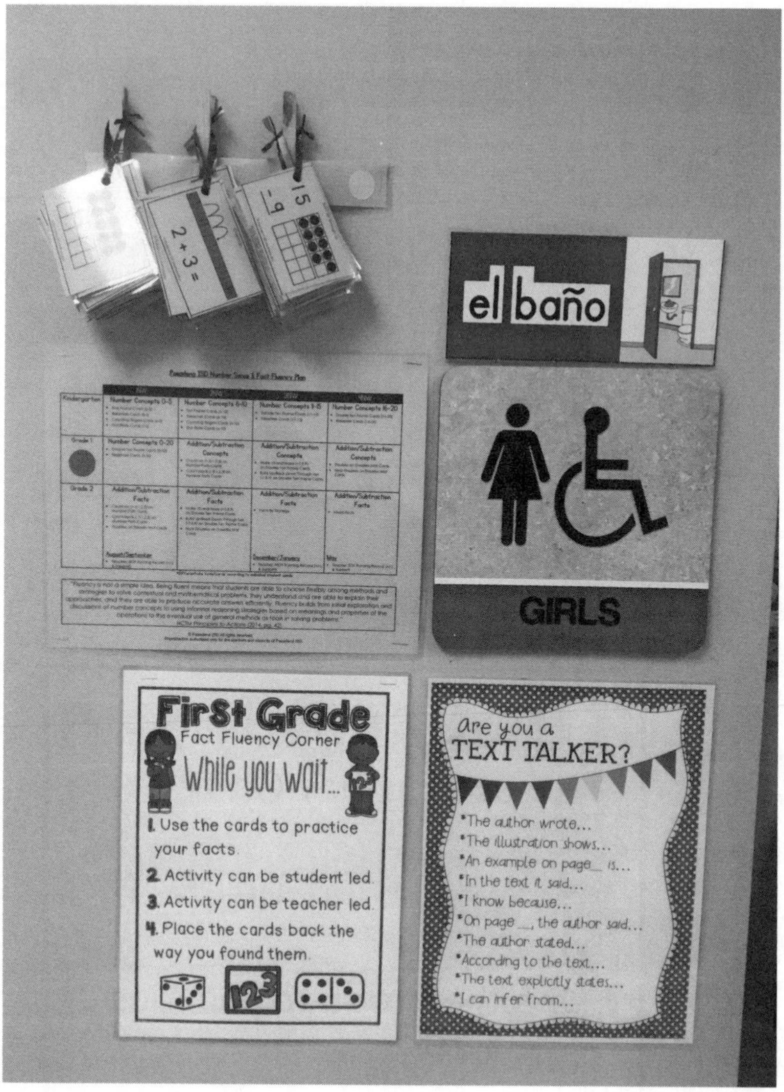

© Pasadena Independent School District 2017

entire school year (see Figure 5.9). I organized the flashcards into 9-week periods and hung the flashcards on clothespins rather than the hooks (see Figure 5.10).

Facts Around the Campus: Fact Fluency Videos

As I was getting to know the campus, I noticed that the cafeteria had two TV monitors mounted near the stage that were not being used. I quickly

Figure 5.10 Fact Fluency Flashcards Displayed

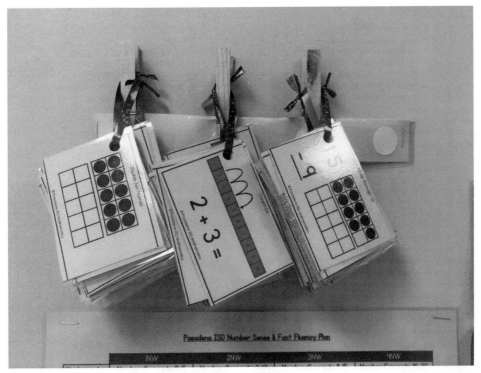

inquired about them, and once I found out that they were working monitors, I decided that I wanted to use them in order to promote math facts! Using PowerPoint, I decided to make short videos that looped facts and could be played during lunch hours (see Figures 5.11, 5.12, 5.13, and 5.14). I decided to make addition and subtraction videos. I thought it was important for the videos to showcase the use of the specific tools listed for each addition and subtraction fact strategy within the district's Scope and Sequence. For example, when teaching facts that include adding a 7, 8, and 9, the tool that is specified in the Scope and Sequence is the double ten frame. By using the double ten frame, students use the "make ten and more" strategy. Due to the difficulty many students in first grade to fourth grade were having with mastering addition and subtraction facts, I knew I wanted to keep my focus on addition and subtraction facts for all grade levels. I was able to train a paraprofessional to get the flash fact videos going and change the videos in order to target specific grade levels as they came into the cafeteria (see Figure 5.15).

Figure 5.11, Figure 5.12, Figure 5.13, Figure 5.14 Examples of Fact Fluency Videos

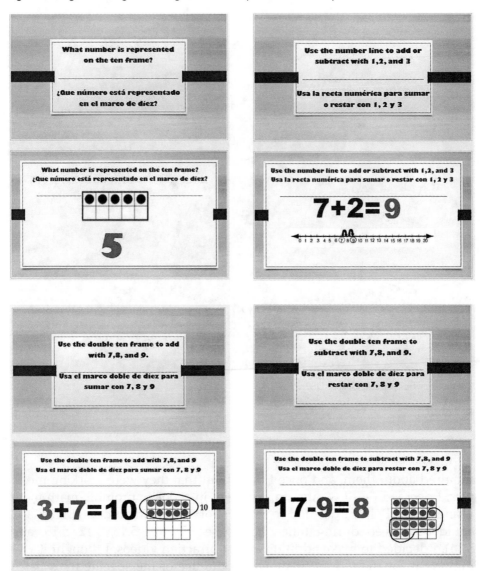

© *Pasadena Independent School District 2017*

The fact fluency videos were a hit. The teachers shared that they really liked the fact that the tools showcased within the videos were aligned to those they were using in the classroom. The teachers asked if they could have access to the videos in order to play them in their classrooms during transitions or just as a brain break. The videos were easily accessed through our campus' YouTube channel (http://bit. ly/2DLQRI2).

Figure 5.15 Fact Fluency Videos Playing During First-Grade Lunch

Facts Around the Campus: Reflections

Making facts visible was a quick and easy way to start mathematizing my campus! Although it took some time to fine-tune the systems that worked best for our campus, these two activities were not difficult to implement and provided targeted exposure and practice for our students. Using the flashcards from our district's Fact Fluency Plan and aligning the tools with the facts on the Fact Fluency Videos has supported a shift in mindsets regarding how fact fluency should be assessed. Rather that assessing the mastery of facts based solely on speed, efforts have shifted to focus on the use of number-based strategies to help students internalize the facts. Having these tools visible around our campus serves as a reminder for both teachers and students that using a variety of tools supports fact fluency development.

> I have seen growth in my students as we focus on using different numeric strategies in order to scaffold student mastery of facts.
>
> Grade 1 Teacher

> Giving students access to different strategies, tools and scaffolds to equip them to tackle fact fluency has given my students opportunities for more success. This type of differentiation is a great way to help students find the tools they are most successful with.
>
> Grade 3 Teacher

School-Wide Mathematics Initiatives: Math Boggle

Once I felt like the "facts around the campus" efforts were off to a good start, I decided to start looking for different mathematics activities to showcase around the campus. The three activities I started with were: Math Boggle, The Answer Is. . ., and Which One Doesn't Belong?

Math Boggle is an open ended-game that allows students to take risks as they make connections with numbers. This activity is similar to the game Boggle®, where players attempt to create words in sequences of adjacent letters. I stumbled across a math version of Boggle® that has been coined as "Math Boggle." I was able to find many examples on Pinterest, and found a variety of freebies on Teachers Pay Teachers. After looking through the endless examples, I decided to create a version of Math Boggle that met our campus needs.

Math Boggle was a perfect activity for our students because it allows students to have an opportunity to share the connections they see with numbers. I decided that our school's Math Boggle (see Figure 5.16) would need to be a simplified version. I started with small numbers and changed the rules such that the connections between numbers did not have to be limited to looking for connections between adjacent numbers. I wanted students to share *any* connections they saw within those numbers whether the numbers were adjacent to each other or not. These adjustments made it possible to have one central Math Boggle board for students in Kindergarten to fourth grade to be able to participate. Our first Math Boggle board

Figure 5.16 First Math Boggle Board

was placed outside of the cafeteria doors. Attached to the boards were dry-erase markers and two laminated posters on which students could write their responses (see Figures 5.17 and 5.18).

> I like playing Math Boggle because it reminds me of a puzzle and it makes me think about numbers that I already know.
>
> Grade 3 Student

> Math Boggle is fun! I like that I can look for addition, subtraction, division, and multiplication facts on it.
>
> Grade 4 Student

Figure 5.17 First Math Boggle Board Response Posters

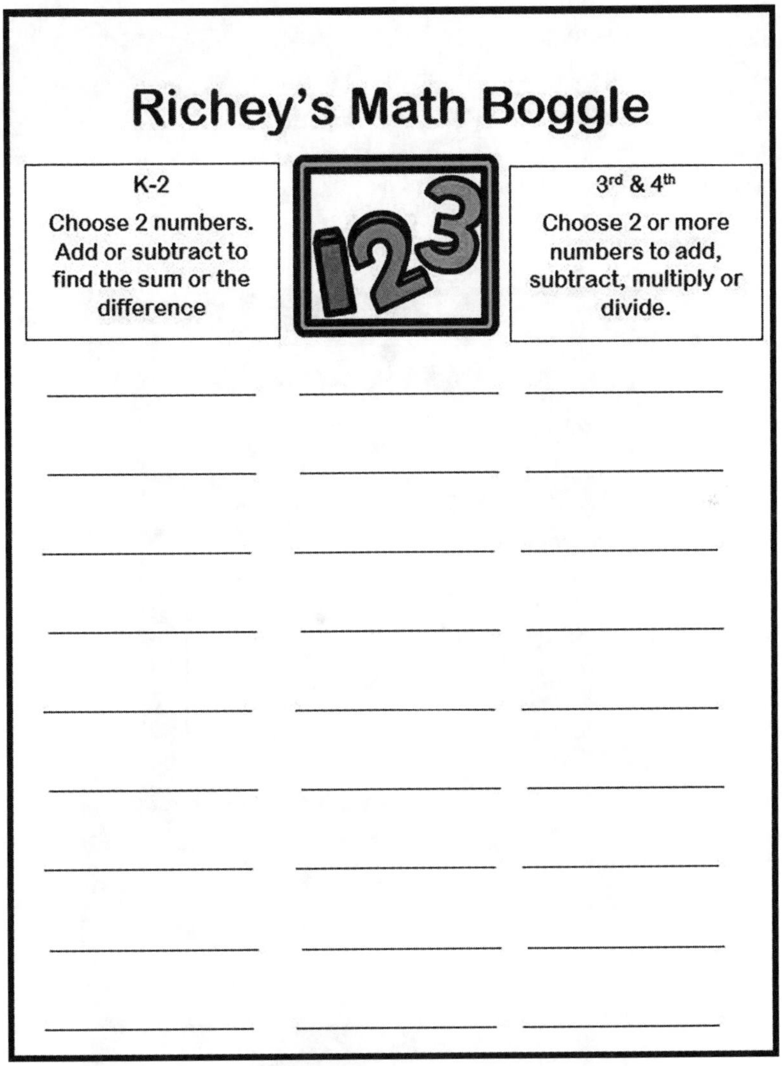

Richey's Math Boggle

K-2		3rd & 4th
Choose 2 numbers. Add or subtract to find the sum or the difference		Choose 2 or more numbers to add, subtract, multiply or divide.

© *Pasadena Independent School District 2017*

Figure 5.18 Posters with Student's Responses

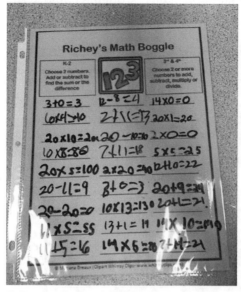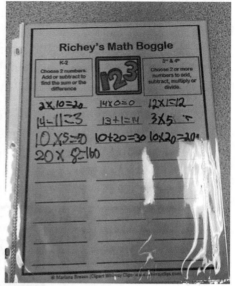

Figure 5.19 Updated Math Boggle Board

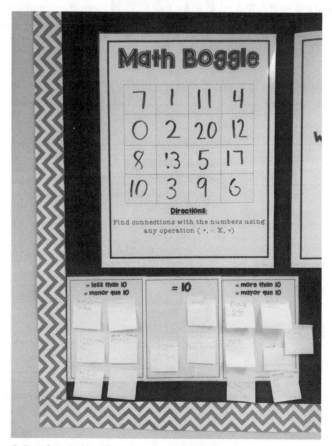

Figure 5.20, Figure 5.21, Figure 5.22 Student Math Boggle Responses on New Board

 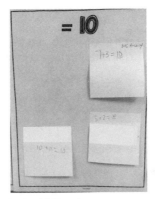 

© *Pasadena Independent School District 2017*

I periodically walked by the Math Boggle board to check in on the responses. If the student's connection was correct, it received a check mark, if it needed to be corrected, it was circled. I changed the board once I noticed that the posters were full, which usually occurred at the end of every month.

As with the math flashcards, I also updated the way Math Boggle was displayed the following school year. The first Math Boggle board was a large display. Each number was printed on an 8.5" x 11" page. In order to change the original Math Boggle board, I had to use a ladder. The following school year I decided to make a laminated poster where I could use a dry-erase marker to write the new numbers when it was time to update the Math Boggle board (see Figure 5.19). This change eliminated the need of a ladder and made the process much more manageable. Since the size of the board had decreased, students now had space to record their connections on sticky notes (see Figures 5.20, 5.21, and 5.22).

School-Wide Mathematics Initiatives: The Answer Is . . .

The Answer Is . . . is an open-ended activity that gives students the opportunity to work backwards. The students are given the "answer" and they are to come up with the question or problem situation that would result in the given answer. This activity can be easily differentiated and can be used across grade levels. Before releasing The Answer Is . . . to the students, I sent an email (see Figure 5.23) to the teachers explaining our new School-Wide Initiative Bulletin Board that was found outside my office and asked the teachers to work with their classes to generate a problem situation with a given answer and deliver a copy of the problem situation to a folder found next to the board. All grade levels were given the same "answer" but Kindergarten to second-grade teachers were asked to work with their classes

Figure 5.23 Email Sent to Teachers Introducing Them to The Answer Is . . .

Teachers,

Outside of the Peer Facilitator's Room (A13) we will begin our School Wide Interactive Bulletin Board. This bulletin board is titled "The Answer is..."

This time around the answer is 24.

Together as a class, come up with a problem situation with the answer/solution being 24. (It can be 24 marbles, pumpkins, or dolls... anything that the class decides on.) This can be done during your Math Stretch/ Math Review time. You can be the scribe, but the class should be a part of creating the problem.

Record the problem situation in the recording sheet that I have placed in your box.

To reflect the instruction in our classrooms, it would be great if K-2 focus on creating an addition or subtraction problem and 3ʳᵈ-4ᵗʰ grade focus on multiplication, division, or a multi-step problem.

There will be a folder next to the bulletin board where you can drop off the recording sheet.

Thank you all so much! Can't wait to see all the fun problems your classes come up with! ☺

Mariana Breaux
Math Peer Facilitator
Richey Elementary School
Extension # 3087

© *Pasadena Independent School District 2017*

to generate an addition or subtraction problem, and third- and fourth-grade teachers were asked to work with their classes to generate a multiplication and division problem (see Figure 5.24).

During the second year of implementing The Answer Is. . ., the process has been released to the students (see Figure 5.25). Students are invited to participate by writing their question/problem situation on a slip of paper (see Figure 5.26) found underneath the board and submitting the paper in a

Figure 5.24 Examples of Kindergarten- 4th Grade Responses to First The Answer Is . . .

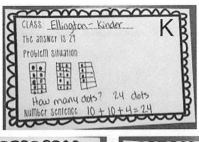

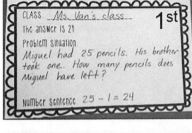

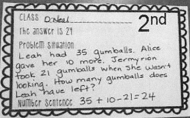

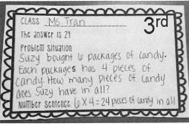

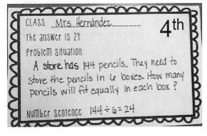

Figure 5.25 New The Answer Is . . . Board

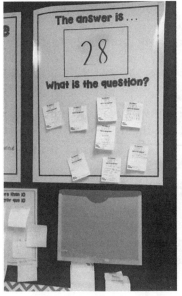

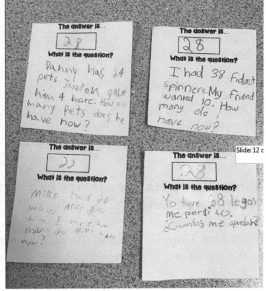

Figure 5.26 The Answer Is . . . Student Response Slip

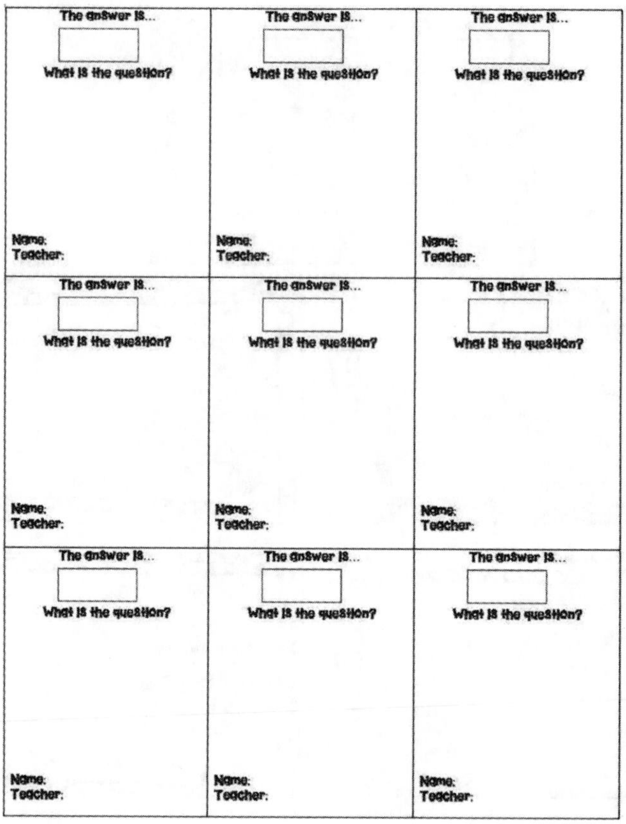

The answer is... What is the question? Name: Teacher:	The answer is... What is the question? Name: Teacher:	The answer is... What is the question? Name: Teacher:
The answer is... What is the question? Name: Teacher:	The answer is... What is the question? Name: Teacher:	The answer is... What is the question? Name: Teacher:
The answer is... What is the question? Name: Teacher:	The answer is... What is the question? Name: Teacher:	The answer is... What is the question? Name: Teacher:

folder for review. The slip they use includes their name and teacher name, and if the response is incorrect they will get a chance to change it.

> The Answer Is . . . is challenging to me. My brain has to think backwards!
>
> Grade 2 Student

> At first I didn't like The Answer is . . . I thought it was too hard and I didn't like to play it. But now that I get it, I like to try it!
>
> Grade 4 Student

School-Wide Mathematics Initiatives: Which One Doesn't Belong?

Which One Doesn't Belong? (WODB) is an activity that I learned about during one of our Mathematics Peer Facilitator meetings. This open-ended activity allows students to be analytical, make connections, take risks, and defend their ideas! The students are given a table with four images or numbers, and the students are to look for which of the four images or numbers do not belong and justify their reasoning (see Figure 5.27). This activity is one of the easiest activities to implement. It's as simple as going on the WODB website (http://wodb.ca/), choosing the activity you like, clicking print, and setting it up by providing students with a way to express their opinion.

> Sometimes my friend and I see different things on the WODB board. I like to see how she sees different things than I do.
>
> Grade 1 Student

When I first introduced this activity, I placed a WODB board in each grade level POD (see Figure 5.28) in order to allow all teachers and students to see it and get familiar with it. I simply created a template where I snipped an image from the WODB website and made sticky notes and pencils available for students to respond (see Figure 5.29). I also included a sentence stem to encourage our students to respond in complete sentences (see Figure 5.30).

Since the WODB boards were all over our campus, I made it a point to check them every time I walked by. When I noticed the boards were filled up, I would take the sticky notes and write down feedback for the students. If the student's connection was correct, it received a check mark, if it needed to be corrected, it was circled and returned to them via their homeroom teacher's box with a short encouragement to try again. The boards were changed once the posters were full, which usually occurred at the end of every month.

Figure 5.27 Examples of Boards Available on WODB Website

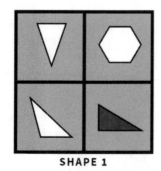

SHAPE 1

from Mary Bourassa

SHAPE 18

from Connor, Dorotea, Jessica & Mike

SHAPE 28

from Erick Lee

© *wodba.ca*

Figure 5.28 4th Grade WODB Board

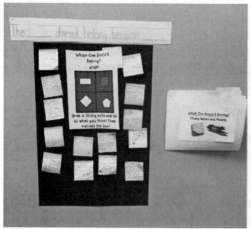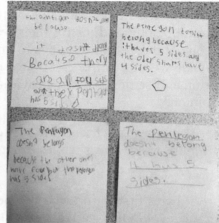

Figure 5.29 Example of WODB Template

Which One Doesn't Belong?
Why?

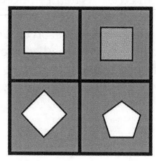

Grab a sticky note and tell us what you think! Think outside the box!

Figure 5.30 Sentence Stem Provided on WODB Board

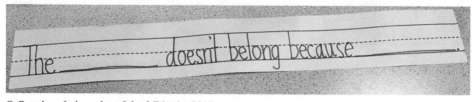

The _____ doesn't belong because _____

School-Wide Mathematics Initiatives: Reflections

Showcasing school-wide mathematics initiatives using activities such as Math Boggle, The Answer Is. . ., and WODB are great ways to make math visible on your campus. These activities will keep students exposed to mathematics activities as they walk the hallways of your campus. Throughout the first year of implementing these initiatives, I would keep the students' response slips as the different boards were changed. In the spring of 2018, we began to have a monthly drawing using all of the correct submissions to Math Boggle, The Answer Is. . ., and WODB. For this drawing, all slips were placed in a container and four prize winners were named. Students are able to come to the office and choose a math related prize. The prizes to choose from include playing cards, dice, fluency flashcards, and a "Mathtastic" bracelet (see Figure 5.31).

Through the use of these school-wide mathematics initiatives, math has been put on the map at our school. Students and teachers are constantly receiving messages that communicate that math is important!

Figure 5.31 Math Prizes

© *Pasadena Independent School District 2017*

All of the mathematics initiatives that are visible around our campus keep me in the loop of all that's out there, things that I can try with my students. These implementations, and making facts accessible on our campus, make our students more aware and excited about math! Before our journey to mathematize our school walls, math was just another subject to teach each day. Now, the children and I both are excited to talk about math and try new activities. We look forward to our math time, and it's hard to stop!

Grade 2 Teacher

School-Wide Mathematics Initiatives: Mathematician Street

When the journey to mathematize my campus began, The Answer Is. . ., Math Boggle, and WODB were placed in different parts of the campus. It worked out well for a while, but then it began getting harder to update them frequently because they were scattered all over our campus. In the spring of 2017, I decided to place the activities in one spot near my office to make it easier to maintain. I coined the hallway where my office is located as Mathematician Street (see Figure 5.32).

Figure 5.32 The First Mathematician Street

In the last couple of years, Mathematician Street has expanded (see Figure 5.33). Mathematician Street includes a variety of activities focused on developing our mathematicians' mindsets and love for mathematics.

Figure 5.33 Updated Mathematician Street

© *Pasadena Independent School District 2017*

Making this change has been beneficial in several ways. The fact that all of the activities are together makes it easier to update them. Another benefit from having all of the activities in a central place is that we have a special space designated for mathematics. Students know where they can come to be challenged and express themselves as mathematicians. The greatest benefit from Mathematician's Street is that it allows our walls to send the message to everyone who walks into our campus saying, "Math is valued here! Math is so important to us that we have dedicated a hallway to it!"

Mathematician St. always catches my eyes! It always looks like so much fun! I always want to stop and try the activities!

PPCD Teacher

The implementation of Mathematician St. has positively impacted my students and teachers. Mathematician St. has helped us promote a growth mindset and fun real-life math activities school wide. Most importantly, these initiatives help us instill a love for math in our students.

Campus Administrator

Mathematician Street has also inspired the development of a Readers' Boulevard and a Writer's Way where students have access to interactive reading and writing activities around the campus.

> Mathematician St. is contagious!! If it wasn't for Mathematician St., I would have never thought of creating a Readers Blvd. which in turn inspired our Writing Peer Facilitator to create a Writer's Way. Our walls honor mathematics, reading, and writing alike.
>
> Reading Peer Facilitator

One of the great things about mathematizing your campus is that there are so many ways to do it! There is no wrong way to do it! It's all about making math visible and accessible to our students. Below are some examples of how different campuses have taken activities such as Math Boggle, WODB, The Answer Is. . ., and Mathematician Street and made it their own in order to meet the needs of their campuses (see Figures 5.34, 5.35, and 5.36).

Figure 5.34 South Belt Elementary School's (Pasadena ISD) Mathematician Street

Robin Sanders
@RobinSa20476784

Follow ∨

Ready for our awesome mathematicians and bookworms! #PISDMathChat

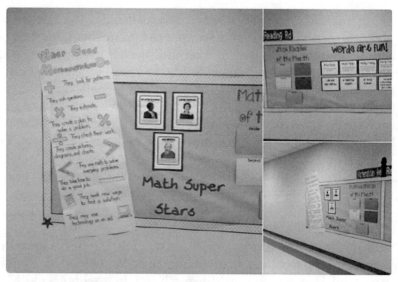

8:20 AM - 15 Sep 2017

1 Retweet **8** Likes

Figure 5.35 Young Elementary School's (Pasadena ISD) Mathematician Street

 **Jessica Garza**
@JessicaCGarza

Following ∨

Mathematician st is here and ready to go!!!
#PISDMathChat

3:19 PM - 19 Sep 2017

Figure 5.36 John Haley Elementary School's (Irving ISD) Mathematician Street

Lessons Learned

- Don't be afraid of trying new things.
- If possible, find one central location for the activities.
- Adjust the activities to meet the needs of your campus.

Getting Started Checklist

- Assess the message the walls at your campus are sending.
- Listen to the conversations about math that are happening around you.
- Get inspired! Explore resources such as Twitter (#PISDMathChat, #ElemMathChat, #Mathematize) and Pinterest.
- Decide on which activities you want to start with and use templates to get started!
- Designate a space that will be dedicated to display math activities!
- Start somewhere, start small!

Key Points

- Mathematizing your campus communicates that math is valued.
- Mathematizing your campus encourages risk-taking.
- Mathematizing your campus makes mathematics accessible.

Summary

Mathematizing your campus can only begin after you take an honest inventory to assess the message that the walls are communicating about the importance of mathematics. It is important to listen to the conversations around you, as the conversations will reveal how teachers and students really feel about math. Once you are ready, you can begin mathematizing your campus with two simple types of activities—making facts visible and one of the campus-wide mathematics initiatives.

Reflective Questions

1. What do your walls say about the importance of mathematics on your campus?
2. What are the conversations between teachers and students like in regards to mathematics on your campus?

3. Why is it important to mathematize your campus? What are the benefits of mathematizing your campus?
4. Which of the activities presented in this chapter could you see yourself implementing and maintaining in the next school year?

Resources

- Richey Elementary YouTube Page (http://bit.ly/2DLQRI2)
- WODB (www.wodb.ca)
- Campus-Wide Initiative Poster Freebies (http://bit.ly/2xBuj4S)
- Chronicles of a Math Coach Blog (https://chroniclesofamath-coach.wordpress.com/)
- Pinterest—Dr. Nicki Newton (www.pinterest.com/drnicki7/)
- Pinterest—PISD Mathematics (www.pinterest.com/PISDMathematics/)
- Twitter—PISD Mathematics (https://twitter.com/pisdmathematics)
- Clipart for Fact Fluency Corner and Richey's Math Boggle—Whimsy Clips (www.whimsyclips.com/)

6

Mathematizing Your Classroom

Kirsta Paulus is a third-grade teacher in a self-contained classroom of a Title 1 elementary school in Pasadena ISD. Her school has over eight-hundred fifty students campus enrolled in pre-kindergarten through fourth-grade. Kirsta's classroom contains students identified as English language learners, students in need of inclusion support, and students identified as gifted/talented. Kirsta has participated in district-curriculum writing efforts as a writer of instructional resources and assessment items for third-grade mathematics. She has also facilitated professional development sessions for mathematics at her campus as well as for the district, and has presented at regional and statewide mathematics conferences sessions. (Connect with Kirsta on Twitter: @KirstaPaulus)

Jessica Garza is a second-grade bilingual teacher at an elementary school in Pasadena, Texas. Her school has approximately 600 students. A large percentage of the students are Hispanic, come from lower income households, and have high mobility rates. Her classroom includes students identified as English language learners and students in need of special education support. Jessica has been teaching mathematics for four years and supports mathematics at her campus by serving on her school Math Committee. Jessica has participated in district-curriculum writing efforts as a writer of instructional resources to support students in second-grade mathematics. She has presented mathematics conference sessions at the regional and state level, as well as with students in a higher-education setting. (Connect with Jessica on Twitter: @JessicaCGarza)

Samantha Cortez is a first-grade bilingual teacher in a self-contained classroom in Pasadena, Texas. She works in a Title 1 school that serves approximately 600 students from pre-kindergarten to fourth grade with the majority of the students receiving free or reduced lunch. Her classroom includes students identified as English language learners, students identified as gifted and talented, and students in need of special education support. Samantha taught in a monolingual classroom for one year and has been a first-grade bilingual teacher for two years. She supports mathematics instruction at her campus by serving on the Math Committee. Samantha has participated in district-curriculum writing efforts as a writer of instructional resources to support students in first-grade mathematics. She has presented sessions at regional and state level mathematics conferences. (Connect with Samantha on Twitter: @SCortez7178)

Introduction

If your classroom could speak, what would it say about mathematics? During our first years teaching, we spent a lot of time looking around the classrooms at our schools for a reference and a guide as to how to set up our own classrooms. We noticed a trend. Our colleagues' classrooms were literacy-rich with extensive classroom libraries, reading nooks, and anchor charts focused on literacy skills, but there was little guidance regarding how to create a mathematically rich classroom.

We wanted to create classroom environments that communicated to students, administrators, families, and every other visitor that mathematics was valued in our classroom and that we were all part of this evolving mathematical community. We wanted to give students positive opportunities to grow and learn as mathematicians. We wanted to eliminate the fear of mathematics and encourage our students to be risk-takers and curious mathematicians. So we asked ourselves, "How can our Math Workshop become meaningful, creative, and purposeful?"

We took defining steps to transform our walls, our students' mindsets, and our use of data in order to better meet our students' needs. Our main goal was to have a student-centered mathematics classroom so that our students would find value in their learning and be successful, purposeful mathematicians. We wanted there to be value in the tools that we implemented in our classrooms, but those efforts can be difficult when there is no guide as to how we should implement those tools. Mathematizing our classrooms came from finding value in the tools that we implement in our classrooms such as anchor charts, interactive math journals, data binders, and differentiated workstations. The pages that follow describe how these tools have been used to mathematize our classrooms.

Tools to Mathematize Your Classroom: Anchor Charts

In my role as a third-grade teacher, I (Kirsta) am constantly seeking ways to encourage my students to be more independent learners. I want to develop capable problem solvers, and I began to see my classroom walls as an opportunity to promote this skill. While our class anchor charts first began as a way to be more transparent in our learning of mathematics and emphasize the importance of our classroom as a learning space for mathematics, the anchor charts have developed through the years to serve an even greater purpose. Our math anchor charts now allow students opportunities to seek answers to questions, to confirm their thinking, and to find ideas and strategies to apply in their attempts at tackling mathematics. Our anchor charts have become an essential tool for students to reference as they grow as mathematicians.

Anchor Charts: Co-constructed With Students

Anchor charts should be co-constructed with students because the process gives the students a sense of ownership over the material. If students are not able to provide input into the creation of the anchor chart, they are less likely to reference the anchor chart while working independently. Sticky notes are an easy way to incorporate student input. Giving students a practice problem on a sticky note and attaching it to the anchor chart is a quick, simple way to remind students of times when they successfully applied the student expectation to a problem situation. In the following example (see Figures 6.1 and 6.2), students worked with a partner to determine if a given number was even or odd and then justified their thinking using divisibility rules.

Including student quotes and scribing students' thoughts during classroom discussions is another way to quickly include student input on an anchor chart. In Figure 6.3, students shared their ideas for objects that would best be measured with the given unit, the class discussed and agreed upon an estimated weight for each object, and the teacher scribed notes from the conversation.

This purposeful effort to include students in the creation of anchor charts has resulted in an increased use of the anchor charts by students.

We use our anchor charts every day.

Grade 3 Student

Figure 6.1 Anchor Chart with Student Input

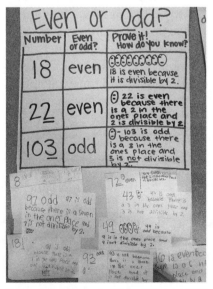

Figure 6.2 Student Work from Anchor Chart

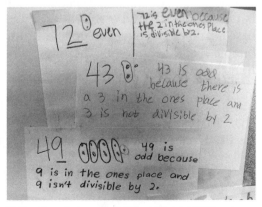

© *Pasadena Independent School District 2017*   © *Pasadena Independent School District 2017*

Figure 6.3 Student Input on Anchor Chart

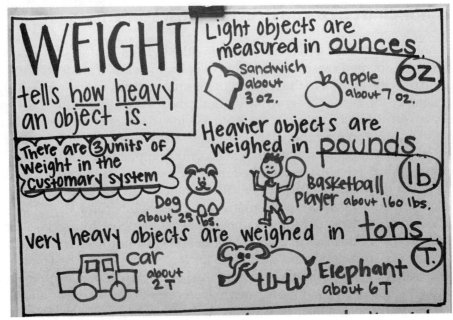

© *Pasadena Independent School District 2017*

Anchor Charts: Clear Focus

Anchor charts should have a clear, concise title accompanied with an "I can" statement because these features help students to quickly and easily identify the focus of each anchor chart. Including sentence frames on the anchor chart models the correct use of academic language and encourages the expectation that students do the same. In the following example (see Figure 6.4), students can clearly see that the focus is place value relationships and the expectation is that students will be able to describe mathematical relationships in the base ten place value system up to the hundred-thousands place. The thinking bubbles capture students' thoughts, while the sentence stem at the bottom translates these thoughts into academic language.

The purposeful effort of using a specific title and "I can" statements has resulted in students spending less time trying to figure out which anchor chart to use for their specific need, and the inclusion of sentence stems has resulted in an increase of the correct usage of academic language.

> Just look at the title and you know if it's the one you want! It takes like two seconds to know.
>
> Grade 3 Student

Figure 6.4 Anchor Chart with "I Can" Statement

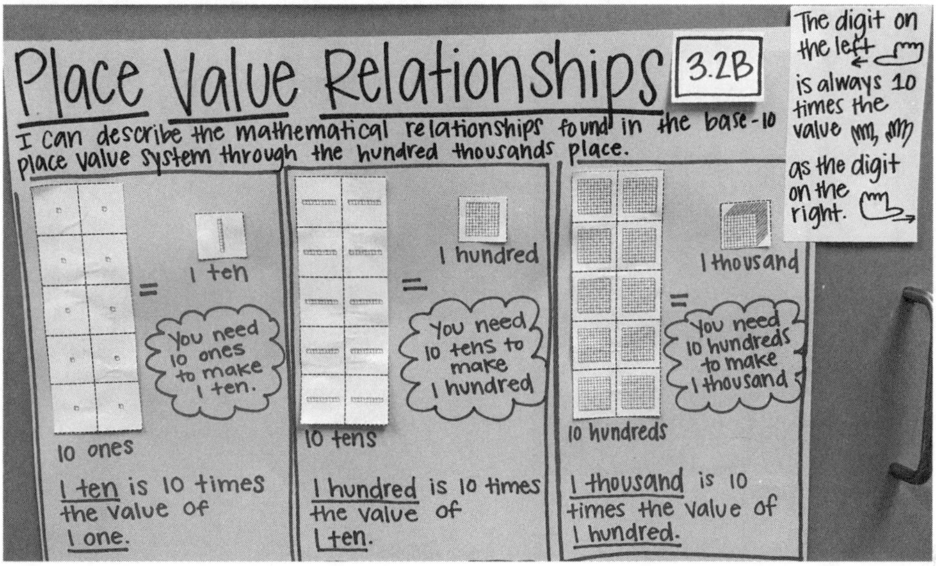

© Pasadena Independent School District 2017

Anchor Charts: Procedural Steps

Anchor charts should include steps for procedures. Including steps for procedures helps students as they work to apply procedures independently. In the example (see Figures 6.5 and 6.6), step-by-step directions accompany each strategy and example so that students can follow exactly what to do, as well as see an example of how to complete the procedure. For example, in "Expanded Algorithm," step 1 reads, "Line up the numbers using place value. Put the 2-digit number on the top." This step is next to where 54 is written lined up above 7 in the algorithm example. Step 2 reads, "Multiply the ones and write the product." This step is next to where 4 is multiplied by 7, and the product is written, again lined up using place value. The steps continue, concisely explaining what to do next to an example of what the step looks like when it is applied.

This purposeful effort of including step-by-step directions on anchor charts has helped students apply complex procedures more independently.

> The anchor charts have directions to follow so you can get help when you're stuck.
>
> Grade 3 Student

Figure 6.5 Anchor Chart with Procedural Steps

Figure 6.6 Anchor Chart with Procedural Steps Close Up

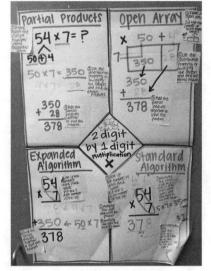

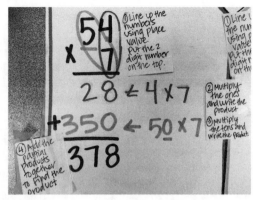

Anchor Charts: Color-Coding

Anchor charts should be color-coded to allow students opportunities to make connections between concepts. As so many student expectations include varying ways to show the same concept (for example, different ways to represent multiplication facts, different strategies to solve an addition word problem, etc.), students' understanding of the larger concept is deepened when they can see and understand how the different representations are related.

In the following example (see Figure 6.7), color-coding is used to differentiate the values of each digit. For example, every representation of the thousands is in purple. This allows students to see what three thousands looks like in standard form, pictorial form, expanded notation, word form, and expanded form. This is continued as every representation of the hundreds is in red, every representation of tens is in blue, and every representation of the ones is in orange. The color-coding allows students to easily see the value of the digit and how it is represented in each of the different forms.

This purposeful effort has resulted in students being able to better see connections between multiple representations.

Anchor Charts: Graphics and Visuals

Anchor charts should include images because visual images help illustrate concepts. In the example (see Figures 6.8 and 6.9), a color-coded pictorial model illustrates the use of the distributive property. The visual of the array

Figure 6.7 Anchor Chart with Color-Coding

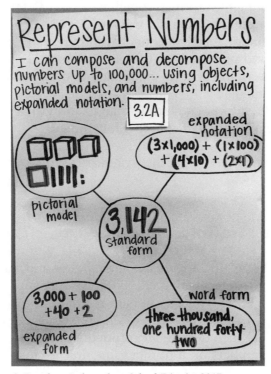

Figure 6.8 Anchor Chart with Images

Figure 6.9 Anchor Chart with Images Close Up

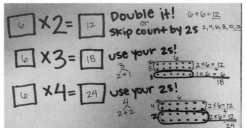

helps students to see how breaking apart a multiplication fact into two facts and then adding the products together can be used to find the original product. For example, students can think of 3 × 6 as (2 × 6) + (1 × 6). This pictorial representation on the anchor chart reminds students of when they initially learned and practiced the distributive property by making arrays with concrete objects and bridges the models to the abstract representation with only numbers.

The purposeful effort of including images and visuals has resulted in a more thorough explanation of concepts for students.

The pictures show you what the words are saying.

Grade 3 Student

Anchor Charts: Scaffolds and Supports

Anchor charts should include relevant scaffolds and supports, such as hundreds charts, math fact tables, etc., because these supports will encourage students struggling with concepts to reference the anchor chart with greater frequency. In the following example (see Figures 6.10 and 6.11), rounding charts are included to help students find consecutive multiples when rounding numbers on a number line. In the close up, students are

Figure 6.10 Anchor Chart with Scaffolds

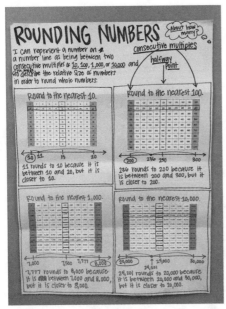

© Pasadena Independent School District 2017

Figure 6.11 Anchor Chart with Scaffolds Close Up

© Pasadena Independent School District 2017

able to see how the circled line on the chart can be used to create a number line for rounding (with a benchmark number on either end and a halfway number in the middle), which can be seen immediately below the chart. Again, a sentence stem is included to help students justify their thinking using academic language.

This purposeful effort of including scaffolds encourages those students who need additional support to refer to the anchor chart. As students become more confident in their ability to apply the skill without the scaffolds, they will reference these anchor charts, or these pieces of the anchor charts, with less frequency.

You don't need to always use them, only when you need them.

Grade 3 Student

Anchor Charts: Question Stems

Anchor charts should include question stems because this helps students make a connection between classroom learning and how they are expected to demonstrate understanding and mastery of a student expectation. In the example (see Figure 6.12), the question stems on the anchor chart model the language that would be used to assess student understanding of the concepts so that students have a better understanding of what test questions are asking and the steps they can take to solve the problems. The question to the right of the table, "How could the relationship between the number of students and the number of teams be described?" models the language that may be used to ask students the relationship between number pairs in a table. The question at the bottom of the anchor chart, "Based on the relationship between the number pairs, how many teams could be organized from 35 students?" models how students might be asked to extend a table's pattern.

Oftentimes, students don't understand what is being asked of them when they read a question, or even when teachers tell them "Show your work!" The purposeful effort of including question stems on anchor charts sets an expectation for students of what showing work should look like and helps set students up for success.

Anchor Charts: Increasing Student Usage

The goal in creating anchor charts is for students to refer back to the anchor charts as a scaffold to support their ability to apply the student expectation to their independent work and math workstations (see Figure 6.13).

Figure 6.12 Anchor Chart with Question Stems

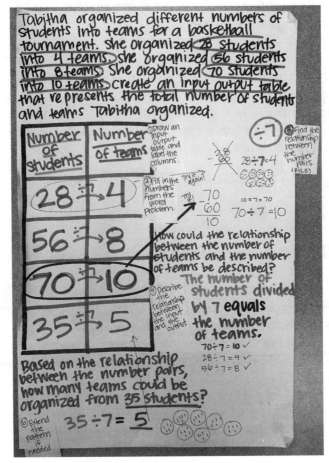

© *Pasadena Independent School District 2017*

If teachers want students to use anchor charts, the anchor charts must be student-friendly. Anchor charts must also be co-constructed with students so that students are familiar with the content and reviewing the anchor chart reminds them of an earlier concrete learning experience.

If teachers want students to use anchor charts, then teachers must model for students exactly how an anchor chart can help them with their independent work and draw attention to the steps outlined to complete a procedure. This can be a brief reminder, but the reminders should be done with consistency as a frequent reinforcement.

Teachers must reference anchor charts and their location often. This can be seamlessly done at the beginning of a lesson to summarize the previous day's learning and introduce the new day's learning. Introducing a new workstation is another time when teachers can highlight where the relevant anchor chart is located and how the content can help students as they work. Teachers must also refer students to anchor charts with consistency. Instead of just verbally

Figure 6.13 Student Usage of Anchor Charts

answering a student's question during the math block, teachers can take them on a "field trip" to find the answer on an anchor chart and show students how their question can be answered by referencing this tool. Although these efforts may take longer initially, it builds students' capacity and enables them to help themselves in the future. Including reminders during independent work or within workstation directions to refer to relevant anchor charts with questions is also a quick, helpful reminder for students and sets the expectation that students first try to help themselves before seeking help from others.

Activities such as scavenger hunts or "Find Someone Who Can. . . " (see Figure 6.14) can be done at the beginning of the year when routines and procedures are being introduced. These simple, engaging activities force students to familiarize themselves with the location of anchor charts as well as their content.

The increased student use of anchor charts has promoted more independent learners in my classroom. Students have come to see anchor charts as a valuable resource they can consult when they have questions or need help.

> The anchor charts give you examples so you can go and look when you have a question or you don't understand something so you know what to do.
>
> Grade 3 Student

Figure 6.14 Anchor Chart Scavenger Hunt

Find Someone Who
(math wall edition)

Find someone who can...

	Student Initials
...show you where to find what good mathematicians do. Have them write down the one they think is the most important below.	
...show you where you can look if you forget how to represent a number using expanded form. Have them explain the steps using the number 5,408 and write it in expanded form below.	
...show you where you can look if you want to learn about place value relationships. Have them write the relationship between 1 hundred and 1 ten below.	
...show you where you can find what station you go to next. Have them write down your next station and their next station below.	
...show you where to find the meaning of unknown math words. Have them copy the card they think is most useful below.	

© *Pasadena Independent School District 2017*

Lessons Learned

- An anchor chart should have a clear, singular focus to avoid student confusion.
- Prewrite the title and "I can" statement on an anchor chart to save instructional time. Make this clear and concise so students can easily identify which anchor chart is relevant to their needs.
- Make anchor charts with students and include their input. Anchor charts are meant to capture students learning and remind them of

previous instruction and examples. Anchor charts made without students will rarely be referenced.

- Preplan what should be included on the anchor chart (steps to follow, an example, etc.) and have a framework in mind. Disorganized anchor charts are difficult to follow, and students are less likely to refer to them when they need help.
- Limit the amount of text on anchor charts and include visuals or graphics when possible. An anchor chart with too much text overwhelms students and discourages them from using the anchor chart. Images are more attractive to students and catch wandering eyes.
- Model how to use anchor charts. and refer students to anchor charts to encourage their continued use. Without modeling and reminders, students will not know how to use anchor charts or use them with consistency.

Getting Started Checklist

- Find a designated place in the classroom to consistently hang class-created anchor charts.
- Collect the materials necessary to create an anchor chart: markers, chart paper or large construction paper, any needed graphics (images of manipulatives, tools, etc.).
- Prewrite a concise, descriptive title on the anchor chart.
- Prewrite an "I can . . ." statement (the student expectation stated in student-friendly language) on the anchor chart.
- Preplan the content of the anchor chart for smooth, timely, and efficient creation by considering the following questions:

  - What is the focus of the anchor chart?
  - What information (content, procedures, vocabulary, sentence stems, images, etc.) needs to be included?
  - How will I organize the information?
  - How will I engage students in creating the anchor chart with me?

Tools to Mathematize Your Classroom: Interactive Math Journals

As a second-grade bilingual teacher, my (Jessica) main goal is to give students the right guidance, experiences, and tools to become independent learners. This means developing students' sense of ownership and giving them purposeful opportunities to learn and grow as mathematicians. I started using interactive math journals as tools to portray the growth of each child in my class throughout the school year, and 3 years later the journal has evolved into much more (see Figure 6.15). Now this journal is an essential tool. The journal is a vehicle to differentiate instruction, collect data, and develop students' number sense as well as math reasoning. This journal is an essential piece to mathematizing the classroom. Most importantly, the journal has given students the platform to become active participants of their own learning and has given them purpose as mathematicians.

Figure 6.15 Students with Interactive Math Journals

© *Pasadena Independent School District 2017*

Interactive Math Journals: Getting Started

In order to use the interactive math journal successfully it is important to establish expectations and a positive culture of mathematics from Day 1. During the first few days of school there are specific conversations that need to be had with students in order to set a purpose for the year. The first and second day of school we discuss essential characteristics of mathematicians and place them under one of three categories:

1. What are mathematicians?
2. What do mathematicians say?
3. What do mathematicians do?

As a class we highlight how mathematicians persevere, ask questions, use vocabulary, share ideas, take risks, make mistakes, and keep practicing. Once students are aware of their role in the classroom, they are given a graphic organizer where they have an opportunity to reflect and choose the characteristics of mathematicians on which they would like to focus for the year (see Figure 6.16). On Day 3, students create

Figures 6.16, 6.17, 6.18 First Steps: Interactive Math Journal

© *Pasadena Independent School District 2017*

their journal cover by taping down the graphic organizer created on the previous day (see Figure 6.17). The process of physically constructing a journal gives students a sense of ownership and independence. The purpose of the journal cover goes beyond aesthetics, it gives students the notion that they are expected to be active participants in their education and that they are capable of being independent learners (see Figure 6.18).

The journal has four sections: data and goals, mini-lesson, problem solving, and math writing (see Figure 6.19). In the weeks ahead students will glue tabs in the journal as each section of the journal is introduced.

In order to avoid confusion, all of the sections of the math journal are not introduced in the same day. I wait to introduce each tab or section of the journal until it is relevant to the students' learning process. For example, students learned about the data section of their journal after their first assessment. This way it was easy to model how students record their scores and how the scores will be used to guide their learning. Throughout the school year the journal becomes a space for them to practice and grow as mathematicians; therefore, it is important that students understand each section of the math journal and why it is meaningful. The goal is for students to be independent learners and to learn how to use their interactive mathematics journal as a resource.

Components of an Interactive Math Journal: Mini-Lesson

The mini-lesson section of the interactive journal is composed of student-made anchor charts and guided practice samples that are entered on the right side of the journal called the "input" (see Figure 6.20). During the first semester, the anchor charts are made in a guided setting. I have a journal that is identical to my students' journals and together we write the title of the mini-lesson, important vocabulary, and examples of the skill being learned. The titles are written at the top of the page and circled so that

Figure 6.19 Tabs for the Interactive Math Journal

© *Pasadena Independent School District 2017*

Figure 6.20 and Figure 6.21 Mini-Lesson Input Examples

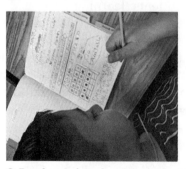 

© *Pasadena Independent School District 2017*

students are able to refer back to the titles to look for specific skills. The information may be written on the page itself or may be done as a foldable and then glued onto the page. It all depends on the skill and the amount of information they need to master the skill. For example, the mini-lesson on addition with regrouping was done on a foldable in order to clearly define the various strategies that could be used (see Figure 6.21). Since most of the skills spiral during the second semester, students are given opportunities to create their own anchor charts. I believe this is an important step since

Figure 6.22, Figure 6.23, Figure 6.24 Mini-Lesson: Output Examples

 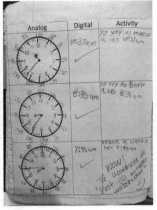 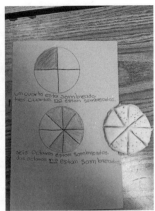

most people learn more about a subject if they are teaching it to others. It is important to note that students need to be involved in the anchor chart process in order to gain true understanding of the concepts.

The "output," located on the left side of the journal, is a space where students can create a product to show their level of mastery with the concepts captured on the right side of the journal. The output is essentially the independent practice portion of the Math Workshop and can be differentiated to meet students' needs. In order to give students time to practice with the concept, the output is not created on the same day as the input. When the output is created, I want students to feel pride and enthusiasm while creating their product; therefore, I try to give students some choice for their outputs. For example, as an output for *generating word problems*, students wrote and solved their own word problem using three different strategies (see Figure 6.22). In a second output students chose to describe an activity from their daily routines by showing it on an analog and digital clock (see Figure 6.23). Student choice may be small such as choosing their own word problem or more significant such as choosing between two projects or assignments. I find that allowing students to choose gives them a sense of ownership and responsibility. Outputs should also be creative and hands-on. Students are more likely to understand and retain a skill if they have experienced it in a fun and creative way. For example, students used playdough to represent fractional parts. Afterwards, they recorded a picture and then named the fractions in a booklet (see Figure 6.24). The booklet was then glued into their journal as an output for *describing, generating, and naming fractional parts*.

By organizing the input and output students are able to use their resources more efficiently. The students know that if they need to look back to a previous lesson, they can find the lesson easily and will be met with

Figure 6.25 and Figure 6.26 Example of Completed Input and Output

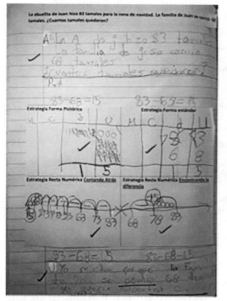 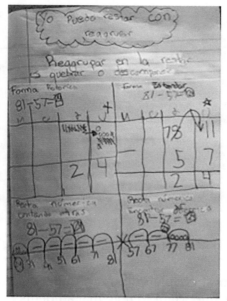

an overview of the skill or concept on the right and their own examples on how to apply the skill on the left. For example, Figure 6.25 shows guided examples of how to solve subtraction problems with regrouping using pictorial representations, standard form, and the number line (input). Figure 6.26 shows a student creating and solving a subtraction word problem using all four strategies (output).

The mini-lesson section of the journal has become a powerful resource for my students. Students know they have full access to their journal and have learned to use the journal whenever they need a refresher on a skill or vocabulary term. The journal has changed the way my students react when they are confused during workstations or independent practice. It is amazing to see a student confidently search within his/her own resource to guide their learning. Because of this process, students have gained a sense of ownership and feel a sense of accountability for what they are learning.

> When children write in journals, they examine, express, and keep track of their reasoning, which is especially useful when ideas are too complex to keep in their heads. By reading their journals, you can evaluate their progress and recognize their strengths and needs. The math journal thus becomes a great learning tool for your students—and you.
> Burns & Silbey (2001, p. 1 *Instructor Magazine*)

Feedback is a vital part to the mini-lesson section of the journal because it gives students an idea of their strengths and what they need to explore further, and gives them an opportunity to reflect as mathematicians. I use an interactive math journal to remain in constant communication with students. I write questions such as, "How can you justify choosing subtraction as your operation?," "What is your reasoning behind this strategy?," and specific praise such as, "I can see that drawing base ten blocks inside the place value chart helped you solve the subtraction problem" (see Figure 6.27 and Figure 6.28).

The feedback should be specific, be positive, and encourage student self-reflection. Students are given time to address questions and comments during guided math instruction or conferencing sessions. Feedback allows others to see the specific strengths and needs of a student when discussing a student's progress during parent conferences or intervention meetings.

Components of an Interactive Math Journal: Student Data

Finding meaning in the learning process is essential for students' learning and growth. In an interview, a Grade 2 student expressed which section of her journal she found most important, "I would pick data because it shows you what you made on your test and what to practice and if you know your math facts so you can use it in math facts station." This 8-year-old mathematician understood the importance of tracking her own growth. She would conference with me after an assessment, identify the skills she needed to practice, and would set goals to keep track of her progress (see Figure 6.29). Once she knew what to practice, her workstation time became more meaningful because she had a purpose and a goal. If she scored low on *comparing numbers to 1,200* then she would choose a workstation that targeted that skill. She was no longer doing an activity because I told her to, she was now self-reflecting and choosing to work on an area of needed growth.

I also used math running records created by Dr. Nicki Newton to assess students' math fact fluency (see Figure 6.30). By using the three-part running record, I am able to assess students' automaticity, flexibility, and number sense. I evaluate their results and place them on a specific math fact level. Students record their level in the data section of their journals (see Figure 6.31).

The math fact fluency data helped the Grade 2 mathematician know exactly what strategies she had mastered and what strategies she had yet to master. This allowed her to practice specific strategies during her fact fluency workstation. In the beginning of the year the Grade 2 mathematician was proficient in adding 0, adding 1, and adding within 5; however, she

Figures 6.27, 6.28 Examples of Student Feedback

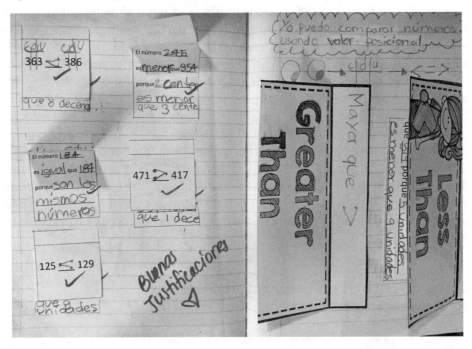

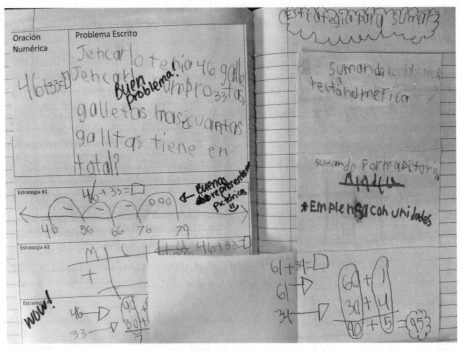

Translation for Figure 6.27: Great job justifying your comparisons.
Translation for Figure 6.28: Great word problem and pictorial representations!

Figure 6.29 Example of Data Graph

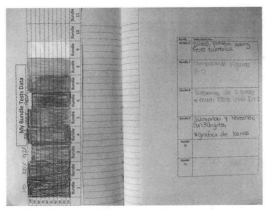

Figure 6.30 Example of a Math Running Record in Action

Figure 6.31 Example of Student Data Recording Sheet: Running Records

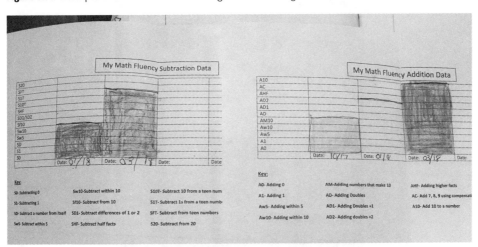

still needed practice adding within 10. Giving her a specific math fact level to practice discouraged her from choosing games that practiced what she already mastered. Many students tend to practice the easier facts because they want to remain in their comfort zone. Giving her a specific math fact fluency level also allowed her to practice at her instructional level without moving on to higher skills prematurely, a step that can discourage a student during the learning process.

Independent learners are active participants of their education, not spectators. When we provide activities and instruction without purpose the learning becomes meaningless. Students need to know why they are learning and what they need to learn to become stronger mathematicians. When students are given purpose and a clear path to success they will work hard to achieve their goals.

Components of an Interactive Math Journal: Math Writing

The math writing section of an interactive math journal is composed of open-ended questions that encourage students to use their mathematical reasoning skills, number sense, and math vocabulary when recording an answer (see Figure 6.32). Most questions asked in the classroom are done in whole group where only a few students get to share their thinking and other students are unable to share because they have not had the appropriate wait time to respond. Math writing is a space for

Figure 6.32 Example of Math Writing

© *Pasadena Independent School District 2017*

students to take their time and write out their thoughts while using the vocabulary learned in class.

> When children write in journals, they examine, express, and keep track of their reasoning, which is especially useful when ideas are too complex to keep in their heads. By reading their journals, you can evaluate their progress and recognize their strengths and needs. The math journal thus becomes a great learning tool for your students—and you.
>
> Burns & Silbey (2001, p. 1 *Instructor Magazine*)

Students' math writing can give insight into their thinking, a misconception, or a need for further growth. It also develops students' ability to give reasoning behind their strategies and understanding. Math has a language, and students need opportunities to develop that language. When analyzing a student's math assessment we have to ask ourselves, did the student miss the question because they did not understand the skill or did they miss the question because they did not understand what the question was asking in the first place? When students are given opportunities to interact and apply math vocabulary, the academic language used on an assessment is less intimidating and understandable.

> A math journal is one of the best ways to introduce writing into your math class. It helps students stretch their thinking and make sense of problems that can sometimes leave them confused or frustrated.
>
> Burns & Silbey (2001, p. 1 *Instructor Magazine*)

As a second-grade teacher, I know the importance of number sense development; therefore I design questions that will provoke students to make connections. One of the questions I like to start with is, "What can you tell me about the number ____?" Along with the question I include a word bank full of vocabulary we have used in class (see Figure 6.33). I challenge my students to answer the question while using as many vocabulary words as possible. This type of question gives me insight into their view of place value and their ability to think beyond the digits in front of them.

I also use math writing to assess my students' math reasoning skills. I do this by giving them a question and asking them to justify their thinking (see Figure 6.34). For example, "Sergio baked an apple pie and cut it into four equal parts. Jonathan baked a same sized peach pie and cut it into eight equal parts. Sergio states that his pie has the largest sized slices. Explain why you agree or disagree with Sergio." This type of questioning gives students the opportunity to think about why their answer makes sense. Many students see mathematics as a random set of rules and procedures because

Figure 6.33 Examples of Math Writing (Place Value)

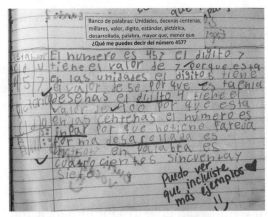

Translation:

Word Bank: ones, tens, hundreds, thousands, value, digit, standard, picture form, expanded form, word form, greater than, less than

Question: What can you tell me about the number 457?

Student response: The number is 457. The digit 7 has a value of 7 because it is in the ones place. The digit 5 has a value of 50 because it is in the tens place. The digit 4 has a value of 400 because it is in the hundreds place. The number is odd because it does not have a partner. The expanded form is 400 + 50 + 7 and in word form it is four hundred fifty seven. (Student included pictorial representation of the number.)

© *Pasadena Independent School District 2017*

Figure 6.34 Examples of Math Writing (Defend Your Answer)

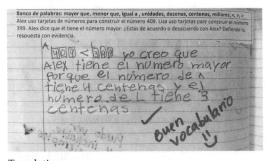

Translation:

Word Bank: greater than, less than, equal to, ones, tens, hundreds, thousands, <, >, =

Question: Alex used number cards to build the number 409. Lisa used number cards to build the number 399. Alex states that he has the greater number. Do you agree or disagree with Alex? Defend your answer with evidence.

Student response: (Students drew and labeled a picture of the number cards.) Alex has the greater number because A (Alex's) number has 4 hundreds and L (Lisa's) number has 3 hundreds.

© *Pasadena Independent School District 2017*

we do not give them the opportunities to process and make connections. I want my students to understand mathematics, and therefore I have to move beyond questions that just look for a quick answer, to questions that provoke a process of thinking and reasoning.

Describing a number in different ways and explaining why an answer makes sense does not come naturally for students. Therefore, it is important to model how to use a word bank and how to respond to questions. The first couple of times we did math writing, we completed the writing activity as a whole group. I gave students opportunities to explain their thinking verbally with a partner first and then modeled how to write it. The modeling sessions took about 15 minutes. Once I saw that my students felt comfortable writing on their own, I gave them similar prompts and had them write in their own journal. Now I give my students approximately 5 to 7 minutes to complete a math writing prompt independently.

Students complete a math writing piece twice a week towards the end of Math Workshop. They enjoy answering these prompts and add an additional challenge of seeing how many vocabulary words they can use in their writing or who can come up with the best explanation. I have found that this writing activity gives them more confidence because they are no longer intimidated by vocabulary words. Math has a language, and math writing gives the students the opportunity to become fluent in that language.

Components of an Interactive Math Journal: Problem Solving

The last section of the interactive math journal is problem solving. Many students struggle with problem solving because it requires students to read the problem, analyze the information, identify a solution strategy, and use the strategy to solve the problem. If any of these components are rushed or missed, then a student might not be successful. Students need to constantly be exposed to problem solving and be given a quality toolbox of strategies with which to critically think through each problem. In this section of the journal, I model how to solve a problem using our district problem-solving model (see Figure 6.35). The problem-solving model aligns to our state standards and supports students from Kindergarten to twelfth grade. It is designed to encourage students to go through a specific thought process when solving problems. I start off the school year by modeling how to use the district problem-solving model.

As a whole group we have conversations describing what analyzing, solving, and justifying a problem looks like (see Figure 6.36). I start by using problems that the students are familiar with from the previous grade level.

Once students are familiar with the problem-solving model, they start to solve problems independently. Every time students are introduced to a

Figure 6.35 District Problem-Solving Model

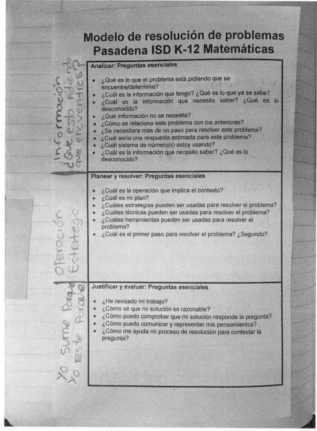

Translation:

Analyze:
- Visualize the problem (act it out or read it as a story)
- State important information
- What is the problem asking you to find?

Plan and Solve:
- Number Sentence
- Use one or two strategies to solve

Justify:

State why did you add or subtract

© *Pasadena Independent School District 2017*

new problem type (example: single-step word problem, multi-step word problem) I model how to solve the problem using the problem solving model.

Why is it important to have a whole section dedicated to problem solving? The first reason is to ensure that problem solving is a constant component of our Math Workshop. Students solve subtraction and addition word problems at least two to three times a week (see Figure 6.37 and Figure 6.38). The second reason is to provide valuable data to me, the teacher. If I have

Figure 6.36 Problem-Solving Model with Problem to Review Previous Grade Level Concepts

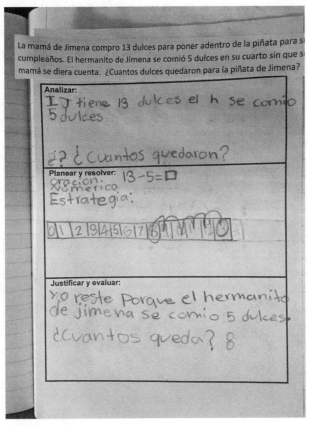

Translation:
Jimena's mom bought 13 candies for a piñata. Jimena's brother ate 5 candies. How many candies are left for Jimena's piñata?

Analyze:
- J has 13 candies
- B ate 5 candies
- How many candies are left?

Plan and Solve:
    Student used the number path to solve.

Justify:
    I subtracted because Jimena's brother ate 5 candies.

© *Pasadena Independent School District 2017*

a collection of student work samples, I am able to explore the samples and identify common misconceptions, strengths, and weaknesses among my students. If a student solved the problem incorrectly, I can identify if the issue was a computational error or a misidentification of the operation or problem type. This information helps me when planning my guided math sessions and intervention sessions.

Figure 6.37 Problem-Solving: Subtraction

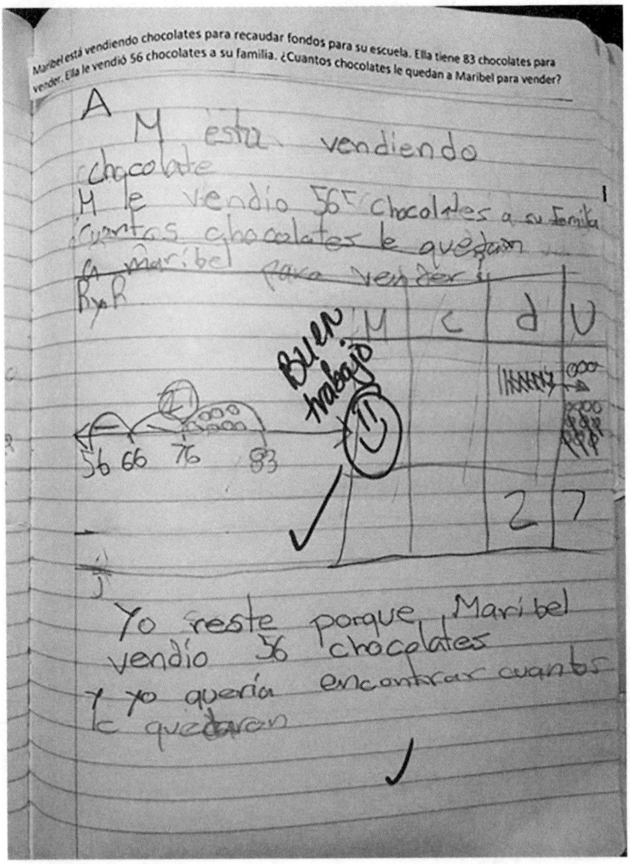

Translation:

Word Problem: Maribel is selling chocolates to raise funds for her school. She has 83 chocolates. She sells 56 chocolates to her family. How many chocolates does Maribel have left to sell?

Analyze:
- M is selling chocolate
- M sold 56 to her family
- How many chocolates does M have left?

Plan and Solve:

$83 - 56 = $ ___

Student solved the problem using two strategies. First, the student used the number line to find the difference of 83 and 56 by counting up. Second, the student used pictorial models and the place value chart to regroup.

Justify:

I subtracted because Maribel sold 56 chocolates and I wanted to find how many were left.

What Do Students Think?

Independent learners look beyond the teacher to gain understanding. When I interviewed my students regarding their perspective of interactive math journals I asked, "What do you do when you need help in math or you

Figure 6.38 Problem Solving: Addition

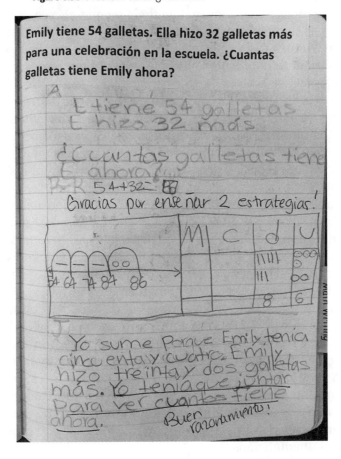

Translation:

Word Problem: Emily has 54 cookies. She made 32 cookies more for her school celebration.
How many cookies does Emily have now?

Analyze:

- E has 54 cookies
- E made 32 more
- How many cookies does E have now?

Plan and Solve:

54 + 32 = _____

Student solved the problem using two strategies. First, the student used the number line by
starting at 54 and adding 3 tens and 2 ones (32). Second, the student used pictorial models and
the place value chart to add.

Justify:

I added because Emily had 54 and made 32 cookies more. I had to join the cookies to find how
many she had in all.

are confused about math?" One Grade 2 mathematician stated, "We write
what we learned and when we don't remember, we can look in our journal." Another Grade 2 mathematician said, "Sometimes I use my journal
in my workstation time because I can learn from it." Overall, 14 students

mentioned using their math journal as their first choice, two students mentioned the interactive math journal as their second choice, three students mentioned it as their third choice, and only one student did not mention the interactive journal as a resource when something has been forgotten.

It is important to note that eleven students did not mention "asking the teacher" as their first, second, or third choice. This shows that the students have grown to be independent learners and are given so many resources that they consider "asking the teacher" as their last option. My students enjoy working in their journal because they are given a space to apply their thinking in a fun way. When I asked one Grade 2 mathematician what her favorite part of the interactive journal was she stated, "I like the mini-lesson because we do activities with all the new things we learn. I like that I can see all of my work. It's fun to use my journal." The interactive math journal has become a meaningful part of my students' learning. Another Grade 2 mathematician expressed that he valued the data section of the journal "because it shows you what you made on your test and what to practice and if you know your math facts so you can use it in math facts station." Students want to learn and when I give them the right tool, their love of mathematics grows.

Overall, the interactive math journal is designed for students to do mathematics and experience mathematics. The expectation is for students to create anchor charts, create student products based on the skills they are learning, self-monitor, create growth plans, explain their thinking, use vocabulary, and solve problems. The teacher's role is to support, guide, question, and model. This tool has revolutionized my students' learning and has created a beautiful mathematics environment in my classroom. My students participate in Math Workshop with a purpose and grow and learn together as mathematicians.

Lessons Learned

- Be purposeful! Modify this journal to meet your students' needs.
- Take it slow. Even if you choose just two sections of this math writing journal it will be a start to mathematizing your classroom.
- Make it fun! Students will love this journal if you approach it in an engaging way.

Getting Started Checklist

- Provide students with a composition notebook and a student-made cover sheet.
- Create tabs (Mini-Lesson, Student Data, Math Writing, Problem Solving).

- Create "Input" anchor charts or foldables that outline important vocabulary and strategies.
- Create "Output" that provides students with an opportunity to display their understanding of the skill.
- Create data charts for students to self-monitor their work on assessments.
- Create math writing prompts that are open-ended with a word bank to encourage vocabulary use.
- Create word problems that target areas of needed growth.

Tools to Mathematize Your Classroom: Data Binders

During my (Samantha) first year of teaching, my team members shared various methods with me for keeping student data. I had student folders numbered in alphabetical order, and I would keep reading and writing data in those folders. When I needed certain assignments or notes, I sometimes had to go through the whole folder to find the needed documents and this process often took a significant amount of time to complete. In our district we have Reading Data Binders, and so I thought, "Why not have a Math Data Binder as well?" I took the concept of the Reading Data Binder and used it to create my Math Data Binder.

In the binder I created a section for anecdotal notes to be recorded on file folders, a pocket divider for each student in which I would keep students' assessment documents (see Figure 6.39). I was now able to have all my mathematics data in one place and have the data accessible for when I was facilitating guided math instruction. I would be able to keep samples

Figure 6.39 Data Binder at the Beginning of the School Year

of my students' work that was completed during guided math instruction, samples of my students' assessments that would be filed after each student's tab, and my report card scoring rubrics would be kept in pocket dividers. All of the student artifacts from instruction and assessment would be kept in one binder.

Now that my Math Data Binder was assembled with tools for organizing student data, I was ready to start using the data binder to guide instruction. This section of the chapter describes how I take this valuable tool that was created and use it to mathematize my classroom instruction.

Action 1: Use the Data Binder to Form Guided Math Groups

During the first 20 days of school, I take anecdotal notes during my whole-group instruction (see Figure 6.40). I start my whole-group instruction by having my students participate in a number talk. I will write a number sentence such as 3 + 1 on the board and ask the students to solve the problem. I then have them turn to their elbow partner and talk about how they solved the problem and the strategy used. I walk around and listen to each group's conversations. I sometimes have sticky notes in my hand and I use these sticky notes to record brief notes on their thinking.

Figure 6.40 Example of Anecdotal Notes: Number Talks

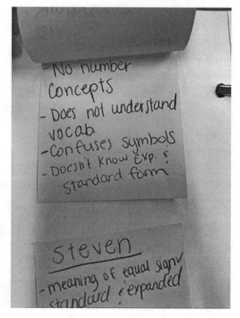

© *Pasadena Independent School District 2017*

After our number talk, I will continue with our math mini-lesson. I use various tools to introduce the concept and when my students turn and talk, I walk around again and take more anecdotal notes regarding the students' responses and thinking (see Figure 6.41). The anecdotal notes I take tend to focus on the students who are not yet understanding the concept. Having these data allows me to determine what I need to modify in my lesson so that all of the students will understand the concept. The anecdotal notes that I take go into the anecdotal notes section of my data binder so that the notes can be analyzed and used to start forming my guided math groups.

Figure 6.41 Example of Taking Anecdotal Notes During Mini-Lesson

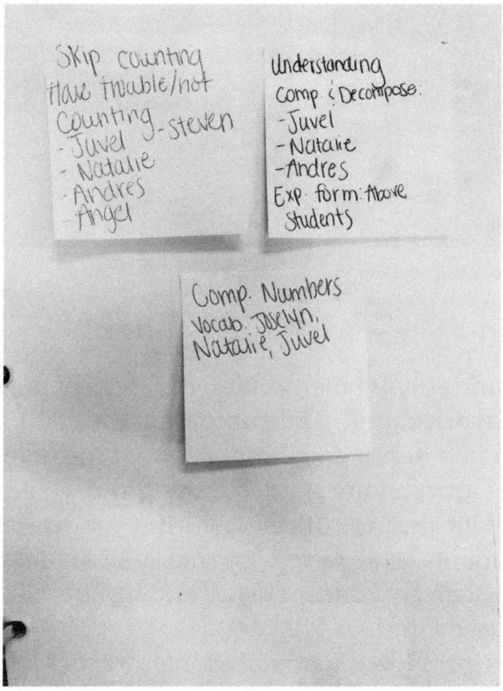

© *Pasadena Independent School District 2017*

During the third week of school, I introduce workstations to my students. I group my students heterogeneously and display the groups on a pocket chart. The concepts in the workstations are concepts that they learned in Kindergarten and concepts they learned the first week of school. I introduce the workstations during my guided math group to make sure the students understand what to do at the workstation. As my students are working at the workstations, I walk around and take anecdotal notes to record which students are understanding the concept and which students might still be struggling with the concept (see Figure 6.42). I observe the students and I will also ask the students questions such as having the students

Figure 6.42 and Figure 6.43 Example of Taking Anecdotal Notes During Workstations

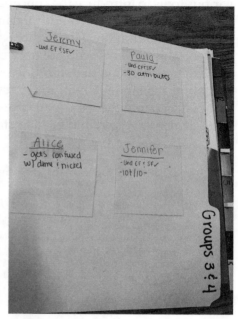

© *Pasadena Independent School District 2017*

explain their thinking and solving methods on the concept that the students are working on in the workstation. The anecdotal notes that I take go into the anecdotal notes section of my data binder so that the notes can be analyzed and used to start forming my guided math groups (see Figure 6.43).

Another form of data that is collected during the first 3 to 4 weeks of school includes students' completed journal assessments and journal entries that focus on the current concept being taught, as well as our district common assessments (see Figure 6.44).

The journal entries provide data as students practice concepts being taught, while the district common assessments provide data regarding what the students have learned over a 2 to 3 week period. These data points are stored in the student tab section of the data binder.

Once I gather all of the data, I use the data from our number talks, whole group instruction, mini-lessons, workstations, journal entries, and bundle assessments to form my guided math groups (see Figure 6.45). First I focus on the students who need more practice on a concept with extensive reteaching and group those students together. The next two groups are formed using students who are able to demonstrate understanding of a concept on their own with minimal reteaching. The final group of students is formed based on the students' ability to learn the concept without any reteaching. This process has been effective because it allows me an opportunity to work with students based on their individual needs. Once my

Figure 6.44 Example of Journal Data and Common Assessment Data

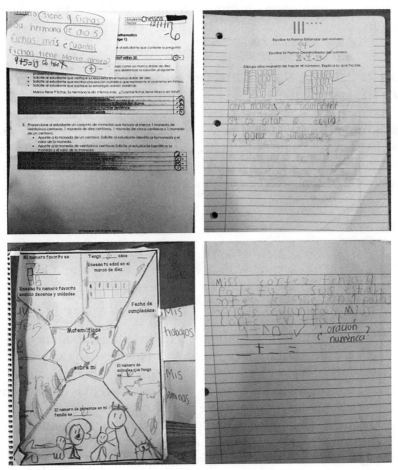

Figure 6.45 Example of Guided Math Groups

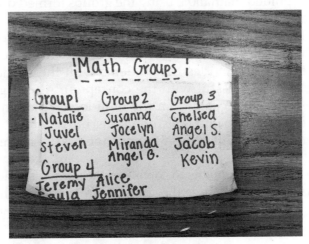

guided math groups have been formed, I am able to begin my small group instruction. The guided math groups remain flexible so that I can adapt instruction according to each student's level of proficiency with a concept.

Action 2: Use the Data Binder to Guide Whole Group Instruction

Using the data that were gathered to form my guided math groups, I devised a plan as to how I was going to facilitate whole group and guided math instruction in a way that would meet the individual needs of my students over the course of the next five days.

Day 1

Our Math Workshop begins with my students doing a number talk or a math stretch, which is usually about a concept they learned the previous week. After the prompt is given, the students write the answer in their math journal and then we discuss their answers as a whole group. During journal time, I walk around, ask the students questions about how they are determining the answer, and take anecdotal notes. I put the anecdotal notes in my data binder. This process does not have to be completed every day, as I usually record the anecdotal notes when the concept is one that most of the class is missing. These efforts give me an opportunity to observe which students are understanding the student expectations and which students are not. The whole process takes about five to 10 minutes.

After the number talk or math stretch has been completed, I begin the mini-lesson. While the students are sitting on the carpet, I teach the new student expectation to the whole group. The mini-lesson is used to introduce the new concept and to create an anchor chart that captures key concepts. Once the mini-lesson is over, the students start their workstations and I call students to my guided math table using the groups formed during the first weeks of school.

On Day 1 I work with my students who have yet to develop proficiency with the concept. I work with the students who need more reteaching because it provides the students with the needed guidance and practice to be successful with the concept(s). At our guided math table, I have the anchor chart from the mini-lesson hanging beside me with sentence stems to encourage student discourse. I review the anchor chart and remind students to use the anchor chart as a reference (see Figure 6.46).

I give the students problems to solve and the students practice the concept using manipulatives. While the students are working, I have my data

Figure 6.46 Example of Reviewing the Anchor Chart and Sentence Stems

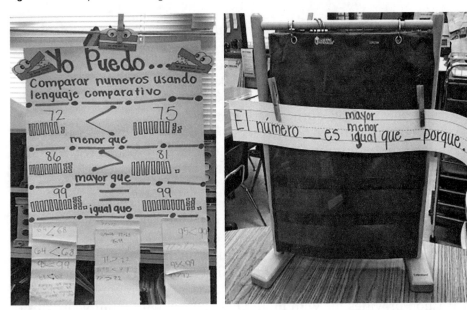

Translation:

Anchor chart with comparing numbers. The sentence stem is stated to say: The number ___ is greater than/less than/equal to _____ because _____.

Figure 6.47 Example of Taking Anecdotal Notes During Guided Math: Day 1

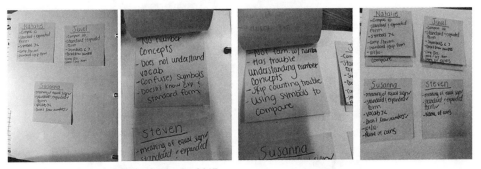

binder open to the group's tab and I take anecdotal notes (see Figure 6.47). I write down the aspects of the concept(s) with which the students are having difficulty. I usually do not record what the students understand because I want to have notes that capture what I need to modify during my whole group instruction the following day.

Day 2

I continue my whole group review of the concept that the students are learning. On this day I do examples with the students or the students complete a flip chart. Based on the groups of students I worked with on the previous day and the anecdotal notes taken, I modify the lesson and focus on the parts the students did not understand the previous day even after reteaching the concepts during guided math.

After I have facilitated the modified lesson and focused on the needs of the students from the previous day, the students go into their workstations. I then pull the next two to three guided math groups, which are the students who needed minimal reteaching. I repeat the same process as I did with the previous group of students and have the students complete the practice problems. I take anecdotal notes in my data binder as I am observing the students during their time of practice (see Figure 6.48).

My work with these two–three guided math groups tends to be less than the time spent working with the first guided math group, as these students need minimal reteaching of the concept. This modified amount of instruction provides me with more time to work with multiple groups of students in one day.

Figure 6.48 Example of Taking Anecdotal Notes During Guided Math: Day 2

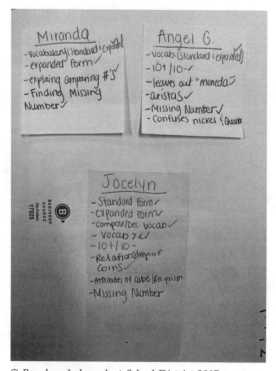

© *Pasadena Independent School District 2017*

Day 3

I continue with whole group instruction on Day 3, and again I use the anecdotal notes I recorded in the data binder during the previous day's guided math groups to modify the lesson. I have the students complete an activity or flip chart and then transition into their workstations. I pull the next guided math groups to my table. If I did not get to all of the groups on Day 2, I sometimes use Day 3 to finish seeing the last group. After I finish working with the last group of students, I begin differentiating instruction to meet the individual needs of students.

Based on the anecdotal data and/or observational data that I took from the first two days of instruction, I look over the notes from the entire class to see which students were struggling on the same concept and I pull those students to work at the guided math table. This group of students may not be from the same guided math group, as I am not working with any students who have yet to demonstrate proficiency with the concept. For example, when I pull students who were struggling with word problems, it may be one student from Group 1 and two students from Group 3. I then reteach the concepts and have the students complete practice problems on an index card (see Figure 6.49). The index card becomes a data point that now goes in the data binder.

Figure 6.49 Student Work after Reteaching Concept in Differentiated Groups

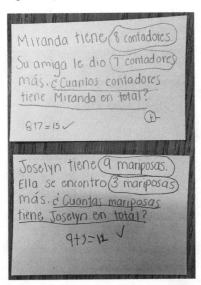

© *Pasadena Independent School District 2017*

Translation:
Word Problem: Miranda has eight counters. Her friend gave her seven more counters. How many counters does Miranda have now?

Days 4–5

After Day 3, I look to see which students still need more guidance based on the anecdotal notes recorded in the data binder and then I continue with differentiated instruction on Days 4–5. I might have students who need one-on-one support, so these two days provide an opportunity to work with the students in a one-on-one setting (see Figure 6.50). During this time, I have the student practice the concepts and then complete work on an index card so that I have additional data that can be added to the data binder (see Figure 6.51).

Figure 6.50 Example of One-on-One Teaching

 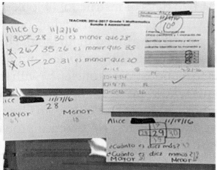

© *Pasadena Independent School District 2017*

Figure 6.51 Example of Student Work on Reviewed Concepts

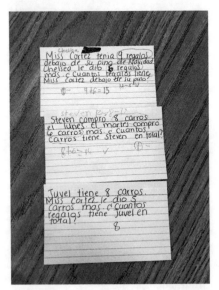

© *Pasadena Independent School District 2017*
Translation:
Word problems used to reteach the
concept.

Action 3: Using the Data Binder to Individualize Instruction

Every 2 to 3 weeks the students complete a common assessment. These common assessments are included in the district Scope and Sequence and assess the students on the student expectations they have learned during the past 2 to 3 weeks. During guided math group time, I pull students individually and administer the common assessment. I prefer to do the assessment individually because it allows me to talk to the student and assess the students' knowledge about the concepts learned. Once all of the students have completed the common assessment, I take the data and analyze what concept was missed the most or what misconceptions the students might have (see Figures 6.52, 6.53, and 6.54).

Figure 6.52, Figure 6.53, and Figure 6.54 Example of Data from Common Assessment

 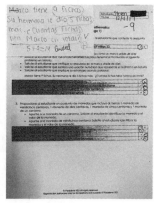 

During Days 4–5, I pull the students based on the common questions missed on the common assessment and I reteach those concepts (see Figure 6.55).

Figure 6.55 Reteaching Concepts from the Common Assessment

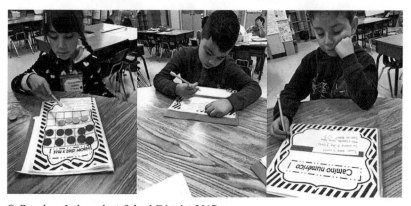

I then have the students work problems on index cards and I save the data points in the student's tab inside the data binder (see Figure 6.56).

During this time I note the students' progress with concepts by checking the report card indicators and record a score accordingly. If a student misses a question on the bundle assessment, I am unable to note in the rubric that the student has mastered the concept. Once I have retaught the concept and the students have demonstrated mastery, I can check the indicators on the student's report card scoring rubric (see Figure 6.57).

If the students still have yet to demonstrate proficiency with the concepts, then I will work with the students in a one-on-one setting at the guided math table.

Figure 6.56 Example of Student Work after Reteaching Missed Concepts

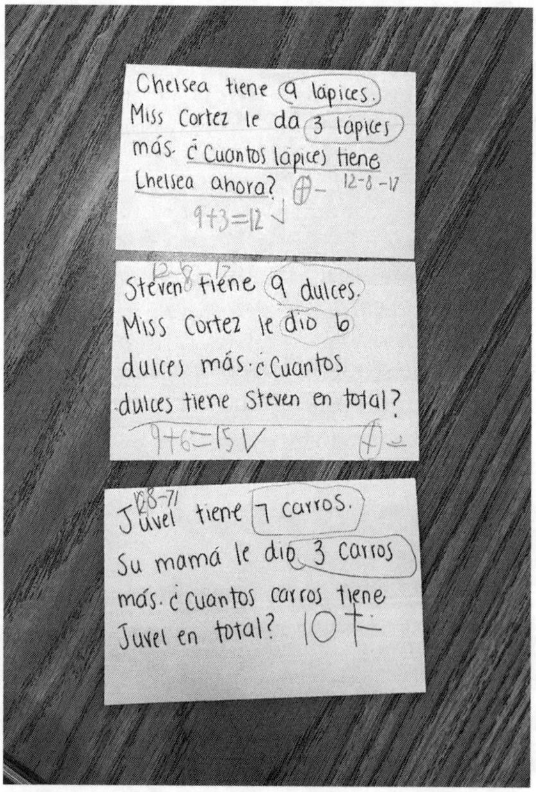

Translation:
Word problems used to reteach the concept.

Figure 6.57 Report Card Indicators

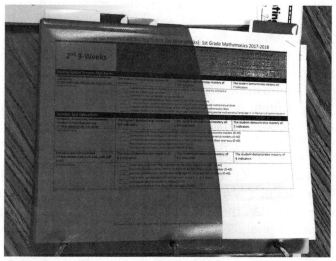

Action 4: Using the Data Binder to Document Student Learning

In my data binder, I keep each student's individual report card scoring rubrics on the back part of the pocket divider (see Figure 6.58).

Figure 6.58 Example of Student Report Card Scoring Rubric

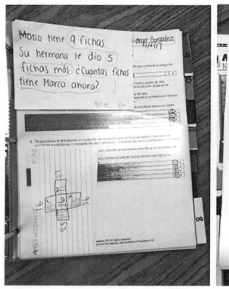 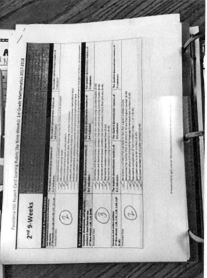

At the end of the 9-weeks we determine the students' scores based on the indicators noted on the district-provided report card scoring rubrics. During the 9-week grading period, I used the multiple data points saved in the Math Data Binder (the common assessments, the index cards, the anecdotal notes, and report card scoring rubrics) to provide me with the needed data to check which concepts each student has mastered. If a student has yet to demonstrate mastery of a concept, I reteach the concept and determine if the student now fully understands the concept. If the student has transitioned to being proficient with the concept, I return to the report card scoring rubrics and check the concepts that have now been mastered.

At the end of each 9-weeks, the students take the district-provided Curriculum-Based Assessment (CBA). After the CBA has been graded, I take all of the data that were captured in the data binder from the 9-week and merge the data with the Curriculum-Based Assessment data to determine each student's final score for the standards-based report card. Because these multiple data points are easily accessible through the use of the data binder, I am able to gather student data easily because the data are organized in each student's tab, and I am able to use the data to assign the student's final score for the standards-based report card.

Lessons Learned

- A Math Data Binder should be a frequently used tool.
- For a Math Data Binder to be purposeful, the binder has to be used consistently to inform instruction.
- When recording anecdotal notes, only writing the concepts that the student is struggling with prevents having too much information in the binder.
- Record and keep the data *inside* the binder (rather than as loose pieces in various locations) so that the data are available and ready to be used.
- Only keep data points that will inform instruction to enhance student learning.
- Use the data points to maintain an ongoing record and knowledge base of each student's level of mastery with concepts.

Getting Started Checklist

- Determine the purpose for the data binder and outline the needed sections and materials.
- Collect the needed materials to start a data binder (3-inch binder, pocket dividers—one for each student, file folders—enough for

every group of 3–4 students, sticky notes for anecdotal notes, scoring rubrics—if applicable).

- Create the binder with the needed tools (before data collecting begins).

Tools to Mathematize Your Classroom: Differentiated Workstations

When creating workstations for my students, I (Samantha) have always been focused on finding workstations that prompted students to practice the concepts we had explored during class. I observed several teachers who had workstations that they found on Pinterest or Teachers Pay Teachers that were fun for the students, and so that is where I went to get ideas for my workstations. When the workstations were implemented, all of the students were doing the same activity and I noticed that some students were finishing the workstation rather quickly. Once these students had finished the workstation, they were getting bored and this was causing them to start playing or talking. I also noticed students who were just sitting there and didn't appear to be getting much accomplished during the workstation time. If the workstation was fun, I didn't quite understand why I could not get the students to stay focused or be productive until I attended a Guided Math Bootcamp by Dr. Nicki Newton.

During the two-day Guided Math Bootcamp training I learned about the benefits of having workstations that were differentiated to meet the students' individual needs. Here I was thinking that all I needed to have were fun workstations for my students, but in reality the fun workstations were not beneficial to the students struggling with a concept or the students who had already demonstrated proficiency with a concept. I had thought about the idea of differentiated workstations, but did not know enough about the process to get them started until I attended the Guided Math Bootcamp. During the drive home, I began thinking about the workstations I already had in place and chose two workstations to start differentiating. I began brainstorming ideas and as soon as I got back to work, I began the process of differentiating my workstations to meet each of my students' individual needs. The paragraphs that follow reflect the steps I took and the steps I continue to take to differentiate my workstations.

Getting Started: Use Data to Generate Activities

To differentiate my workstations, I first look at the data from my Math Data Binder as well as the students' work in their Interactive Math Journals. I look at the data to see which students are demonstrating proficiency with the concepts and which students are having difficulty understanding the concepts (see Figures 6.59, 6.60, and 6.61).

Figure 6.59, Figure 6.60, and Figure 6.61 Example of Data Use When Planning Differentiated Workstations

Based on the data I create three different levels of workstations:

- Level 1: Developing (students who have yet to develop proficiency with a concept)
- Level 2: Proficient (students who have demonstrated proficiency with a concept)
- Level 3: Exceeds (students who have mastered a concept and are ready for an extension)

I look at the student expectation and think about how I can differentiate the workstation so that all of the students are practicing the student expectation on their current level of understanding. I either color coordinate the workstations or label each workstation with a different shape so that I know the intended level of proficiency (1, 2, or 3) for each workstation. I use the color orange or a circle to identify a Level 1 workstation, the color yellow or a square to identify a Level 2 workstation, and the color green or a triangle to identify a Level 3 workstation.

Thinking about the end in mind and what I want my students to know and be able to do, I come up with an activity for the specific student expectation. Everyone will do the same activity in general, but the activity will be tiered based on the students' readiness levels. I start with the Level 1: Developing workstation and create an activity with a lot of visual supports and tools such as double ten frames and manipulatives. For the Level 2: Proficient workstations, I examine the data for the students demonstrating understanding on the proficient level. I might minimize the visual supports, though the visual supports are not removed. Students will still have access to tools such as double ten frames and manipulatives if this aligns with the student expectation. For the Level 3: Exceeds workstation, the activity will be more complex and more open-ended. The students will have to do more problem solving with less visual supports than in the Level 1 and Level 2 workstations. Each workstation includes an "I Can" statement so that the students understand what the intended outcome is of each workstation (see Figures 6.62 and 6.63).

Figure 6.62 and 6.63 Example of Differentiated Work Station

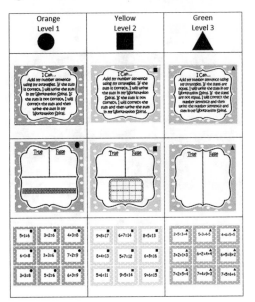
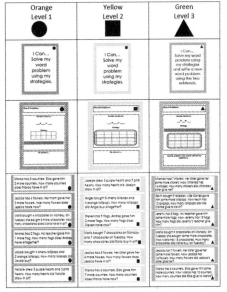

© *Pasadena Independent School District 2017*

Getting Started: Organizing the Workstations

My workstations are organized in different tubs on a bookshelf. The tubs are labeled: Station 1, Station 2, Station 3, Station 4, and Station 5. Station 6 is computer-based supplemental instruction so it does not need a tub (see Figures 6.64 and 6.65).

On each tub the students' names are written to identify the differentiated workstation with which they will work (see Figure 6.66).

Each tub includes the tools and manipulatives needed for the students to successfully complete the workstation (see Figure 6.67).

My students are heterogeneously grouped while working in their workstation (see Figure 6.68).

Figure 6.64 and Figure 6.65 Organization of Work Stations

Figure 6.66 Color-Coded Names to Identify Workstation Level

Figure 6.67 Tools and Manipulatives Needed to Complete the Workstation

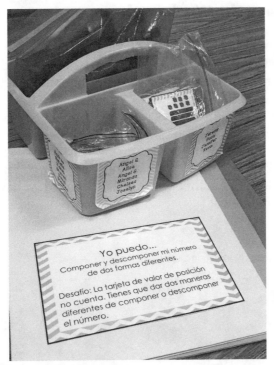

Yo puedo...
Componer y descomponer mi número de dos formas diferentes.

Desafío: La tarjeta de valor de posición no cuenta. Tienes que dar dos maneras diferentes de componer o descomponer el número.

Figure 6.68 Pocket Chart with Heterogeneous Groups

Implementing the Workstations

To successfully implement the workstations, I start by introducing the workstations to the students (see Figure 6.69). I only introduce the level on which the students are working and have the students practice the workstation during our guided math time.

I take about two to three days to let the students explore the workstations during guided math. Once I see that the students understand what to do, I put the workstation out for use during workstation rotations (see Figures 6.70 and 6.71). Once the students are working in their stations, I walk around to make sure the students understand what they have to accomplish and take anecdotal notes.

Figure 6.69 Introducing the Workstation During Guided Math

© *Pasadena Independent School District 2017*

Figure 6.70 and Figure 6.71 Students Practicing their Differentiated Workstation

© *Pasadena Independent School District 2017*

Evaluating the Workstations

To make sure my students are understanding the expectations identified in the workstations, I check their Workstation Spirals (see Figures 6.72 and 6.73). Each student has a workstation spiral that they use during the workstation time. The students write the answers from the workstation activities in the spiral. This action and tool holds the students accountable for their work and provides me with anecdotal data regarding the students' proficiency with the concepts. I check the workstation spiral randomly, so students never know when I will be checking their work. This random check of their work also encourages the students to stay on task with their work! When I check the workstation spiral, I am able to see if I need to re-explain the activities or if additional intervention is needed to support a student's mastery of a concept. Checking the spirals also allows me to evaluate the workstation and see how efficient the workstation is for my students at their differentiated levels.

Differentiating my workstations has been very beneficial for my students and the workstation efforts in my classroom. I have fewer classroom disruptions because the students are working and engaged instead of misbehaving because a workstation might be too hard or too easy. My students look forward to working in math workstations because they get to have fun learning at their academic level (see Figure 6.74)!

Figure 6.72 and Figure 6.73 Examples of Student Work in Workstation Spirals

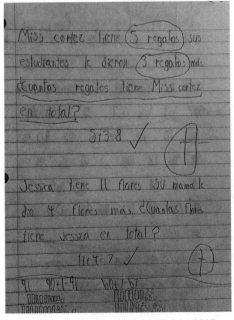
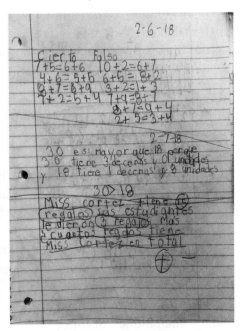

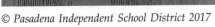

© *Pasadena Independent School District 2017*

Figure 6.74 One Happy Mathematician!

© *Pasadena Independent School District 2017*

I like my math workstations because they make by brain think a lot. It makes me think everyday. My brain thinks and it knows what to do. Makes my mom happy to know that I know what to do in my math workstations.

Grade 1 Student

Lessons Learned

- It takes purposeful planning to create differentiated workstations.
- It is essential to have a clear understanding of what students need to know and how students will demonstrate understanding of a concept.
- A differentiated workstation needs to have clear directions that the students can understand, as well as the needed tools to complete the workstation.
- All students are practicing the same concept during workstation time, though at different levels.

Getting Started Checklist

- Identify a location to store the workstations.
- Create a dedicated work space for workstation groups.
- Use color-coding or symbols to identify the level of the tiered workstations.
- Use data to determine what workstations need to be created.
- Consider differentiating the workstations in three levels: developing, proficient, exceeds.

Key Points

- Anchor charts are co-created reference tools that encourage students to become more independent learners.
- Interactive math journals serve as a tool to differentiate instruction, promote math reasoning skills, and develop students' sense of ownership and accountability.
- Data binders are a data collecting tool used to help modify instruction for students to meet individual needs.
- Differentiating workstations allow students to be engaged because the students are working on their appropriate academic level.

Summary

To mathematize a classroom is to empower students and give them ownership of their learning. The walls, the culture, and the experiences should communicate that math is valued and meaningful. The presence of anchor charts will transparently communicate mathematics learning to students and classroom visitors. These anchor charts will serve as scaffolds and reference tools for students, allowing them to reference procedures and examples as needed.

The interactive math journals will give students the opportunity to learn, communicate, and reflect as mathematicians. The journal will become a true reflection of the math identity and growth of every individual mathematician in the classroom. Having a purposeful collection of data from formative and summative assessments provides a quick and useful reference when working to grow each student as a mathematician.

Data binders are a valuable tool to support these efforts and allow teachers to respond in a timely manner to students' needs. Differentiated workstations allow students to perform at their individual student academic levels. The differentiated workstations allow the students to be productive and engaged because the students are working on the level that is academically appropriate for them. The purposeful use of anchor charts, interactive journals, data binders, and differentiated workstations will challenge students and encourage growth. Implementing these tools will help students identify themselves as genuine mathematicians.

Reflective Questions

1. As you read about mathematizing the classroom environment, what interested you the most? What is a first step that you could take to create a mathematically rich classroom environment?
2. Reflect on the anchor charts you have in your classroom. Which anchor chart(s) have you seen students use? What do these anchor charts have that sets them apart from the ones students rarely reference? How could the attributes of anchor charts listed in the chapter be applied to future anchor charts in order to encourage student use?
3. What sections of the interactive journal did you find most important? How could you modify the journal to fit the needs of your students? Which section could you start to incorporate in your classroom?
4. What is the value of using a Math Data Binder in your classroom? What steps do you need to take to start implementing a Math Data Binder?
5. How can differentiated workstations be beneficial for the students in your classroom? How could you "start small" with this effort?

Resources

- Anchor Charts

  - Colleagues' classrooms can be a resource for anchor chart ideas—go look around and get inspired!
  - https://blog.teacherspayteachers.com/anchor-charts/
  - www.weareteachers.com/anchor-charts-101-why-and-how-to-use-them-plus-100s-of-ideas/
  - www.teachingwithamountainview.com/p/anchor-charts.html
  - www.truelifeimateacher.com/p/anchor-charts.html
  - www.pinterest.com/weareteachers/math-anchor-charts-number-sense/

- www.pinterest.com/weareteachers/math-anchor-charts-fractions-and-decimals/
- www.pinterest.com/3rdgradeinco/anchor-charts-primary-elementary/
- www.pinterest.com/3rdgradeinco/anchor-charts-upper-elementary/

- Interactive Math Journals

  - Engaging Mathematics, Volume II www.region4store.com/catalog.aspx?catid=347952
  - *Instructor Magazine* (Scholastic)
  - Math Running Records in Action by Dr. Nicki Newton https://guidedmath.wordpress.com/math-running-records-videos/

- Data Binders

  - www.pinterest.com/lianec/data-binders/
  - www.pinterest.com/pin/22940279331543640/

- Differentiated Workstations

  - www.pinterest.com/drnicki7/
  - www.pinterest.com/drnicki7/addition-games-activities-within-20/
  - www.pinterest.com/drnicki7/addition-games-and-activities-within-10/
  - www.pinterest.com/drnicki7/comparing-numbers/
  - www.pinterest.com/drnicki7/composing-and-decomposing/
  - www.pinterest.com/drnicki7/1st-grade-ccss-math-standards/
  - www.teacherspayteachers.com

- Teacher Blogs

  - https://guidedmath.wordpress.com/
  - http://themoffattgirls.com/may-fun-filled-learning/
  - http://missgiraffesclass.blogspot.com/2016/01/making-10-to-add.html
  - www.recipeforteaching.com/2016/04/subtraction-smash.html

7

Mathematizing Your Students

Mariana Breaux has been a mathematics instructional coach for three years at an elementary school in Pasadena, TX that serves students pre-kindergarten through fourth grade. 95% of students on the campus qualify for free and reduced lunch. Prior to being an instructional coach, Mariana taught first-grade for three years and third-grade for two years. She has written mathematics curriculum to support district efforts focused on student discourse, engaging instructional activities, and purposeful review for state assessments. Mariana has presented mathematics professional development sessions at the campus and district level while also serving as a Master Trainer for district-wide professional development. She has also presented at numerous regional and state mathematics conferences and at Dr. Nicki's Guided Math Boot Camp in San Antonio. (Connect with Mariana on Twitter: @MarianaBreaux)

Introduction

After learning about Jo Boaler's research on developing a growth mindset in mathematics and hearing Dr. Nicki Newton share that most students develop their math identity by the early elementary years, I felt forced to examine the mindsets we were developing in our students. It amazed me to think that by the end of the early elementary years, a student's math identity is formed and that students often leave as early as first grade having already determined if they feel they are good at math or not (Newton, 2016). I wondered if we were helping our students see themselves as the young mathematicians that they are. I wondered if our students who struggle with mathematics were receiving messages that encouraged them to keep working hard because of their potential as young mathematicians. Upon reflecting, I felt compelled not to leave these ponderings up to chance, but to do something about them on my campus!

At our Campus Leadership Retreat that took place in May 2016, I presented the idea of celebrating our young mathematicians through a "Mathematician of the Month" school initiative (see Figure 7.1). When I presented this idea to the leadership team, I had no idea what that would look like but I knew we needed to start getting our students focused on having a growth

Figure 7.1 Leadership Meeting Agenda

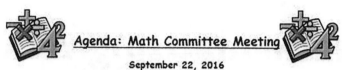

Agenda: Math Committee Meeting
September 22, 2016

K	1st	2nd	3rd	4th	Admin.
Ms. Juarez	Ms. Rodriguez	Ms. Valdez	Ms. Tran	Ms. Aranda	

1. Share Celebrations in Place Value!
- Each team share:
  - ✓ What are the students expected to learn in regards to PV in grade _____?
  - ✓ Things that went great while teaching Place Value
  - ✓ Areas where students struggled this year
  - ✓ Student strengths from last year to this year

2. Strategy Binders- Campus Wide Alignment of Tools & Strategies
- Tools
  - ✓ What tools does your grade level use to teach/ reinforce Place Value?
- Strategies
  - ✓ What strategies does your grade level use to teach/reinforce Place Value?
- Vertical Alignment
  - ✓ Agree on tools that will be aligned K-4 that will be included in the Strategy Binders

3. Mathematician of the Month
- Who are Mathematicians? (District Provided Poster)
  - ✓ Looking for students who exhibit Growth Mindset in mathematics
  - ✓ Narrow down indicators on check list
- How will it work?
  - ✓ Each grade level will turn in 2 names each month
    - ☐ Each teacher will choose 2 mathematicians that exhibit characteristics from the check list
    - ☐ All teachers in a grade level will place their 2 names in a bowl and draw a boy and a girl to be recognized as the grade level's mathematician of the month
    - ☐ Names will be due on the last Monday of the month to Mrs. Breaux- Ms. Breaux will come and take pictures of the Mathematicians and deliver a certificate. Their pictures will be posted on a bulletin board.
    - ☐ Mathematicians' names will be posted on a slide on the announcements before the Brain Smart Dance on the last Tuesday of the month

mindset in mathematics. The response from the leadership team was a positive one, and they were excited to see it come alive in the following school year. At that time, I was also certain that I would simply go on Pinterest or Teachers Pay Teachers and find what I needed to launch this initiative because surely someone was doing this already! To my dismay, when I searched for

Figure 7.2 Math Committee Meeting Agenda

Richey's Next Steps in Mathematics
2016-2017

1. Continue with using the District PLC model for Math Planning Meetings

Nine Weeks Planning Days

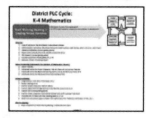

S.E. Planning Days

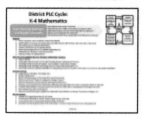

Recommendations from Cindy Garcia

- Start shifting from one teacher presenting an overview of the lesson plan to having the team read the lesson plan individually before the meeting or at the start of the meeting and then bring up questions, suggestions, or changes that they might want to make.
- It would be positive if more time during the meeting was spent on practicing and modeling for each other some of the strategies. For example, bringing out coins and modeling to each other how you would help a student show that 5 nickels equals one quarter.
- It would be beneficial for teachers who have taught that grade the year(s) before to share *"This is how I taught it last year, what I told my students was, one way I modified ____ was by, my students did ____."* For example when teaching fractions, time, perimeter that will require use of manipulatives and number based strategies it will be of great benefit for them to be able to share *how* they taught those SEs they could review/learn/refine instructional strategies from each other by modeling for each other.
- It would be positive if more time during the meeting could be spent on practicing some of those strategies that were shared. Have a sample problem on the board and practice "thinking aloud" what you say to students and showing each strategy with a problem task that will be used in the classroom.
- One recommendation for Grade 3 & 4 is using some of their planning time after STAAR to figure out their plan for the next school year. *What will be the structure? What will be the expectations? Is all shared work on the S drive? What can they prepare in the summer (if they want to get ahead)? Are there lesson plans accessible so that refinements can be made next year?* If possible, I suggest the teams leaving for the summer with the first one to two weeks of school already planned out. Although we will make adjustments to the Scope & Sequence, Place Value will most likely remain in Bundle 1. If teachers attend 1NW Focus, they can replace an activity or make any quick adjustments to their lesson plan as needed.

2. Guided Math- Book Studies
   - Math Workshop in Action
   - Guided Math Conferences
   - Guided Math in Action (NTA)
3. Continue implementation of the K-4 Problem Solving Model

4. Richey Strategy Binders- Collection of Math Strategies (K-4)

5. Ideas to Mathematize Campus			
The answer is...	Math Boggle	Cognates Word Wall	Campus 100's Day Countdown
Hallway Number Line	Bell Ringers- Monthly System	Shape of the Month Bulletin Board	Mathematician of the Month (2 per grade level each month)

guidelines and templates to begin the process, there was nothing like this out there! However, since I had presented the idea to the leadership team and felt committed to the process, it was time to get to work!

Fast forward to our first Math Committee meeting of the 2016–17 school year (see Figure 7.2). It was during this meeting where a process began to take shape. Our district specialists provided all elementary mathematics teachers

Figure 7.3 "How do Mathematicians work?" Poster

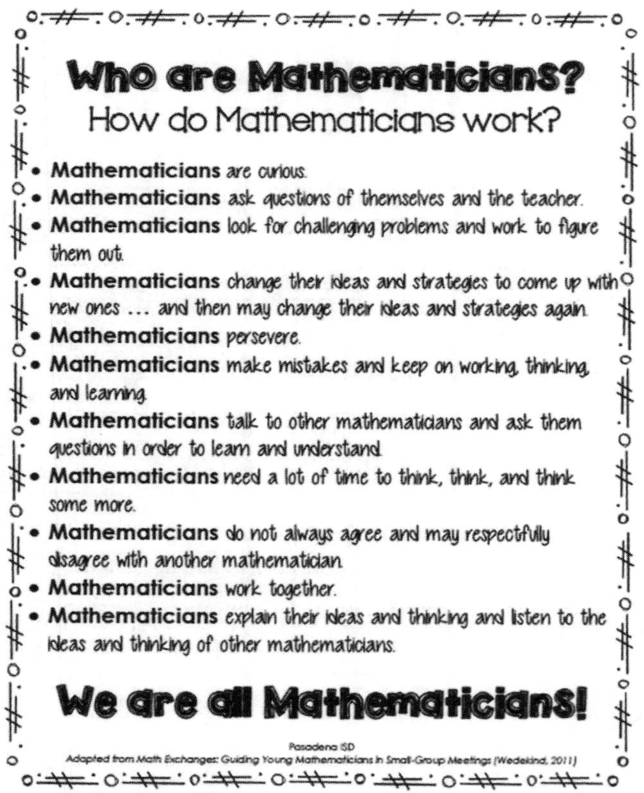

Who are Mathematicians?
How do Mathematicians work?

- Mathematicians are curious.
- Mathematicians ask questions of themselves and the teacher.
- Mathematicians look for challenging problems and work to figure them out.
- Mathematicians change their ideas and strategies to come up with new ones ... and then may change their ideas and strategies again.
- Mathematicians persevere.
- Mathematicians make mistakes and keep on working, thinking, and learning.
- Mathematicians talk to other mathematicians and ask them questions in order to learn and understand.
- Mathematicians need a lot of time to think, think, and think some more.
- Mathematicians do not always agree and may respectfully disagree with another mathematician.
- Mathematicians work together.
- Mathematicians explain their ideas and thinking and listen to the ideas and thinking of other mathematicians.

We are all Mathematicians!

Pasadena ISD

Adapted from Math Exchanges: Guiding Young Mathematicians in Small-Group Meetings (Wedekind, 2011)

© *Pasadena Independent School District 2017*

Figure 7.4 "How do Mathematicians Talk?" Poster

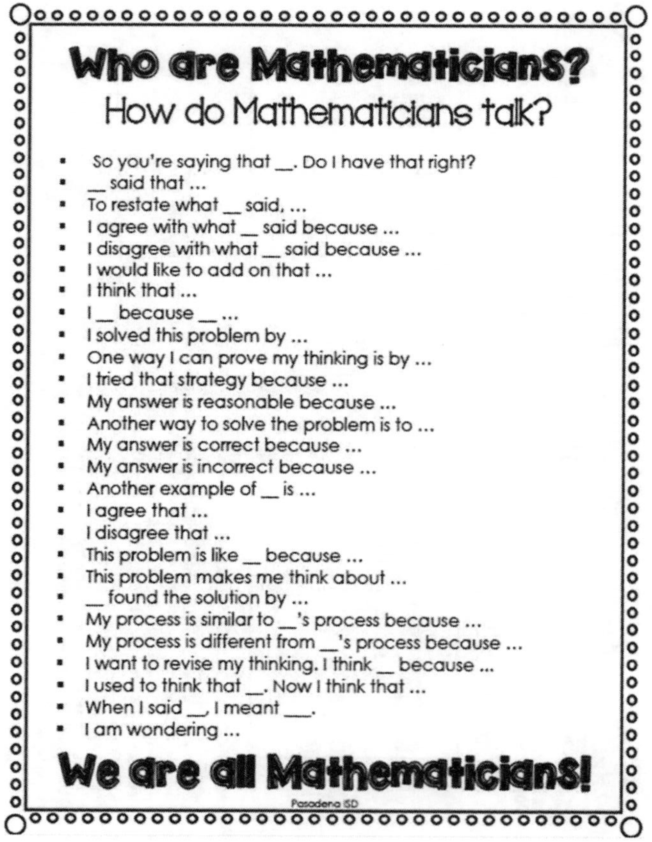

Who are Mathematicians?
How do Mathematicians talk?

- So you're saying that ___. Do I have that right?
- ___ said that ...
- To restate what ___ said, ...
- I agree with what ___ said because ...
- I disagree with what ___ said because ...
- I would like to add on that ...
- I think that ...
- I ___ because ...
- I solved this problem by ...
- One way I can prove my thinking is by ...
- I tried that strategy because ...
- My answer is reasonable because ...
- Another way to solve the problem is to ...
- My answer is correct because ...
- My answer is incorrect because ...
- Another example of ___ is ...
- I agree that ...
- I disagree that ...
- This problem is like ___ because ...
- This problem makes me think about ...
- I found the solution by ...
- My process is similar to ___'s process because ...
- My process is different from ___'s process because ...
- I want to revise my thinking. I think ___ because ...
- I used to think that ___. Now I think that ...
- When I said ___, I meant ___.
- I am wondering ...

We are all Mathematicians!

Pasadena ISD

© *Pasadena Independent School District 2017*

with posters outlining the behaviors that mathematicians exhibit and we used these documents to guide our planning conversations (see Figures 7.3 and 7.4).

As a math committee, we worked together to examine these documents and decide what they meant for us and the students at our campus. Once we decided what characteristics our mathematicians should exhibit, we came up with an action plan for the Mathematician of the Month initiative and the campus protocol for selecting and honoring our mathematicians.

Figure 7.5 Richey Elementary's Mathematician of the Month Characteristics

Richey Elementary's Mathematician of the Month

Each grade level will choose 2 mathematicians (1 boy & 1 girl) using the following characterisitcs.

- ☐ Is curious about mathematics
- ☐ Asks questions of him/herself and the teacher
- ☐ Looks for challenging problems and works to figure them out
- ☐ Changes their ideas and strategies to come up with new ones as they learn
- ☐ Perseveres- doesn't give up!
- ☐ Makes mistakes and keeps on working, thinking, and learning
- ☐ Talks to other mathematicians and asks them questions in order to learn and understand
- ☐ Takes his/her time to think, and think, and think some more
- ☐ Does not always agree and respectfully disagrees with other mathematicians
- ☐ Works together with other mathematicians
- ☐ Explains his/her ideas and thinking to other mathematicians
- ☐ Listens to the ideas and thinking of other mathematicians

Adapted from poster provided by PasadenaISD- <u>Who are Mathematicians?</u>

Math Exchanges Guiding Young Mathematicians in Small Group Meetings (Wedekind, 2011)

It was in that math committee meeting that our school's Mathematician of the Month was born! After the meeting, I captured the conversations from the math committee meeting into one document that included the characteristics of mathematicians and how the mathematicians would be selected (see Figures 7.5 and 7.6).

Once the document was completed, I emailed a copy to each math committee member. Each committee member was responsible for sharing the document with their grade level team members and communicating the process on which the committee agreed. The committee members also agreed to collect feedback from the teachers on their grade level teams regarding

Figure 7.6 Richey Elementary's Mathematician of the Month Campus Protocol

Richey Elementary's Mathematician of the Month

How will it work?

✓ Each teacher will choose 2 mathematicians (I boy & I girl) from their classroom that exhibit characteristics from the check list

✓ All teachers in grade level will place their 2 names in a bowl and draw a boy and a girl to be recognized as the grade level's mathematician of the month

✓ Names will be due on the last Monday of the month to Mrs. Breaux- Ms. Breaux will come and take pictures of the Mathematicians and deliver a certificate. Their pictures will be posted on a bulletin board.

✓ Mathematicians' names will be posted on a slide on the announcements before the Brain Smart Dance on the last Tuesday of the month the proposed process and email me the following week to share if the team had approved our initiative. All of the teams approved the initiative, and the following month our first "Mathematicians of the Month" were recognized.

Mathematician of the Month: The Process

Mathematician of the Month is a monthly acknowledgment and celebration of mathematicians in Pre-Kindergarten through Grade 4, though the process can be used with students from any grade level. At the beginning of each month, every teacher in each grade level selects and nominates two mathematicians from their homeroom who exhibit the characteristics outlined in our school's Mathematician of the Month document. Then the grade level teachers come together and select one boy and one girl from the entire grade level to honor as the Mathematician of the Month. One representative from each grade level, usually the math committee grade level representative, emails the names of the mathematicians to me. Once I have the names of the mathematicians, I prepare a certificate for each mathematician (see Figure 7.7).

Each mathematician comes to my office, and I interview them using questions inspired by Dr. Newton's Mathematical Disposition: Quick

Figure 7.7 Mathematician of the Month Certificates

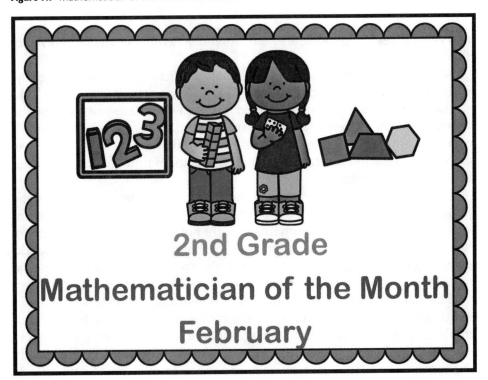

Figure 7.8 Dr. Newton's Mathematical Disposition Quick Interview

Part 3 Mathematical Disposition: Quick Interview
Do you like math?
What facts are easy? Which facts do you just know?* (Point to the benchmark problems).
What facts are tricky? Do you use any strategies on the tricky problems?
What do you do when you get stuck?

Interview, a resource found in *Math Running Records in Action* (Newton, 2016, p. 50; see Figure 7.8).

I begin our discussion by asking each mathematician questions 1–4 from the Mathematician of the Month Interview Questions document (see Figure 7.9).

After the mini interview, we read through the Mathematician of the Month indicators together and I inform them that they have been selected as their grade level's Mathematician of the Month. I ask them how they feel about being selected for this honor and allow them time to articulate their feelings and emotions.

I take some time to affirm them and tell them that being chosen as the Mathematician of the Month is something that they should always remember. I tell them that even though math might not always come easy to them, they have the skills to learn and grow as mathematicians if they keep working hard and never give up. At this point, they receive a certificate, a special bracelet, and they are photographed (see Figures 7.10 and 7.11).

The picture is then posted on our Mathematician of the Month bulletin board (see Figure 7.12). Once all of the mathematicians have been photographed, a PowerPoint with the images is sent to our technology liaison to be looped on the morning announcements for the remainder of the month. The technology liaison also uploads the video to our school's website in order to allow parents to view the slideshow video (see Figure 7.13).

Figure 7.9 Mathematician of the Month Interview Questions

Mathematician of the Month

Sample Questions for Mini-Interview

1. How do you feel about math? What do you like about math?

2. Does math come easy to you, or is math difficult at times?

3. What do you do when things get tough or you face a problem that you can't solve easily?

4. Which characteristics of a mathematician do you exhibit?

5. How do you feel about being selected as the Mathematician of the Month for your grade level?

© *Pasadena Independent School District 2017*

Table 7.1 Mathematician of the Month Mini-Interview Responses

Which characteristics of a mathematician do you exhibit?
"When I get to a hard problem, I don't give up. I use my strategies that my teacher showed me." Grade 2 Student
"Sometimes math is easy for me and sometimes it's hard. But I try my best." Kindergarten Student
"I like talking about math. And I defend math. Sometimes my friends tell me that they don't like math and that math is not important. But I always tell them that math is very important! I asked them 'What do you want to do when you grow up?' One of them said he wanted to build homes. So I told him that he was going to need math to build safe homes for people." Grade 3 Student

Table 7.2 Mathematician of the Month Mini-Interview Responses

How do you feel about being selected as the Mathematician of the Month for your grade level?
"I am so excited to be the mathematician! I like math and I use my strategies." Grade 3 Student
"Yes! I was hoping it would be me! I've been working hard to make it on the math board." Grade 4 Student
"I can't believe it! I was finally picked!" Grade 2 Student

Figure 7.10 Mathematician of the Month Bracelet

© *Jones School Supply*

Figure 7.11 Mathematicians of the Month

© *Pasadena Independent School District 2017*

Figure 7.12 Mathematician of the Month Bulletin Board

Figure 7.13 School Website Showcasing the Mathematicians of the Month

Mathematician of the Month: Refining the Process

At the beginning of the 2017–18 school year, the math committee met to discuss the next steps in our Mathematician of the Month initiative. We made three major adjustments to our protocol in response to suggestions and feedback from teachers.

The first thing we re-evaluated and adjusted was our selection process. Some teams wanted to change the selection process in order to make sure that mathematicians were selected from all homerooms throughout the school year. Most teams opted to make a team schedule outlining whose turn it was to select the mathematicians for every given month (see Figure 7.14), while others decided to follow the original selection protocol. As a committee we decided that each team had the freedom to choose the selection method with which they were the most comfortable.

Figure 7.14 Mathematician of the Month Selection Sample Schedule - Kindergarten

© *Pasadena Independent School District 2017*

Second, we implemented a Mathematician of the Month nominees list (see Figure 7.15). The goal of the nominees list is to honor every student in every homeroom who has been nominated regardless of being selected as the grade level's Mathematician of the Month. Some grade level teams posted the names of their grade level nominees in a special Mathematician of the Month bulletin board in their PODs. Other teams began to photograph all of the students who were nominated as Mathematicians of the Month within their homerooms and also created a bulletin board where the pictures from each month are posted (see Figure 7.16).

Another major adjustment we made was to be sure to include all students in our building in the Mathematician of the Month initiative, including students in our SUCCESS (Students Utilizing Curriculum

Figure 7.15 Mathematician of the Month Nominees List

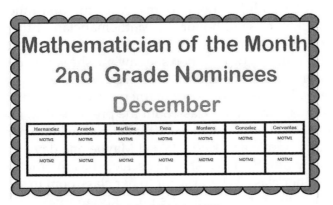

Figure 7.16 Mathematician of the Month Nominee Bulletin Boards

Concepts for Succeeding in Society) and PPCD (Preschool Programs for Children with Disabilities) homerooms. After the first time that I went into the SUCCESS class to honor the Mathematician of the Month who was selected, I was stopped by one of the students the next day when we crossed paths in the hallway. When she saw me she stopped me and said, "Hey! You were in my classroom!! Why were you there?" I explained to her that we had started honoring mathematicians on our campus and that when she saw me in her classroom the previous day, it was because I was there to honor her classmate. After I explained it to her, she looked at me with a big smile and said, "Wow! Maybe one day I can be picked too!" Just a few months later, she was selected as the Mathematician of the Month for her class. When I went to her classroom to share the good news with her, she turned around so quickly and gave me the biggest smile! She was so excited! She cheered the whole way towards me. The teachers from those special groups have also expressed the same enthusiasm as the student did!

> I love that we began something so inclusive of all of our students. My PPCD students also get to be in the spotlight for their efforts and love for math.
>
> PPCD Teacher

> "Mathematics is not about numbers, equations, computations, or algorithms: it's about understanding." (William Paul Thurston) This quote is a perfect example of one of my students that was chosen for mathematician of the month. This particular student struggled for so long trying to figure out numbers, one to one correspondence, addition etc. She struggled day after day but I continued to work with her and encourage her along the way and one day she just clicked and was able to understand what addition was and how to compute addition problems. The look in her eyes was something I can't explain. When this happened I knew I had to select her to be mathematician of the month because she had worked so hard and never gave up when I pushed her to her fullest potential because I knew she could do it!
>
> SUCCESS Teacher

Mathematician of the Month: The Benefits

Our campus has benefited greatly from the Mathematician of the Month. By acknowledging and affirming our young mathematicians' efforts, we have seen more students excited about mathematics and willing to take risks. When the mathematicians are interviewed, they can't contain their excitement and pride. It is amazing to think that as a result of this initiative, each year more than 120 students from Pre-Kindergarten through fourth grade will have had an experience where it has been affirmed that they are mathematicians! What makes them mathematicians is that *they are good at math*—not because they get 100's on all of their math assignments, but because they ask questions, demonstrate endurance, think outside the box, work well with other mathematicians . . . because they have a mathematical mindset! Additionally, the mini-interviews allow these 120 students the opportunity to articulate that they are good at math and that when things get difficult for them, they will not give up. In our journey to mathematize our students and honor our young mathematicians, we have had to work together, communicate, reflect, and make adjustments.

Because of this initiative, the conversations on our campus have also begun to shift. Even just a year ago, most students would articulate that they are not a "math person," but because of the positive experiences with mathematics, we hear more and more students express that they love mathematics! Teachers have also contacted me to share that students are creating math-centered goals. Some of their goals include "making it to the math wall." One instance that occurred in January stands out. After returning from the winter break, the fourth-grade students were discussing New Year resolutions. One of the teachers came by my room to share that one of her students expressed that his resolution was to make it to the Mathematician of the Month wall. I strongly believe that through this initiative we are planting seeds that will yield a harvest of learners with great math-esteem!

I have had the honor and privilege to share about our journey to mathematize our students through the Mathematician of the Month initiative at different events such as the Region 4 Education Service Center Mathematics Conference, Dr. Nicki Newton's Guided Math Boot Camp, as well as an after-school professional development session in my district. It has been amazing to see how every person who has implemented this in their campus or classroom puts their own twist on it (see Figures 7.17, 7.18, 7.19, 7.20, and 7.21). In the end, it doesn't matter how our mathematicians are honored. What matters is that we are intentional in recognizing our students' efforts and showcasing them in order to send the message that they ARE mathematicians in training!

> The Mathematician of the Month initiative has made a positive impact on our campus because we have seen students work hard during math to be able to reach the "Math Wall." It has motivated students to set goals of becoming a true mathematician thus improving their listening and retention skills during instruction.
>
> Grade 2 Teacher

Figure 7.17 Matthys Elementary School's (Pasadena ISD) #MathematicianOTM

Martha Banda
@MBanda17   *Following*

The Mathematician of the Month, # of the day and Countdown to 100th Day Wall-done! Next:pictures for Mathematicians at Work #PISDmathchat

© *Pasadena Independent School District 2017*

Figure 7.18 Murnin Elementary School's (San Antonio ISD) #MathematicianOTM

Allison & Hanke
@MurninMath   *Follow*

Soon...very soon!!!
#MathematicianOfTheMonth
#MotM

8:43 AM - 29 Aug 2017

1 Retweet 10 Likes

© *Pasadena Independent School District 2017*

Figure 7.19 Ms. Garza's Mathematician of the Week

Jessica Garza
@JessicaCGarza   *Following*

Getting ready for my mathematicians! First lesson: characteristics of a mathematician 🧑 #PISDMathChat

8:23 PM - 14 Aug 2017

2 Retweets 11 Likes

© *Pasadena Independent School District 2017*

Figure 7.20 Ms. Cortez's Mathematician of the Month

samantha
@SamuelCUS   *Follow*

Math Wall of Champions, Anchor Charts, Workstations, Math Data Binder, and our Mathematician of the Month! Mathematics Class!
#PISDMathChat

© *Pasadena Independent School District 2017*

Figure 7.21 Ms. Tran's Mathematicians of the Week

© *Pasadena Independent School District 2017*

Implementing "Mathematician of the Month" has increased our students' awareness of what it takes to be an accomplished mathematician. "Mathematician of the Month" rewards students who use their strategies, explain their thinking in a deep and rational way using academic vocabulary, and exemplifies the traits of having a growth mindset. This encourages higher-level thinking skills as well as an atmosphere of healthy competition where students can enjoy explaining what they know and why they know it. Students are always excited to see who will receive "Mathematician of the Month" and see their picture on the bulletin board.

Grade 3 Teacher

The pride and excitement that is seen in the children that are chosen for the honor of being the Mathematician of the Month is evident of the importance that is placed on math in our school. Children from other grade levels have come up to me in the halls and let me know, with pride, that they have been chosen for this honor. I think that it is important that we are honoring all levels of children at Richey, not just those with the highest grades. This is just the boost that some children need to raise their confidence level so that they can be successful.

Grade 2 Teacher

At Richey Elementary, general education, special education, and Pre-K students have an opportunity to be nominated and recognized as Mathematician of the Month. Our campus really enjoys celebrating our future mathematicians!

Principal

Lessons Learned

- Define and agree upon the characteristics of a mathematician.
- Create a system that works for you and your campus.
- Reflecting on the process is key!
- Do not be afraid to ask for feedback from teachers and committee members.

Getting Started Checklist

- Decide on the behaviors that each teacher will be looking for in the mathematicians, and compile a list of those characteristics.
- Decide on the selection process that meets your campus needs and preferences (ex. Select mathematicians from each homeroom

within each grade level. Select two mathematicians, one boy and one girl, from each grade level.)

- Assign a point person in each grade level who will send the names of the Mathematicians of the Month to the person in charge of printing certificates and interviewing the mathematicians.
- Designate wall space to display the pictures of the Mathematicians of the Month.
- Download or create a template for the certificates and the photo frames.
- Order Mathematician of the Month student bracelets.
- Download and print Dr. Newton's Mathematical Disposition: Quick Interview.

Key Points

- The Mathematician of the Month Initiative develops students' growth mindset.
- The Mathematician of the Month Initiative builds students' math-esteem.
- The Mathematician of the Month Initiative affirms students as young mathematicians.
- The Mathematician of the Month Initiative develops a positive math identity.

Summary

The Mathematician of the Month is an initiative geared towards identifying and encouraging students on a monthly basis for their efforts as mathematicians. The initiative can be implemented in any grade level and allows research to be brought to life! As the mathematicians are honored, students have opportunities to articulate a positive math identity and be recognized for growth mindset and mathematical mindset qualities. As students' pictures are taken and displayed, students are honored and their math-esteem is developed.

Reflective Questions

1. What initiatives does your campus have in place that promote the love of mathematics?
2. How could you adapt "Mathematician of the Month" to fit the needs of your campus?

Resources

- *Math Running Records in Action* by Dr. Nicki Newton
- Dr. Nicki Newton's Math Running Records in Action Blog (https://guidedmath.wordpress.com/math-running-records-videos/)
- Dr. Newton's Mathematical Disposition: Quick Interview (http://bit.ly/2E32lHu)
- *Mathematical Mindsets* by Jo Boaler
- Chronicles of a Math Coach Blog (https://chroniclesofamath-coach.wordpress.com/)
- Mathematician of the Month Freebies (www.teacherspayteachers.com/Store/Chronicles-Of-A-Math-Coach)
- Clipart for Mathematician of the Month Documents—Whimsy Clips (www.whimsyclips.com/)
- Mathtastic bracelets (www.jonesawards.com/Shop/Details/SBMTCBL/)

8

Mathematizing Your Intervention and Enrichment

Debra Garcia is the intervention teacher for an elementary campus in Pasadena, Texas a suburb of Houston. Debra's campus has about 800 students and the majority of the students are from high poverty homes and more than half of the students are in bilingual classrooms. For the past four years, Debra has been working with all of the students at her campus through the campus-wide intervention and enrichment program. Before serving as an intervention teacher, Debra taught for 17 years in first-grade, third-grade, and fourth-grade bilingual classrooms. She has presented conference sessions for mathematics at the regional and state level and presented at Dr. Nicki's Guided Math Boot Camp in San Antonio. (Connect with Debra on Twitter: @DebraGar1972)

Rogelio Guzman is the mathematics instructional coach for an elementary campus in Pasadena, Texas. The majority of the students at the campus are second-language learners and come from high poverty households. Rogelio has 22 years of teaching experience with 15 years serving as a classroom teacher and seven years serving as an instructional coach. Rogelio has presented professional development for mathematics at the campus and district level. (Connect with Rogelio on Twitter: @RGDiesel2011)

As more and more schools incorporate the professional learning community (PLC) process into their team meetings, the third and fourth questions of the PLC process become a regular topic during team conversations.

- How will we respond when our students don't learn?
- How will we respond when our students do learn? (DuFour, DuFour, Eaker, Many, Mattos, 2016 p. 163)

To answer these questions, teacher teams must consider how to adjust daily schedules to provide intervention for those students who have yet to develop proficiency with a concept/standard and enrichment for those students who have already developed proficiency with a concept/standard. With the diverse needs that students bring to the classroom and the varying paces at which students develop proficiency with concepts, it is not uncommon for additional support to be provided by other teachers within the grade level or campus or through alternative settings.

Is it possible to create some sort of an alternative setting where students in need of intervention receive additional support while students in need of enrichment also receive additional support? The chapter that follows describes how one campus used a data-driven need to create an alternative setting to meet the diverse needs of their students . . . a setting where all of the young mathematicians could have fun while receiving needed support in mathematics.

The Math Lab: Why?

The idea of the Math Lab stemmed from several conversations among our teams of teachers regarding how to reach our students struggling with concepts on common assessments and state assessments. As the conversations progressed and we uncovered gaps in our students' proficiency with various concepts, another trend emerged among the data. Many of our students had yet to develop proficiency with grade level mathematics facts, and this lack of proficiency seemed to pose a hindrance to students and their confidence with solving problems. We concluded that we needed to create a fun and engaging way to facilitate purposeful practice of mathematics facts with our students and instill a sense of confidence in our students regarding their proficiency with facts and solving problems.

The Math Lab: First Steps

To facilitate the purposeful practice of mathematics facts in a fun and engaging way meant that we needed a plan regarding how to make this happen! And for this plan to happen, we needed the support and approval from our campus administrators to facilitate these efforts! We gathered data from campus and state assessments, classroom observations, teachers' anecdotal notes, and teachers' feedback to develop a purpose and goal for additional time to be set aside to support the development of fact fluency. The purpose aligned with a campus initiative already in place to target and develop fact fluency within the appropriate grade levels. The purpose also addressed our need to provide additional support where the data showed our students still lacked proficiency with specific grade level standards.

Armed with this information, we presented our idea and the data to the campus administration team and all of the team members were quickly on board with the idea of additional, purposeful practice for our students. The administrators approved the use of a campus space for the efforts, allowed a small budget to support the efforts, and allocated personnel to support the efforts. Now that we had the approval to create some sort of additional support for mathematics instruction, we started brainstorming and determining the needed logistics to make the plan a reality.

The Math Lab: Where?

What would fun, engaging, and purposeful practice look like? What kind of environment would instill confidence in our students and allow them to grow in a way that allows each student to be successful? How could we provide opportunities for all students to engage in these efforts with an already-packed daily schedule and an instructional calendar that allowed little flexibility due to the constraints of district and state assessments? We needed a space on our campus to create a safe, numeracy-rich environment where students could roll up their sleeves and get much-needed practice with mathematics. We needed a space on our campus where we could supplement our students' core instruction with purposeful hands-on activities that targeted math fluency, automaticity, and the review of previously taught concepts.

We examined any available spaces on the campus and determined that one of the rooms in a portable building could be used for these efforts . . . and the "Math Lab" was born. We called the room a lab because much like a science lab, students needed opportunities to learn through hands-on exploration of concepts. We called the room a Math Lab because we needed a space where students focused solely on mathematics, and in this case, proficiency with mathematics facts. We knew that a Math Lab would be a great resource for our students, but we didn't know *yet* how we were going to implement the idea of a Math Lab, what resources students would use while visiting the Math Lab, and how we could get our students to use the Math Lab with fidelity. As a campus we decided to make the Math Lab part of our daily campus schedule and added the Math Lab to our PIE (Planned Intervention and Enrichment) schedule.

The Math Lab: When? Who?

As our campus became immersed in the professional learning community process, our campus incorporated a 40-minute planned intervention and enrichment (PIE) time into the school day for students in each grade level. During this PIE time, our teachers use data to determine which students might need additional small group instruction on core instructional concepts. The instruction in these intervention groups is facilitated and monitored by the grade level teachers. The remaining students in each grade level who might not need additional instruction at that time are divided amongst three enrichment activities. The three enrichment activities are chess, a computer-based reading program, and our newly created Math Lab (see Figure 8.1)!

Figure 8.1 Schedule of PIE Time Enrichment Activities

WIN Schedule Kindergarten – 4th

Week 1	Monday	Tuesday	Wednesday	Thursday	Friday
Red	Math	Chess	Computer	Math	Chess
Blue	Chess	Computer	Math	Chess	Computer
Green	Computer	Math	Chess	Computer	Math

Week 2	Monday	Tuesday	Wednesday	Thursday	Friday
Blue	Math	Chess	Computer	Math	Chess
Green	Chess	Computer	Math	Chess	Computer
Red	Computer	Math	Chess	Computer	Math

Week 3	Monday	Tuesday	Wednesday	Thursday	Friday
Green	Math	Chess	Computer	Math	Chess
Red	Chess	Computer	Math	Chess	Computer
Blue	Computer	Math	Chess	Computer	Math

Kinder	First	Second	Third	Fourth
12:30 – 1:00	9:25 – 10:05	11:00 – 11:40	7:50 – 8:30	1:20 – 2:00

© *Pasadena Independent School District 2017*

Students are assigned a color and rotate through these activities (one activity per day) according to the schedule. Over the course of a week, students will visit each enrichment rotation for approximately 80–120 minutes. The addition of the Math Lab to the PIE schedule allowed approximately 600 students the opportunity to receive additional support with mathematics concepts and in particular, with mathematics facts. We call our planned intervention and enrichment program WIN (What I Need) time, and we have seen the results of WIN time improve our students' overall academic success and confidence as learners.

Math Lab: How?

From the first moment that students would be walking through the door to the Math Lab, I wanted them to feel how important mathematics is. With that in mind, we mathematized the walls of the Math Lab with tools such as number lines, posters, anchor charts, and bulletin boards with mathematics resources (see Figures 8.2–8.6).

It's like immersing yourself in a world that speaks of mathematics!

Grade 3 Teacher

Figures 8.2, 8.3, 8.4, 8.5, and 8.6 The Mathematized Walls of the Math Lab

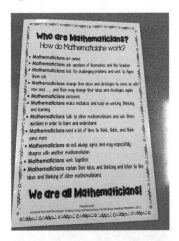

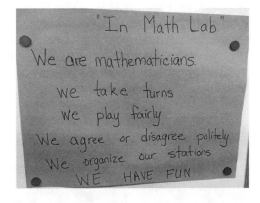

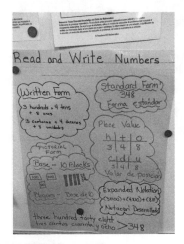

We arranged the tables and the chairs in the Math Lab so that students would be encouraged to work in cooperative groups (see Figures 8.7 and 8.8). This purposeful seating arrangement would allow students to build "mathematical friendships" in a risk-free environment.

We placed baskets on each table with everyday tools such as calculators, 100s Charts, dry-erase markers, and felt that could be used as erasers (see Figures 8.9–8.12). Having these tools nearby would provide students with

Figure 8.7 Arrangement of Tables and Chairs in the Original Math Lab

© *Pasadena Independent School District 2017*

Figure 8.8 Arrangement of Tables and Chairs in the New Math Lab

© *Pasadena Independent School District 2017*

the tools to complete activities as well as to self-check their answers and justify answer choices during the workstations.

We knew that rules and procedures are important in any classroom, and that the use of rules and procedures would be particularly important in the Math Lab. We created some basic "rules" for all of our students to abide by while working together in the lab (see Figure 8.13). We created and

Figures 8.9, 8.10, 8.11, and 8.12 Table Baskets with Everyday Materials

© *Pasadena Independent School District 2017*

Figure 8.13 Behavioral Expectations for the Math Lab

- Get started quickly
- Work the whole time
- Smooth Transitions
- Clean up quickly

© *Pasadena Independent School District 2017*

discussed expectations and procedures for behaviors like taking turns, getting materials out, and putting materials away. We knew that emphasizing these expectations on the front end would alleviate wasted time and possible headaches (teachers and students) in the future.

The Math Lab: What?

We wanted to utilize our students' time in the Math Lab to target fact fluency and grade-specific concepts. With this in mind, we created games that targeted fact fluency and previously taught concepts for which additional review would be beneficial to the students. To find these games we used all of our available district resources, we browsed websites such as Pinterest and YouTube, and we consulted with our campus teachers. We wrote a grant to www.donorschoose.org/, and we received several items generously donated from strangers. We selected games that use everyday classroom items such as dominoes, cards, dice, or spinners. The games are meant to be fast paced, competitive, and most often self-checking. We had to make the majority of our games for the Math Lab, as we had a limited budget and we needed activities that covered five grade levels of student expectations.

Two of the games that we used to support fact fluency for all grades levels are Zap and Power Tower (see Figures 8.14–8.17). Zap is a very simple game that the students love to play. To prepare Zap we wrote basic math facts on Popsicle sticks and placed them in a long slender container. For about every ten Popsicle sticks we place one that says Zap! To play the game the students pull a stick, read the math fact and solve it (we have a calculator that the students use to check each others' answers). They pass the container around, and if a student grabs the ZAP stick they must return all their Popsicle stick winnings back to the container. This is great for everyone. The students love to get ZAPPED. The prep time and storage is minimal, which makes it easy to make several and differentiate by grade level or student need.

Power Tower is another fun game that students are in love with and never get tired of. You get small 4 ounce cups (I use about 30 Dixie white

Figure 8.14 and Figure 8.15 Example of Games to Support Fact Fluency: ZAP and Power Tower

© Pasadena Independent School District 2017

Figure 8.16 Example of Power Tower

Figure 8.17 Example of Games to Support Fact Fluency

cups for this activity). To prep we write basic math facts on the outside and the answer on the inside. Place them in empty Pringles containers for storage, and they are ready to go. The students work in pairs and use the cups like flashcards to quiz each other. The student who is asking for the answer is looking inside so they can easily self-check. If the student gets the correct answer they use that cup to build their tower. If they are incorrect the other student keeps the cup for themselves. The student with the largest cup tower at the end wins! This is an easy, inexpensive way to practice basic facts while keeping the students engaged. One quick tip is to use a sharpie to write the math facts and then we take it off with rubbing alcohol and recycle the cups. This way we are constantly changing the game so the students can look forward to new challenges and it helps keep them excited about the game.

Power Tower is my favorite. It's fun and challenging.

Grade 4 Student

Two of the games that we used to spiral previously taught concepts were Numbers in Many Ways and Roll and Build (see Figures 8.18–8.21).

Figures 8.18, 8.19, and 8.20 Example of a Game to Revisit Previously Taught Concepts: Numbers in Many Ways

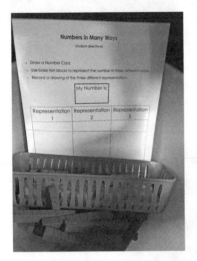
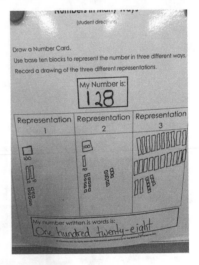

© *Pasadena Independent School District 2017*

Numbers in Many Ways reviews composing numbers for our first and second graders. The students either draw cards to get a number or they use spinners to build one. Either way, when they do they then write it down and represent their number by drawing or using base ten models three different ways. This is a very important educational standard for our students that is often taught at the beginning of the year. Reviewing this concept in Math Lab improves and builds our students basic number sense.

Another game we use to review number sense is Roll and Build. Our kindergartners use this game a lot. This again is a huge foundational skill. The students roll a dice, count the dots, and look for their number on the activity mat. Once they locate the number, they use unifix cubes to build the number and place it on the mat. The students really enjoy this activity because it is very hands on. As the year goes on we will include mats that have bigger numbers and keep challenging the students.

To maintain student interest and continue providing needed support for grade level standards, new games were introduced on a monthly basis. These games were chosen based on students' needs, as evidenced in data from common assessments. An example of a game that was incorporated into the workstation rotations because of the student data from a comment assessment is Decimal Power (see Figure 8.22). This game was used for our fourth graders since they were struggling with decimals and that is an essential standard for that grade level. Using this game in the "Math Lab" supported our students and our teachers. For Decimal Power students reach into a container and pull out a handful of coins. They draw a model, write the amount in fraction form, decimal form, and then shade in the grid to match the amount. The students really connect with this game because it specifically supports their classwork. It is always different because they randomly grab any amount of coins so the activity is unpredictable, and they get to use the dry-erase markers that they always love.

Figure 8.22 Example of Decimal Power

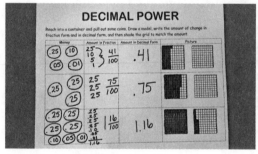
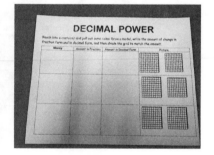

© *Pasadena Independent School District 2017*

Math Lab is never boring, they put the math in a fun way. Power Tower helps us learn our facts.

Grade 3 Student

Math Lab helps our students build skills using hands-on activities. Math Lab is a life-saver.

Grade 4 Teacher

The Math Lab: Daily Logistics

The schedule accommodates visits to the Math Lab from about 20 students at a time. When the students enter the Math Lab, they grab a Popsicle stick from a cup holder as they walk in. The stick is color-coded and numbered.

These show the students the exact group and seat number that they will sit in for the day's lab (see Figures 8.23 and 8.24). Next, the lab instructor goes over rules and procedures. If they are introducing a new game, it will take about 10 minutes to introduce and practice the new game in whole group. The students rotate every 6 minutes so that they experience two workstations focused on fact fluency and two workstations focused on previously taught concepts. The lab instructor uses a timer and when time is up a bell is rung. The first ring is the signal to pick up their station. The second is for them to line up by their station, and the third ring they make the transition to their next station.

While the students work, the lab instructor is constantly monitoring the students, asking questions and reteaching skills as necessary. Since we started the Math Lab a few years ago we have not only grown in games and size, but we also have grown in personnel. We now have two dedicated paraprofessionals to help out; while one is working with the groups the other lab instructor pulls students back one-by-one and does math running records with the students. This provides us great information on the students' mathematical abilities. We use this information for differentiation; we provide a copy to the teachers to make decisions and necessary interventions when needed.

> Students are always excited about the stations and having stations that reinforce what the students are learning in class is a great benefit for both the student and teacher.
>
> Math Lab Instructor

Figures 8.23 and 8.24 Example of a Daily Schedule of Workstations

The Math Lab: Storage

As more and more games were created to support the Math Lab efforts, we developed systems for storing the materials. We collected a variety of containers such as chip cans, small boxes of household materials, and baskets to store the manipulatives and games (see Figures 8.25–8.31). With time, we stored the workstations in color-coded baskets that were labeled with the grade level or skill. We stored the baskets in cabinets, bookshelves, and on tables.

Figures 8.25 and 8.26 Original Systems to Store Manipulatives and Games

© *Pasadena Independent School District 2017*

Figure 8.27 Current Systems to Store Manipulatives and Games

© *Pasadena Independent School District 2017*

Figures 8.28, 8.29, 8.30, and 8.31 Example of Workstation with Grade Level or Skill Identified

© Pasadena Independent School District 2017

Having the workstations organized in this way allowed for minimal preparation time and made it easy to differentiate the workstations among grade levels. Also, the lab instructor was able to quickly locate the needed workstations and materials for the next grade level (see Figures 8.32, 8.33, 8.34, and 8.35).

Math Lab: The Benefits

One benefit of the Math Lab has been the increased use of mathematics vocabulary and academic language as students interact with one another. The Math Lab is by no means a quiet place. Within the walls of the Math Lab, you will hear mathematical discussions and student laughter. You will hear the use of sentence stems such as "I agree with your answer because" or "I disagree with your answer because" as students share their thoughts with one another. As one Kindergarten student said, "You get to learn math and grow your brain."

The Math Lab has grown over the past 4 years and has allowed mathematics to be spotlighted on our campus and has been integral with our

Figures 8.32, 8.33, 8.34, and 8.35 Pictures from Math Lab

© *Pasadena Independent School District 2017*

efforts to mathematize our campus. The Math Lab has provided a safe place where all students can practice skills on their level and experience success in mathematics. As mathematicians we are always trying to make sense of numbers, find patterns, and see the mathematics in the world around us. The Math Lab has provided this benefit for our students because of its hands-on approach and investigative nature. We have immersed our students in a mathematically rich environment where learning math is "fun." The activities are engaging, short in duration, and well-suited for developing number sense, developing fact fluency, and reviewing previously taught concepts and skills. Our Math Lab has helped our students experience mathematics in a different way.

> I can see how my students apply effortlessly what they have practiced in math lab in my class and vise-versa.
>
> Kindergarten Teacher

The math lab offers students opportunities to practice math skills and have fun at the same time!

Campus Administrator

Lessons Learned

- Planning is key to maintaining the Math Lab.
- Keep activities engaging and challenging to maintain student interest.
- Finding a location can be difficult; therefore, start small and consider setting up a mini-lab in your classroom.
- Find personnel to facilitate the Math Lab; talk to your administrators about finding you help.

Getting Started Checklist

- Find a designated room or location on your campus.
- Come up with a schedule to meet your needs.
- Find personnel (teacher, paraprofessional, school volunteer, etc.).
- Provide various activities (competitive, collaborative, and team games).
- Include important stations (basic math facts, hot topics, word problems).
- Maintain expectations and structures to make the most out of your and your students' time.

Key Points

- Hands-on, engaging activities.
- Number sense, fact fluency, and previously taught standards.
- Manipulatives, tools, and procedures.

Summary

The Math Lab is an exciting and fun way to provide additional math support to your students in a safe, learning environment. The Math Lab allows the students to practice math in a different way, thus encouraging them to explore number concepts, build fact fluency, and develop academic language through activities and games. We chose games because "games are an important part of practice. They help students to practice thinking and reasoning about math with strategies" (Newton, 2016, p. 66).

Our campus saw the need to get our students interested in mathematics and increase their success with mathematics. After we implemented the Math Lab, we saw a huge difference in our students' attitudes toward math and the overall success of our campus. The task has been challenging but well worth it!

Math Lab is the most fun I have all day!

Grade 3 Student

Reflective Questions

1. What are the benefits of having a designated space, in addition to the classroom, to develop fluency with mathematics facts?
2. How could a Math Lab, or an adaptation of a Math Lab, be facilitated at your campus?
3. How do you currently provide your students the opportunities to practice math concepts during school?
4. What system do you currently have in place that provides number sense and fact fluency practice?
5. Do you think your students feel confident in their computational skills? If so, how did you establish that feeling of confidence? If not, how could a Math Lab be used to promote student confidence?

Resources

-   *Math Running Records in Action* (Newton)
-   *Learning by Doing* (DuFour, DuFour, Eaker, Many, Mattos)
-   www.pinterest.com/drnicki7/addition-games-and-activities-within-10/
-   https://youtu.be/SlmJIUOYcB4
-   http://frogsandcupcakes.blogspot.com/
-   Donors Choose (www.donorschoose.org/) to request support with resources such as manipulatives (ex. place value number cubes, protractors, etc.) and tools (fraction number lines, dry-erase boards, cardstock, etc.)
-   www.youtube.com/results?search_query=dr.+nicki+newton

9

Mathematizing Your Parents

Dr. Nicki Newton, Jacquelyn Kennedy, Jessica Garza, Janet Nuzzie, Lara Roberts, and Rogelio Guzman

Several of us have collaborated on this chapter: Dr. Nicki, Jacquelyn, Jessica, Janet, Lara, and Rogelio.

Introduction (Dr. Nicki and Janet)

Support from students' homefront can be a key element in the teaching and learning of mathematics. Parents and guardians are trying their best to help their children, but many of them need help with the different ways in which we are teaching math these days. There are really great ways to get parents/guardians on board. Tools such as mathematics handbooks and Mathematics Toolkits can be provided to support parents' efforts in helping their children. Facilitating Family Math Events, along with a variety of other activities, can help parents be in tune with the math that their child is studying. Other events can include opportunities for parents to come into schools, work with teachers and students, and have access to the resources that can scaffold learning. In the end, we must all consider ways to include parents in our efforts to mathematize our students and schools.

Building Parents' Capacity: Mathematics Handbooks (Jacquelyn, Dr. Nicki, and Janet)

Mathematics instruction has changed significantly in recent years with the adoption of new state standards. In addition to the new standards, *how* we teach mathematics curriculum has changed significantly in comparison to how our students' parents were taught mathematics in elementary school. The content is more rigorous, strategies are based on number sense, not procedures, and the number of strategies students are expected to learn has increased. Many students struggle with mathematics. With the increased level of rigor and the recent emphasis on multiple strategies and representations for learning mathematics, it is often challenging for parents to help their child at home. Teachers often brainstorm ideas of how to provide students with more access to practice mathematics skills both in and out of school. Teachers tutor students before school while students eat their breakfast. Teachers work with students during school through small group, differentiating instruction as frequently as possible. Teachers differentiate student workstations to meet the individual needs of each student. Most teachers have adopted some form of Math Workshop in an attempt to provide more targeted instruction to meet students where they are and in hopes of getting them where they need to be. Beyond school hours, teachers participate in campus extended day tutoring and develop individualized homework plans for students depending on their individual areas of need. The one component that is often missing is the opportunity to teach parents how to help their children.

As teachers, we know how crucial parent involvement is to students' academic achievement, but many parents work late hours or multiple jobs and so it can be difficult for them to attend additional meetings at school. So another way to reach out to parents who cannot attend meetings is to create and share a mathematics handbook. If the parents cannot come to us, we can send the information home to them. A mathematics handbook can be a great resource for parents. To avoid overwhelming parents, create a mathematics handbook for each unit or cluster of standards taught.

Mathematics Handbook: Reference Guide for Priority Standards

Schools should provide parents with a grade level mathematics handbook that specifically goes over the priority standards and discusses what students are expected to master during the school year. Parents should not only know what their students need to know, they should be given the tools to help them learn it. Many parents are unfamiliar with these ways of doing math so we have to show it to them. They should have a quick reference guide for all the big ideas in a unit of study (see Figure 9.1).

Mathematics Handbook: Mathematics Vocabulary

The mathematics handbook should include key vocabulary words that students must know to be successful, including vocabulary terms that have been used on past state assessments. It is most beneficial when students can make a visual connection to a new vocabulary term they are learning. The Pasadena ISD Weebly Glossary page can be used as a reference for vocabulary terms (https://sites.google.com/view/pisdmathematicsglossary/home). When possible, visual models or photos of classroom anchor charts

Figure 9.1 Quick Reference Guide

Big Idea: Students should be able to multiply in a variety of ways. We focus on strategies and models for teaching students multiplication with multi-digit numbers in 4th grade.	**Big Idea:** Students should be able to divide in a variety of ways. We focus on strategies and models for teaching students division with multi-digit numbers in 4th grade.

What: Open Array

This is a rectangular model based on using the area of a rectangle to break apart numbers. When we break apart numbers we call this (Partial Products) because we are solving the problem by finding part of the quotient at a time.

For example: 12 × 13

What: Open Array

This is a rectangular model based on using the area of a rectangle to break apart numbers. When we break apart numbers we call this (Partial Quotients) because we are solving the problem by finding part of the quotient at a time.

For example: 254/6

We look at 254 and think how many hundreds can we take out of 254. None. So then we think how many tens can we take out. Well we could take out 40 and then we would have 14 ones left. Well we could take out 2 more sets of 6 and then our remainder would be 2.

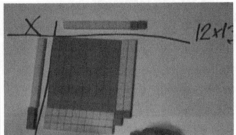

We do this with our base ten blocks and then we do it with a drawing.

	40 + 2
	240	12

Remainder 2

×	10 +	2
10 +	100	30
3	20	6

100 + 30 + 20 + 6 = 156

should be included to help parents understand content or instructional strategies. For example, a mathematics handbook on the concept of capacity could include photos of what a cup, pint, quart, and gallon of liquid look like for both parents and students to reference. A mathematics handbook on multiplication strategies could include visual cues for students to remember the difference between columns and rows.

Mathematics Handbook: Assessment Items

The mathematics handbook should include assessment items. Assessment items should be included so that the child will have additional opportunities to practice the skill in a format that is similar to how they will be assessed. Also, parents will get a glimpse into what it is that their child is expected to do and how they will be expected to demonstrate mastery of the skill. Most states now have unpacking documents that can be used as resources to promote understanding of how and what students are expected to do in order to prove they have mastered the student expectations. This is very helpful because many student expectations are broad and it may be unclear to parents what exactly is expected of students.

Mathematics Handbook: Videos of Mathematics Instruction/Mathematics Strategies

The mathematics handbook should include QR codes, videos, and website links so that parents can see videos that support their understanding of the mathematics standards. There are numerous videos available that demonstrate strategies for various mathematics concepts (see Figure 9.2). Websites and videos provide parents a resource where they can learn information about how to reinforce concepts from the classroom.

Figure 9.2

Pasadena ISD Mathematics YouTube page (https://www.youtube.com/user/PISDMathematics)	School Tube https://www.schooltube.com/	Teacher Tube https://www.teachertube.com/	Dr. Nicki Youtube	MathCuts https://www.facebook.com/pg/mathcuts/videos/?ref=page_internal

Mathematics Handbook: A Deeper Look at Videos of Mathematics Instruction/Mathematics Strategies (Jessica)

"I know how to subtract, I just do not know how to subtract like you do." A version of this statement has been heard by many teachers from students' parents. The fact is there has been a shift in the way mathematics is being taught. Most parents were taught mathematics through memorization and drills. Now, we have realized that memorizing procedures is limited but a student who gains number sense and is able to understand concepts is limitless. Does this mean parents need to be left in the dark? Absolutely not! Teachers may be experts on mathematics curriculum, but parents are experts on their children. Most parents want the best for their children and want to be a part of their education. So how can the gap be closed?

We are living in a new world where one person can connect to another without leaving their house. Computers and smartphones have become household items. There is an app or website for everything! Parents are always on the go; they have work, errands to run, and extracurricular activities to keep up with so how can we reach them without overwhelming their schedules? The answer is simple: use this technology to communicate essential academic needs. Instructional videos that focus on core standards could be used to bridge the gap between parents and students.

ShowMe is one of the many apps that could be used to reach students' parents. It is free and easy to use. The app has a "white board" that teachers use to explain concepts or strategies. The teacher may pre-prepare several white boards and then record his or her voice while going through the lesson. Parents may access the app by logging in to the website www.showme.com/, or the teacher could text or email a link to the video. With this app the teacher is also able to create classes and assign videos to specific students. For example, subtraction with regrouping is an essential skill in second grade. A teacher may choose to make a 5-minute video on strategies used in class to subtract. Once the video is made, the teacher can email or text the link to students' parents. This gives parents insight on how to help their child practice the skill at home.

Instructional videos have many benefits. First, parents will become aware of the strategies used in the classroom and can help students use the strategies with homework. Second, parents will be exposed to the vocabulary used in mathematics. The instructional videos are made by the teacher; therefore the teacher can show parents the importance of using vocabulary words to practice with students. Third, parents can get a glimpse of the rigor in assessments. Again, mathematics instruction and assessment has changed over the years, and many parents are unaware of the mathematics goals for each grade level. If a teacher provides a quick video on how to solve a sample test question then parents can gain a better perspective on their child's expectations. The goal is to connect with parents, give them tools on how to work with their child at home, and include them as a valuable asset to their child's academic journey. Now, it is likely that parents will not watch 100 videos on mathematics, but if they watch five videos that capture essential standards for their child's grade level then the time they choose to spend practicing with their child will become more efficient and have a greater impact on their child's growth.

A second resource is Ready Rosie. Ready Rosie is a website that has videos showing how parents can include mathematics conversations in their everyday life. The videos show interaction between real parents and their children. For example, one of their videos shows a mom grocery shopping with her son. While they are shopping, the mom asks her son questions like, "What 3-D solid is this box?" and "How much do you think this watermelon weighs?" The mom then goes to the scale by the fruit section and weighs the watermelon. These videos are available in English and Spanish. They are 2–4 minutes long and allow parents to see how they can incorporate mathematical vocabulary and concepts within their everyday life. This is just one more way of reaching out to parents, giving them tools, and giving them an opportunity to experience mathematics with their child. The teacher does not have to make videos because they are already made, but the teacher can enroll the class and send parents emails or texts with the video links.

The apps ShowMe and Ready Rosie are just two ways parents can be included in students' mathematical journey. It is important to mathematize students' parents because they are the constant variable in each mathematician in the classroom. They spend more time with students and if given the right tools could become a teacher's greatest ally. It is time to get parents involved and excited for mathematics!

Below are some tips for creating instructional math videos:

- Videos should be short, 3–5 minutes, and to the point.
- Videos should include math vocabulary.
- Videos should provide grade level examples.

Mathematics Handbook: Prompts for Mathematical Discourse

Last, the mathematics handbook should include prompts to promote children's use of academic languages such as question stems and sentence stems. When students can discuss their thinking and explain their thinking to others we know they have mastered it. The academic language we expect teachers and students to use does not come naturally for most educators, so imagine the difficulty for parents. By including even one or two sentence starters in the study guide, parents and their children can practice the use of academic language necessary to achieve at high levels. Mrs. Shannon's class has a PDF available with question stems parents can use (http://mrsshannonsclass.weebly.com/uploads/5/6/7/8/5678537/mathematics_questions.pdf).

Building off the findings from Jo Boaler's book, *Mathematical Mindsets*, the mathematics handbook should also include prompts that encourage students to reflect on what was learned during the day's instruction and/or how the day's instruction was facilitated (yes, reflect on the teacher's instructional strategies, too!). Some possible prompts that could be used to generate these reflective conversations include:

- What did you learn in mathematics today?
- How did your learning today connect with what you learned on the previous day?
- With what concepts/skills from today's mathematics lesson did you feel proficient? Why?
- With what concepts/skills from today's mathematics lesson do you still have questions? Why?
- How could the mathematics learned today be applied to your everyday life?
- What mistakes did you make today in mathematics? What did you learn from your mistakes?
- What new terms did you learn about during mathematics instruction today? How are the terms related to each other?

Rethinking how parents ask their children to think about mathematics when they are away from the classroom has the potential to reshape how our students think about mathematics. We want our students to be reflective thinkers and consider the bigger picture of how mathematics fits into the world around them. We want mathematics to be a topic that can permeate home life, though in a way that allows students to find a balance between home life and school life.

Providing a mathematics handbook for parents can effectively bridge the gap between school and home. We often turn to parents for help with disciplinary problems, but we also need to reach out to parents to support their child's development of mathematical proficiency. The mathematics handbook can provide a positive academic experience for parents, where teachers and parents come together as a team to get their child where they need to be in the world of mathematics.

Building Parents' Capacity: Mathematics Toolkits (Dr. Nicki and Janet)

Tools are an important part of learning mathematics (see Figure 9.3). Schools should make sure that parents have basic tools to utilize when working with their students at home. Tools vary based on the grade level, but some basic tools are a number line, a hundreds grid, a 200 grid, a decimal grid, a decimal number line, and some counters (I use paper mosaics because they are cheap to buy and you can do a lot of different things with them). I also encourage teachers to print out paper number rulers, yardsticks, and meter sticks. Tools can also include virtual manipulatives or apps that include resources such as rekenreks.

Resources to get started:

Figure 9.3

Primary Toolkit ideas: https://guided math.wordpre ss.com/2014/ 08/27/math- toolkits -part- 2-primary- toolkits/	Upper Elementary toolkit ideas: https://guided math.wordpre ss.com/tag/m ath-toolkits/	Toolkit Ideas: https://www. pinterest.com /drnicki7/mat h-toolkits/	Virtual Manipulative s: http://nlvm.us u.edu/en/nav/ vlibrary.html	Online Rekenrek: htt ps://apps.mat hlearningcent er.org/numbe r-rack/	Templates of Manipulative s: https://lrt.e dnet.ns.ca/PD /BLM/table_o f_contents.ht m

Tools can be purchased, compiled from extra sets of manipulatives, or created. Many schools have die-cut machines and die-cut templates that can be used to create manipulatives such as base ten blocks and geometric shapes and solids. Numerous websites include templates to create tools such as geoboards, rulers, pattern blocks, and other manipulatives. Other teachers use websites such as Donors Choose (www.donorschoose.org/) to recruit funding for classroom resources. Many tools can be copied as templates on paper (colored paper is a plus!) and remain as one-page documents or might need to be cut and placed in baggies.

Once the tools have been collected, the toolkits can be compiled in a variety of ways. Mathematics Toolkits can be stored in gallon or 2-gallon sized bags, in consumable items such as shoeboxes, 1-inch binders (with page protectors), and in containers such as plastic bins or tubs. The toolkits might be comprehensive of all of the standards within the year's curriculum or the toolkits might reflect the needed resources for particular units of study such as place value, operations, or measurement.

Creating the perfect, comprehensive toolkit can be overwhelming and almost impossible with all of the resources appearing daily through online venues. With that in mind, determine the minimum tools parents might need to support their child's work with mathematics while at home and create Mathematics Toolkits with the minimum tools. As parents and students become more proficient with using these resources at home, add to the toolbox or send an additional toolkit home that supports other concepts in the curriculum. Because parents might not be used to using tools such as base ten blocks for operations or pattern blocks for fractions, including links to videos that model instructional strategies is critical to supporting parents as they work with their children.

Providing a Mathematics Toolkit is critical to mathematizing our campuses and the parents who send their children to our campuses. Just as our students need tools when introduced to new concepts within mathematics, parents need tools to support efforts that extend the mathematics learned at school into conversations at home about mathematics. A toolkit can be as simple or as elaborate as time and resources allow. The main goal is to equip parents with the needed tools as well as the knowledge on how to utilize the tools while exploring mathematics with their children.

Building Parents' Capacity: Family Math Events (Dr. Newton and Jacquelyn)

Family Math should be incorporated in a serious way into every school's programming calendar (see Figures 9.4 and 9.5). I have done family math work for years, starting in California and then quite extensively when I worked with schools in the Bronx. We would throw these huge Saturday festivals with various themes and parents and students, really whole families, would come out in the hundreds. We would ask the local vendors to help sponsor our events (with some luck). We took any type of donations that we could get. I am going to list a few of the events in the tables below:

Figure 9.4

Monday Morning Math and Muffins	Wednesday Homework Workshop	Dice, Dominoes, and a Deck of Cards
This workshop would be done on Monday mornings (right when school started) and Monday afternoons (right before school ended). It was a way to get parents to come in, have some coffee, tea or water, a muffin and some math. We would teach parents quick games that they could turn around and practice with their students. We would give them whatever they needed to play the game with their students, for example a game board, dice, or dominoes.	Homework is always tricky. So about twice a month we would offer Homework Help at the school where parents could come in and learn how to do the math in the current and upcoming units of study. This is an excellent thing to now move onto an online platform.	This workshop is always great fun because we are all familiar with these items and to show parents how to mathematize them is easy. They get the basic premise so it isn't a stretch to say these are the grade level standards and so this is how you can play games to teach those. For example, let's play a Make Ten game. Pull a card and ask your child to tell you how many more to ten. Or, let's make arrays. Pull 2 cards and make that array (with the mosaics). Now, break it apart. So you can help parents understand the distributive property and then teach it to their students. We would have different types of dice such as dice with 3 in a cube and 10-sided dice. Then, we could show parents how to play place value games and multiplication games. We would use the dominoes for working with addition facts as well as using a domino to make a fraction.

Figure 9.5

Carnivals, Festivals, and Other Family Events
The basic premise of any carnival or festival is that there are 12 stations and the students rotate through them and do different math activities at each station. There were primary activities and upper elementary activities at each station. We did this a variety of ways from giving students tickets for each activity that they finished to eventually just doing a station card and when all activities were done the students would get a goodie bag at the end. This was the easiest and the students loved it.
Infrastructure:
12 Activity Stations 1 Picture Station 1 Graffiti Station 1 Library
We always had a picture station so we would take individual and family and friend photos (and then when students would come the next Monday they would see a wall of pictures of the event). We had a graffiti station so students could write math problems and solve them or write messages about math or the festival in general. We had a library station where students could read math books or books about the various topics and write a Post-it note about the math. The space has to be decorated out of this world! We would go all out on decorations and the activity cards! We were going for fun! We wanted students to enjoy math and have good associations with doing it.
4 Rules:
Rule 1: Every student had to be accompanied by an adult (otherwise parents would send their children alone). Students made their parents come. We would often hear parents say, "She has been talking about this all week. She made me come!" Students would come with whatever adult they could get to bring them so we had older brothers, older sisters, uncles, aunts, and grandparents. Rule 2: You have to do all 12 activities to get the goodie bag at the end. The student must do the activity (parents could help but not do it for them). Rule 3: You gotta have fun! Math is Fantastic! Rule 4: Have food—nothing extravagant, but cookies, chips, pizza, and something to drink (punch) go a long way (give a food ticket so you can control the amount people take).

Figure 9.5 (Continued)

Math Carnival	Math Olympics	Bubble Festival

Math Carnivals are so fun. Every station has a fun math game. We might have math toss where students would try to knock down place value bottles. We would have estimation stations. We would always have a puzzle place (very popular station). Everything was in the form of a game.	For Math Olympics students would come and they would participate in various events that were all tied to the standards. So for example they had to do a meter jump. They had to estimate the weight of rocks. They did paper ball toss (and measured in customary units). These were all "Olympic type" games and students loved them. *We would also do this in the school and have classes do a class Olympics and then the winners would compete in the grade Olympics.	We adapted this from the Lawrence Hall of Science book. So we would set up various stations where students had to measure the size of their bubbles, look at and analyze the shape of their bubbles, make bubble prints, etc. The most popular station by far was the one where they stood inside of a swimming pool in a bucket and the pool and bubble solution and then you take a hula hoop and lift it up so they are actually inside of the bubble! **http://lhsgems.org/ GEM132.html**

Figure 9.5 (Continued)

Dinosaur Festival	Under the Sea	Build It Festival

We made this up! It was so fun! Everybody always came out! The idea is to take everything that kids love about dinosaurs and map it to the curriculum. These were interdisciplinary festivals that included math, language arts, social studies, and science. Students would do things like measure to compare their arm span to that of a pterodactyl. They would look at a map and have to find where there favorite dinosaurs were located in the world. They would go on a dinosaur dig and measure what they found. We would order tons of stuff online to do the dig up. We would also order different cheap models of dinosaurs and some real fossils (ammonites, shark teeth, pieces of dinosaur eggs, etc.).	This festival was focused on the ocean. It was interdisciplinary as well, and students did various things like measure sharks and other fish, guess weights, and do a goldfish toss game (measure how far they could throw a ping pong ball and actually win a goldfish). Students would have to estimate how many fish were in a bowl as well as estimate the length of the largest whale in the world.	This is another Lawrence Hall of Science festival that we adapted. We would do it around Father's Day, but students could come with whomever they wanted. This festival is especially fun because there are various stations set up for students to use their imagination and build different things. We had tons of different building materials, such as Popsicle sticks, chenille stems, playdough, and various other things. Students would have to build these different structures. **http://lhsgems.org/ GEM370.html**

Figure 9.5 (Continued)

Cookie Festival	Test Prep for Grades 3–5: Movie Night & Dance Fever	Grading Period Reviews
	 	**SCHOOL** **CALENDAR**
We would always do a cookie festival in October because this is national cookie month. The cookie festival was the finale of a whole month celebration. During the month of October we would have students vote for their favorite cookie, then each class would make a graph, and then the older grades would aggregate and analyze all the data and make a big school graph. We then would have a cookie sale based on the data. Finally, we would have a cookie festival where parents and students would come and make various cookies. For example, there was a S'more station. There was a Mason Cookie Jar Station (where students would measure out all the dry ingredients and then parents would take that home and add the wet ingredients and bake the cookies).	We wanted parents to attend test prep meetings. They would come, and we would take them through the various standards and work through various problems and give them plenty of games to practice with their students. But the way we could ensure that we had a huge attendance is to tie it to a student event. **Movie Night:** We would set up a movie night for Grades 3–5 (but oftentimes parents would bring all their children), and the students would watch a movie and eat popcorn in the auditorium, and the parents would attend a test prep workshop in the gym or cafeteria. **Dance Night:** We would have a third–fifth grade dance (really only the students at this level could attend), but we might have another activity for the younger siblings in the gym and the parents would attend the workshop.	In order for teachers to meet the needs of their students, it is just as important for students' parents to have opportunities to learn the mathematical content that their children are learning so they can contribute to their child's academic success. This can be done by hosting a grading period review for parents. These grading period reviews can occur in conjunction with the school calendar, such as every 6-weeks or every 9-weeks. During this meeting teachers can collaborate with parents and introduce mathematical vocabulary, teach mathematical strategies to solve problems specific to the standards in the grading period, expose parents to assessment items so they are aware of the level of rigor their child will be expected to demonstrate on future assessments,

Figure 9.5 (Continued)

There was a station with premade sugar cookies and the students had to measure out the frosting and the sprinkles or whatever they were going to use to decorate their cookies. There was a graph-your-favorite-cookie station for the entire festival.		and share mathematical resources such as websites and other online resources to help them learn content and provide extra practice for their child.

Family Math Events: A Deeper Look at Family Math Nights (Lara)

Math family night can be a fun way to share your love of mathematics with the families you serve. It can show parents ways to help their child be more successful in the mathematics classroom. Math night can help to answer questions that parents have about how math instruction has changed over the years. It can help to bridge the gap between how students are taught math at school and how they are taught math at home. This might seem like a difficult challenge, but you will find that if you simplify the activities and focus on concepts on which parents can have the most impact, it can be done!

One idea for a fun and informative math night is Game Night. There are tons of math games that use common household materials such as dice, dominoes, and playing cards. These are simple games to teach parents, and they can recreate them at home. The internet is a quick source of games of this nature, but teachers on your campus may have their own ideas. It is a good idea to give parents a set of instructions on how to play the games so they can remember when they get home. If needed for your population, have the game translated into possible home languages of your students. Be sure to have everything needed to play the games at the event. It is very valuable for parents to have fun with their children and math. It is also beneficial for the teachers to be there guiding the students so parents can hear the academic language used in schools.

Some ideas for games could be Race to 100 for second grade. This game is played with a deck of playing cards with face cards and tens removed. Players turn over two cards, use the numbers to create a two-digit number, then add their sum to zero to begin. Play continues with players adding their new value to the running total. The first player to reach 100 wins. This game is fun and works with adding larger numbers. A possible first-grade activity calls for students to string 20 pieces of ringed cereal on a string to create a necklace. Students then roll a number cube (0–6) to determine how many rings to take away, then record their subtraction sentence.

A good activity for the upper grades can be a multiplication game similar to War using a deck of cards with face cards removed. It helps to create a festive environment if you have enough space for all grade level games to be happening in the same location such as the cafeteria or gym. Families can visit their child's current grade level table as well as the grade above and below. Ask around in the community or see if your school can provide door prizes. A simple idea is to give out sets of dominoes, playing cards, and dice.

Another theme idea is the 100th Day of School. The 100th day of school is a big milestone in an elementary school especially to Kindergarten and first-grade students. February is generally when the 100th day of school falls. All of the activities would have to relate to the concept of 100. Place value and number sense have always been difficult for students, so take the opportunity to find games and activities that would focus on those skills. Kindergarten and first-grade teachers on your campus will have tons of activities centered around 100; the upper grades might be a little more difficult. One option might be to use the hundreds chart to show multiplication strategies. The concept of 100 can also be explored through the lens of measurement. A line of tape that is 100 inches long can be created on the wall or floor, while a second line of tape that is 100 centimeters in length can be created along the same wall or floor. Students can then discuss the similarities and differences between the lines. This process can be repeated with different measurements.

Throughout the week of the 100th day of school, make announcements to build up the excitement. A good way to get kids and teachers excited is to post blank posters in the hallway with prompts like, "100 ways to make 100" or "100 things we love about our school." Leave self-stick notes with pencils near the posters and watch the students do the rest. Leave the posters up and encourage parents to add to the poster. Put out boxes of 100 plastic cups with simple directions to create a 100-cup structure and see what happens. This math night has the potential to become a celebration of math and school.

Another option for math night could be to center it around a holiday such as Halloween, Thanksgiving, or Christmas. An easy Halloween theme is Monster Math. Find activities that target needed skills, but incorporate monsters. To help the younger grades with shape recognition, create shape monsters. These are cardboard cut-outs of squares, circles, triangles, rectangles, and other shapes, with googly eyes. Then ask participants to sort a set of shapes and "feed" the monsters. A fun activity to work on multiplication facts is Multiply a Monster. Students roll two number cubes and record the numbers in blank multiplication sentences. The students then solve the problems. The product of the first problem gives the student the number of legs to put on their monster, the second product represents the number of eyes, and so on until the monster is complete.

Decorate your space with lots of eyes and teeth to gain excitement throughout the week. Another idea is to post clues every day for monster mystery numbers so students could guess the mystery number for their grade level. A new clue can be posted every day, finally revealing the correct answer at math night or the next day. All of the buildup to the math night really helps students persuade their parents to attend the math night.

These are just three examples of possible math nights to host at your school. Many have found that families are more likely to come to math night if there are incentives, giveaways, or food. If it is not possible with the school's budget, ask the surrounding community businesses for donations towards food or door prizes. Plan activities the week of the math night to entice the kids to come. If possible, plan math night to be in conjunction with the book fair in the library.

Parents tend to come for the book fair and stay to have fun at math night. Keep the math activities simple and straightforward. You want parents to leave with the feeling that they can help their student succeed in math by using the activity they just learned. Find activities that focus on fact fluency or number sense. These are often areas of concern for parents, but they don't know how to help their student improve. Lastly, tailor your math night to the needs of the families that will be attending. You do not want to showcase how to use base ten blocks when the families will not have anything similar in their own homes. Instead show them how they can use straw bundles to represent the base ten models. Simple changes like this show parents ways they can ensure their students grow to become better mathematicians.

Family Math Events: A Deeper Look at Dads, Dominoes, and Doughnuts (Rogelio)

Learning mathematics and applying mathematics skills have definitely changed since most parents were in elementary school. The curriculum has become more rigorous and thus is requiring more of our students. We, as teachers, want all of our students to be successful and we believe that everyone can learn mathematics. Sometimes, we feel that we are alone, no parent support, in teaching of mathematics, but we should not feel alone.

Parents also want the best for their children when it comes to learning in school. So why not take advantage of this opportunity and build the capacity of our parents so they too can help their children in their learning? With our rigorous math curriculum ever so changing, it only makes sense to mathematize our parents and provide them with the mathematical knowledge they need to better support their children at home. If parents simply cannot attend after-school events for various reasons, then another idea is to host events or parent workshops early in the morning at the beginning of school. This type of parent workshop is limited to anywhere from 30 to 40 minutes. An example of such an event is "Dads, Dominoes, and Doughnuts."

Dads, Dominoes, and Doughnuts is a 35-minute workshop with the purpose of showing dads how much fun they could have with their children playing games with dominoes that support fact fluency and number sense. It is a win-win situation. Dads get exposure to grade level math games, and children get to play and practice fact fluency and number sense concepts with their dads or grandads. The workshop can consist of a whole-group teach piece, a guided practice piece, and hands-on exploration by the parents. Each activity can be differentiated according to each grade level and fact fluency continuum. During the event, take pictures of the parent and child and allow the parent to walk their child to class. The workshop can take place at any time, though it could be facilitated at times close to holidays such as winter breaks and spring break. Besides teacher input, the use of a district scope and sequence can be used to determine and guide the needs of each grade level.

The materials needed for activities are easy to find! Examples of materials include those noted below as well as doughnuts!

- Kindergarten–Grade 1: dominoes (double six), five frame cards, ten frame cards, two-sided counters, domino parking lot handout, domino handout
- Grade 2: double nine dominoes, domino parking lot handout: doubles, double plus one, make ten, and domino war: addition and subtraction
- Grade 3–4: double twelve dominoes, domino parking lot handout: doubles, double plus one, make ten, and domino war: addition, subtraction, and multiplication

In the end, the workshop is about building the capacity of our parents and showing them how much fun mathematics can be. The workshop is about getting the parents, in this case dads, more involved in their child's mathematical learning. To better support their children with the rigorous content in mathematics, parents need to know how their children learn math, how they practice math, and how they are taught math. It is equally important for parents to know the vital role they play as math parent educators.

Dads, Dominoes, and Doughnuts can be very successful and often spurs comments such as "I enjoyed practicing numbers with my daughter," "Sign me up for the next one," and "I really enjoyed it." The ideas can be adapted into other events such as Muffins and Math With Moms, and Moms and Measurement Cake Decorating Workshop.

Family Math Events: School Math Days

School Math Days are certain days every month where parents and guardians are invited to visit the school and watch and play math in action. For example, every class in the school does math between 10:00 and 11:30 on the second and fourth Friday of every month. During this time, parents are invited to come in and watch the students play math games and play along.

Math Bees and Paper Airplane Competitions and Slime Fests

Math Bees are just like Spelling Bees, but they are around math. You have the whole school participate by grade level, and it doesn't just have to be around solving facts but can have various components such as problem solving and measurement activities. For example, the students could have to solve a word problem by actually measuring out ½ cup of water and ¾ cup of water. They have to prove it with numbers and the actual model. Or students have to solve problems using the various models, so they might get 12 × 15 and have to show it with an open array.

Math competitions can also be done as groups competing with each other by doing different math projects. Paper Airplane Competitions involve science, engineering, art, and perseverance. Students love them and get very intrigued by the task. A Slime Fest is another instantly exciting and rigorous activity that involves all of these things. Students will stick with searching for and trying out the best slime recipe for hours. If this is made into a competition or a family event it can be extremely engaging and strongly tied to standards.

Lessons Learned

- All stakeholders want students to be successful in mathematics . . . and parents are integral to every child's success in mathematics!
- Parents can help their children with mathematics when schools equip parents with the right tools to provide at-home support.

- At-home support can come in many forms, including mathematics handbooks and mathematics toolkits.
- Family Math Events provide opportunities to parents and children to interact with mathematics together.
- Parents will come to Family Math Events if you invite them to an event that is engaging and meaningful.
- Everybody wants to eat, drink, and be merry at the event . . . so plan for fun and have fun!

Getting Started Checklist

- Determine the needed components of a mathematics handbook (ex. identification of priority standards, academic vocabulary, assessment items, instructional videos, apps, and prompts for discourse) and create the handbook.
- Determine the needed components of a Mathematics Toolkit (tools and templates) and create the toolkit.
- Disseminate the mathematics handbook and Mathematics Toolkit to parents.
- Schedule Family Math Events that align with the campus schedule and accommodate the varying hours that many parents work.

Key Points

- Mathematics handbooks.
- Mathematics Toolkits.
- Technology (videos, apps, websites).
- Family Math Events.

Summary

Home involvement is a crucial piece to mathematizing your school. There are so many ways to get parents and guardians connected with the school. Parents want to know how to help their students achieve and inviting them into the school and showing them different ways to do that is a win-win for everybody. Provide resources such as mathematics handbooks and mathematics toolkits. Have lists of outside resources such as videos, podcasts, tweets, and pins on Pinterest that can scaffold student understanding. Definitely provide resources for homework. Do plenty of events that help parents and students to associate math with doing engaging, fun, educational things. Be sure to have opportunities for parents and guardians to participate at different times, before school, during school and after school as well as on the weekends. The bottom line is that if we as educators want our parents and guardians to be more involved, then we must provide the opportunities to help them help their children.

Reflective Questions

1. What resources are you currently providing that encourage parents to support their children's learning of mathematics while at home? What resources are needed?
2. What events do you have scheduled that bring parents into the school to have fun doing mathematics with their children? What events are needed?

Resources

- *Mathematical Mindsets* (Jo Boaler)
- Mathematics handbooks

  - (Texas Standards) Lead4Ward Resources http://lead4ward.com/resources/
  - (Texas Standards) Texas Gateway Supporting Mathematics TEKS www.texasgateway.org/resource/mathematics-teks-supporting-information
  - (Texas Standards) Pasadena ISD Weebly Glossary Page https://sites.google.com/view/pisdmathematicsglossary/home
  - (Texas Standards) Pasadena ISD Mathematic YouTube Page www.youtube.com/user/PISDMathematics
  - (Texas Standards) Pasadena ISD Mathematics Weebly Page https://pisdmathematics.weebly.com/
  - Mrs. Shannon's Class http://mrsshannonsclass.weebly.com /uploads/5/6/7/8/5678537/mathematics_questions.pdf
  - Websites and apps to model instructional strategies https://Showme.com
  - Websites and apps to model instructional strategies https://readyrosie.com
  - www.showme.com/sh/?h=S2vaQ1g (video from Jessica Garza)

- Mathematics Toolkits

  - https://guidedmath.wordpress.com/tag/math-toolkits/
  - https://guidedmath.wordpress.com/2014/08/27/math-toolkits-part-2-primary-toolkits/
  - http://nlvm.usu.edu/en/nav/vlibrary.html

- Family Math Events

  - www.pinterest.com/lararoberts/mathliteracy-night/
  - www.pinterest.com/carriescott759/family-math-night/?eq=family%20math%20night&etslf=10225
  - www.pinterest.com/bethwoods791089/family-math-night/?eq=family%20math%20night&etslf=12727
  - http://theelementarymathmaniac.blogspot.com/2014/02/getting-families-involved-in-math_6.html
  - https://theimaginationtree.com/feed-hungry-shape-monsters/
  - http://firstgradeschoolbox.blogspot.com/search/label/100th%20Day%20of%20School
  - http://rachelktutoring.com/blog/math-games-with-dice/
  - www.teachingwithsimplicity.com/2015/03/family-math-night-for-big-kids.html

- Dads, Dominoes, and Doughnuts

  - www.mathwire.com/numbersense/dominoes.html
  - www.pinterest.com/drnicki7/domino-math/
  - www.multiplication.com/our-blog/jen-wieber/domino-games-4-ways-times-table-practice
  - www.husd.org/cms/lib/AZ01001450/Centricity/Domain/3010/1st%20Grade%20Math%20Games.pdf
  - www.multiplication.com/sites/default/files/files/Times-Tables-Dominoes-x4-Directions(4).pdf
  - www.youtube.com/watch?v=KiYtAyGNtNA

10

Action Planning

The Journey of A Thousand Miles begins with a Single Step.

—Laozi

The way to start is to start. Start small, focused, and specific. Keep yourself honest by attaching deadlines to your dreams. Make sure that all of your goals are measurable. At the end of every chapter we have given ways to get started thinking about the ideas in that chapter. Bringing it all together, think about where you want to go first and how you will get there (see Figures 10.1 and 10.2). Here are some general questions to think about:

- What are the specific conversations that you want to start at your home campus?
- What is the state of mathematical affairs in your classroom, grade level, school, and district right now?

Figure 10.1

Here are some questions to think about for each chapter.			
Chapter 2: Mathematizing Your District	Chapter 3: Mathematizing Your Staff	Chapter 4: Mathematizing Your Campus	Chapter 5: Mathematizing Your Classroom
What is the one thing that you would like to see as a district initiative?	How does your staff react to math? What are some immediate initiatives that you might take to get your staff excited about math?	What is done to cultivate a positive, productive disposition among your students and staff at your school right now?	What is the general "feeling tone" (Hunter) about math among the students in your classroom?

Figure 10.2

Chapter 6: Mathematizing Your Students	Chapter 7: Mathematizing Your Intervention and Enrichment	Chapter 8: Mathematizing Your Parents
What do you have in place right now that cultivates a spirit of risk-taking, perseverance, curiosity, wonder and joy among your students right now?	How is intervention looked at and treated at your school? What are you doing to address the different levels of student achievement at your school?	What parent math initiatives do you have in place right now?

Thank you for joining us on this journey!

- What is your specific goal? Or, where is your point of entry?
- What does this look like to you right now? What do you want it to look like?
- What are you already doing really well?
- What are some of the challenges?
- How will you troubleshoot these challenges?
- What do you need to improve on?
- How will you go about doing that?
- Who will you get to help?
- How will you celebrate incremental steps taken towards meeting your goal?

We have come to the end of our journey in this book but really the journey continues always! We will continue to seek out ways to teach better and learn more so that we may inspire our students, help them see math in the world they live in, feel the joy of it all and improve their achievement. We will continue to read, share, tweet, blog, Instagram, and learn together. Janet always says, "Mathematicians learn and grow together!" It is our deepest and sincerest hope that you have learned some new things in this book and that you will grow professionally because of it. Let's stay connected via Twitter as we all work together to mathematize our districts, staff, classrooms, students, intervention/enrichment, and parents! #MathematizeChat